THE LIFE OF J

The Life of John Wheatley

by John Hannan

Spokesman

First published in 1988 by:
Spokesman
Bertrand Russell House
Gamble Street
Nottingham, England
Tel. 0602 708318

Copyright © John Hannan (1988)

This book is copyright under the Berne Convention. All rights are reserved. Apart from any fair dealing for the purpose of private study, research, criticism or review, as permitted under the Copyright Act, 1956, no part of this publication may be reproduced, stored in a retrieval system, or transmitted, in any form or by any means, electronic, electrical, chemical, mechanical, photocopying, recording or otherwise, without the prior permission of the copyright owner. Enquiries should be addressed to the publishers.

British Library Cataloguing in Publication Data
Hannan, John
  John Wheatley.
  1. Great Britain. Politics. Wheatley, John, 1869–1930.—Biographies
  I. Title
  941.082'092'4

ISBN 0–85124–487–4
ISBN 0–85124–497–1 Pbk

Photoset, printed and bound in Great Britain by
Redwood Burn Limited, Trowbridge, Wiltshire

Contents

Acknowledgements	vii
Introduction	ix
Chapter 1 The Early Years	1
Chapter 2 1906–1910	11
Chapter 3 Council Politics	28
Chapter 4 £8 Cottages	36
Chapter 5 The Rent Strike	43
Chapter 6 The War Years	56
Chapter 7 The 1918 Election	67
Chapter 8 The Post-War Years	72
Chapter 9 The 1922 Election	88
Chapter 10 Into Parliament	95
Chapter 11 Minister of Health	117
Chapter 12 Election and General Strike	139
Chapter 13 Challenge from the Backbench	154
Chapter 14 A Manifesto for Socialists	161
Chapter 15 1929–30	169

Acknowledgements

I would like to thank Cathie and my children for the encouragement given to me with the writing of this book.

I must also acknowledge the help that I have received from the following:

Harold Smith; Richard Storey, Archivist at Warwick University; Department of Economic History – Strathclyde University; Marx Memorial Library; Glasgow Room of the Mitchell Library; Patricia Fanning, Waterford Municipal Library; Donal Brady, Waterford County Library; C. Fahy, National Library of Ireland; Library at London School of Economics; Strathclyde Regional Archives; Records Office, Kew; The late John P. Wheatley; Lord Wheatley; Eileen Coyle; Dunbarton Public Library; Ballieston Public Library; Raphael Samuel.

Introduction

John Wheatley is best remembered for his 1924 Housing Bill. It was considered no mean feat in a minority Government, but it fades in significance with the achievement of the Glasgow Independent Labour Party which, within 20 years of its being, provided the city with two thirds of its elected representatives at Westminster. John Wheatley was the principal architect of this accomplishment and it is as much an enigma as the man himself that this has never been fully recognised.

Wheatley was a Johnny-come-lately to the Socialist movement. He had previously been involved in Irish politics, but he had come to the realisation that Home Rule for Ireland would do nothing to improve the miserable existence of the Irish whom, he knew, would continue to live in Scotland. In his efforts to wean them from nationalist politics and their Liberal attachment Wheatley formed a Catholic Socialist Society. It was condemned by his own church and, in a city bitterly divided by religion, was viewed by some socialists as an attempt to bring sectarianism into the working class movement. The results in Glasgow of the 1922 election, at which the Catholic vote went solidly to Labour, was vindication of Wheatley's policy. There were some who argued that the C.S.S. had hindered Labour's progress, but a survey of the results at the same election in Liverpool – a city not dissimilar to Glasgow – where only an Irish Nationalist victory in the Scotland division prevented a Tory whitewash would weigh against that argument.

Wheatley had tremendous confidence in the ability of a united working class to work out its own destiny, but he recognised that the greatest obstacle to that unity was sectarianism. There would have to be a common cause and he found it in housing. Like the C.S.S., his £8 Cottage scheme was at first scorned, but from it grew an organisation that successfully challenged the Government on rents during the war and in which the women played a major role. Wheatley's influence on the Labour movement increased as the war progressed until he became virtual leader of all left wing opposition on the Clyde. In industrial matters his advice was much sought by the shop stewards and in the City Council, through his leadership, the small Labour group had taken over a great deal of the responsibility for protecting the people against the worst effects of the war. Throughout the war, and in the depression that followed, Wheatley kept the focus directed on housing and rents and it was on that platform that ten Labour men were elected to represent Glasgow in Parliament. It was a phenomenon that had London journalists racing north, but so captivated were they by the cloth caps that they failed to recognise the architect of this achievement.

Wheatley's experience in Government convinced him that the leaders would never commit the Labour Party to a socialist policy and shortly after the 1924 election he retired to the back benches. In the years preceding the second Labour Government Wheatley tried to create a broad base of opinion within the Labour movement sufficient to coerce the leadership into adopting Socialist policies. In this he failed, but the events of those years are interesting because they are not without their parallels today. Then, as now, the Labour Party had been cleverly boxed into the red corner and forced to jettison its militants. The Tory party adopted the Union Jack as its party emblem which Wheatley perceived as a device to divide the nation. Areas which were decidedly anti-Tory Baldwin sought to disenfranchise. Laws were introduced to the advantage of the rich with a complete disregard for the needs of the poor. The Government, choosing the battle ground, engaged the workers in a war of attrition and the worker's leaders hoisted the white flag before the battle had begun in earnest. There was voluble, but no effective opposition in parliament and yet surprisingly the electorate turned again to Labour.

Foreseeing the economic recession Wheatley warned Labour of the dangers inherent in forming yet another minority Government. By that time he had been successfully tagged with the nuisance label and his warning went unheeded. He was dead before his worst fears were realised.

Chapter One
The Early Years

*I Bertolt Brecht came out of the Black Forest
My mother moved me into the cities as I lay
inside her body and the coldness of the forests
will be inside me till my dying day.*
BRECHT

It would have been odd to find a Southern Irishman living and working in Scotland who had not been caught up in the new enthusiasm for the Home Rule for Ireland movement that the centenary of the 1798 rebellion had inspired. It would not have been odd to find a man like John Wheatley as one of the local leaders in this movement. He had all the necessary qualifications: intelligence, courage, skilled in debate with a passionate interest in politics and he was a Catholic of Irish birth. He had been born in 1869[1] a mere 20 years after the famine and nowhere in Ireland had it brought greater distress than his birth-place Bunmahon in the County of Waterford. Of a population of 1,771 more than a third disappeared from the face of the earth.[2] What was odd, when one examines Wheatley's background, was the fact that he was 30 years of age before he became involved in politics of any colour.

Thomas Wheatley, John's father, was one of Ireland's desperately poor, an agricultural labourer. In 1876[3] with his wife Joanna and four children, John was the eldest, he left Ireland to work in the Lanarkshire coalfields. The family settled in Braehead, later known as Bargeddie, a village seven miles east of Glasgow. Thomas worked in a local pit and the family found accommodation in what was typical of a Lanarkshire mining village. It was a one-roomed house in what was commonly called a 'twa-faced raw' or back to back house. It was a row of squat houses through the centre of which ran a straight wall which prevented any through ventilation. The room had two hole in the wall beds, but not a cupboard or any kind of storage space. It was obligatory to buy coal from one's employer at regular intervals and this had to be stored under one of the beds. Beneath the other bed, in addition to dirty washing, was stored the 'Hurley bed' in which the children slept. This bed was wheeled out to the centre of the floor each evening. Sugar bags were often used to cover the stone floor. There was neither drainage nor water supply to the house and water had to be carried from a common supply 100 yards away. An open sewer ran in front of the house and the lavatory, which served twelve families, was on an ash pit facing the windows on the row. It was in accommodation such as this that John Wheatley was to live for nearly twenty years with a family the size of which increased to eleven.[4]

John's education at St. Bridget's chapel school[5] in nearby Baillieston ended at thirteen years of age when economic necessity forced him to join his father in the pits.[6] He was to work there for more than a decade and it was a period in which the mine owners continuously sought to reduce the miners' already poor living standards. In one year[7] alone, about three years after John started work, the owners were successful in reducing the men's wages from 3/6d per day to 2/6d. With an average weekly rent of 4/– and other expenses amounting to about 1/6d there was little left for the miner to provide food and clothing for his family. It was also a time when the Lanarkshire Miners Union was being re-organised under the leadership of men like Keir Hardie, Bob Smillie, and Wm. Small to fight against these conditions.[8] Why was it then that Wheatley, with all his attributes and who later said that these conditions burned deeply into his soul[9], did not join these men in their struggle?

John Scanlon, an intimate of Wheatley and writing while he was still alive, said that 'it was not easy for a little known man to make himself known in the work of the Miners' Union, that the men whose word counted were the already elected officials. It was obvious that the circumscribed work in a Trade Union did not appeal to Wheatley'.[10] It is difficult to imagine a man like Wheatley being unable to make himself known in any company. It is possible that Wheatley's then Liberal views did not match the Socialist demands of these new leaders. Perhaps Pat Dollan's assertion that 'Wheatley's greatest handicap was a defect for team work, that he could only work in small groups in which he was the chief and dominant figure'[11] comes closer to explaining why Wheatley played no obvious part in Union affairs.

In 1893, the year before the great miners' strike, Wheatley left the pits to work in a local pub.[12] By the time of his marriage to Mary Meechan in 1896[13] he had become manager of this pub. Mary was the daughter of Bernard, one of the founders of the Baillieston branch of the Irish National League which had been formed in 1886.[14] The marriage took place in St. Bridget's church

The Early Years

to which the guests were conveyed by coach and pair. It was what was known as a 'Ticket Wedding' that is, the guests paid 5/- for a ticket to the reception, which was held in McInnes's Hall in Baillieston, instead of giving the customary gift.[15] Roughly a year after the marriage Wheatley moved to Springboig,[16] an area of Shettleston, where he went to work with his brother Patrick in the retail grocery business. Patrick had two shops and John managed one of them.[17] It is worth noting that John McGovern, who was to succeed Wheatley as M.P. for Shettleston, began his working life with the Wheatley brothers.[18] It was only after his move to Shettleston, a town touching on Glasgow's eastern boundary, that evidence comes of Wheatley's involvement in politics.

When Wheatley moved to Shettleston that town did not boast of a branch of the Irish National League. The League itself had been in decline following the split in the leadership in the wake of the Parnell affair. The inauguration in 1898 of William O'Brien's United Irish League to commemorate the centenary of the Wolfe Tone rebellion was to prove the unifying factor in the Nationalist movement. O'Brien's League was born out of agrarian unrest and represented the poor tenants in Ireland. It brought with it a resurgence of interest in the Home Rule movement with the result that, in addition to branches of the new League being formed, branches of the older I.N.L. were revivified with an influx of new members.[19] One of the oldest and largest branches of the I.N.L. in Scotland was the Michael Davitt* branch in Coatbridge of which Wheatley's father was a prominent figure.[20] It seemed probable that John Wheatley was caught up in this new enthusiasm for it was at a meeting of the Coatbridge branch early in 1899[21] that we first become aware of Wheatley's active interest in politics.

Although the recently formed Independent Labour Party had given a commitment to a policy of Home Rule for Ireland it was to the Liberal Party that Nationalists in this country largely pledged their support. Home Rule for Ireland had been a major plank of Liberal policy since Gladstone's time. Nevertheless, there were some members of the Party who were less than wholehearted in their support of Home Rule and other Nationalist demands of the time. Dr. Douglas, the Liberal candidate for Lanark North West at the by-election in February that year, was one of those Liberals whose public utterances on the Irish question were, to say the

*Davitt was well known in Lanarkshire having supported Keir Hardie in the 1888 election against the wishes of the I.N.L. He founded the Land League in Ireland in 1879 which, among other things, fought against tenant evictions. His work must have been well known to Wheatley.

least, equivocal.[22] Some Nationalists, including Chisholm Robertson[23] leader of the Scottish Miners' strike in 1894, were averse to pledging the Irish vote to Douglas. It was only after a series of hastily convened meetings that it was agreed to support him.[24] In the event, Douglas was elected with the very slender majority of 359 votes.[25] It was apropos this situation that, at the Coatbridge branch's first meeting in February, Wheatley put forward the following resolution to the branch.

'That the branch does not give its support to any Liberal candidate who will not support:
(1) A measure of Home Rule for Ireland.
(2) The establishment of a Catholic University* in Ireland which will meet the requirements of the Irish people.
(3) The redress of Ireland's financial grievances.
(4) The immediate release of all political prisoners in Ireland.'

The question of a Catholic University for Ireland, while often the subject of timid debate, had never really been seriously contested by the Nationalists in this country and the agitation for the release of political prisoners had been the concern of an I.N.L. hybrid body, Amnesty Association.[26] No action appeared to have been taken on this resolution. No doubt the branch, like most Nationalists of the time, thought it sufficient to press for Home Rule to which all things would be added. While academic, the resolution did point to the fact that Wheatley at this stage could not dissociate Nationalism from Catholicism.

It was in March the following year that Wheatley emerged as a potential force in the Nationalist movement. Following a meeting of Irishmen in the Catholic League of the Cross Hall in Wellshot Rd., Shettleston, a branch of the Irish National League was formed. It was named the Daniel O'Connell branch after the great Irish fighter for Catholic emancipation and Wheatley was elected President.[27] That the branch should choose to be part of the more conservative wing of the Home Rule movement under the leadership of John Redmond is an indication of Wheatley's views at the time. This proved to be immaterial as, in the following June, the different factions of the Nationalist movement were united under the banner of the United Irish League.

In the three and a half years that Wheatley held the office of President he displayed exceptional organisational and administrative skills. It was also a period when his honesty and courage were put to the test. The first task of the branch was to organise

*The University Education (Ireland) Act 1879, while satisfying some, fell short of the Catholic demand for a fully denominational university subsidised by the State.

The Early Years

the Irish vote in the area and for this purpose a registration committee was set up.[28] The job of the committee was to ensure that the electoral register was up to date and that those Irish entitled to the vote had their names on the register. In the course of this work the branch was able to help the Irish in another area. It had been the practice at that time of some landlords to coerce new tenants into paying the balance of rates left owing by the previous tenants and it became part of the work of the new committee to protect tenants against this abuse.[29] It was Wheatley's first skirmish in what was to be, for him, a long and bitter war against landlordism.

Within five months of the inauguration of the Shettleston branch Wheatley became the Nationalist leader in the constituency which had the largest Irish population in Lanarkshire and in the process showed a capacity to make circumstances and events work for him. The Liberals in Scotland were questioning the value of their Party's support for Irish Home Rule and with sound reason. Gladstone's decision in 1886 to back Ireland's demand for Home Rule had led to the defection of Liberal Unionists and the erosion of Liberal dominance in Scotland. Before 1886 Scotland had returned 62 Liberals to Parliament as against 10 Tories. By 1900 the Tories had gained 28 seats and in Glasgow had taken all seven seats from the Liberals. At a branch meeting in July[30] Wheatley voiced his concern at these changing attitudes of the Liberals and it was agreed that he write to Dr. Douglas expressing this concern. To increase the pressure on the M.P. Wheatley felt that it was necessary to have a more coherent Nationalist organisation in the constituency and he proposed at this meeting that there should be a joint meeting of all U.I.L. branches in the division with a view to establishing a North West Lanark Nationalist Council. One month later delegates from eight different branches attended a meeting at Shettleston at which a North West Lanarkshire Council was formed with Wheatley as President.[31] It was obvious that Wheatley had done some canvassing before putting forward the proposal to his own branch.

The Daniel O'Connell branch expanded rapidly and in little over a year could boast of 250[32] fully paid up members and was now meeting in the Catholic School Hall.[33] It was now the political and cultural centre for the Irish in Shettleston. A dramatic society was formed and Gaelic speaking classes were held twice a week.[34] Members were encouraged to give readings on subjects chosen from Irish literature and Irish history. It was apt that Wheatley should himself give a reading on 'Scenes from the Famine'. Famine,[35] Wheatley later said, was an indiscriminate term used to describe a partial failure of the crops as there had been sufficient food produced in Ireland in those years to feed the population.*[36] It had been the practice of the branch to invite guest speakers, but shortly after moving into these premises the Parish Priest began to lay down certain conditions as to the use of the Hall. One of these conditions was that no outsiders be invited to give lectures. Wheatley objected strongly to this on the grounds that the U.I.L. was a political and not a religious organisation.[37] Anxious, as he said, to keep politics clear of the parish building, the branch decided to move to rooms in Wellshot Rd. It was to be the first of many conflicts Wheatley was to have with the clergy and it showed a definite shift in Wheatley's attitude to politics and religion.

The move to Wellshot Rd. proved to be a prudent one since, after the Lanark North East by-election when the U.I.L. came out strongly in favour of Bob Smillie, branches of the U.I.L. which had been using Catholic Schools were requested by the Priests-in-Charge to find alternative accommodation.[38] Wheatley also supported Smillie but the reasons he gave did not suggest that he had moved in any way towards the Socialist camp.[39] However, the rooms at Wellshot Rd. were inadequate to cater for the huge membership and Wheatley proposed that the branch launch a fund that would enable it to build its own premises.[40] This project brought Wheatley into further conflict with the Parish Priest and had far-reaching consequences, but it also demonstrated an ability to get things done. By the middle of 1902 the branch was firmly established in its own premises in William Street and more surprisingly, the entire cost of the project had been met.[41] Unfortunately for Wheatley, Father Andrew O'Brien had himself built a parochial hall and was not at all happy to see another hall in the parish which he considered as being in competition with his.[42]

There were many of the Catholic clergy in Scotland who refused to separate the Irish cause from Catholicism and so Father O'Brien could only see the Nationalists' hall as a Catholic hall over which he had been denied the authority to administer. Complaints began to be levelled at the administrators of the U.I.L. hall, both from the pulpit and the Catholic press, as to irregularities in its use.[43] The most serious was that the hall was deliberately being kept open during the times when services were being conducted in the church, thus encouraging the faithful not to attend these services. It was also being hinted that the hall was being used for the sale of Socialist literature. In the

*An agricultural census for 1847 showed that the value of produce in Ireland was £45 million, sufficient to meet the needs of the population twice over.

The Early Years

controversy that followed from these complaints the reason that Wheatley had originally given for leaving the School Hall was being turned upside down. It was said that the Parish Priest had only objected to outside speakers because Wheatley had insisted that their names be publicised from the pulpit and that it had been the Parish Priest who had been the one anxious to keep politics clear of the parish building. Wheatley's public denial of these charges did not endear him to a section of the Catholic community.[44]

On what he considered to be a matter of principle Wheatley would not bow to any authority. The building fund that he had launched had not only covered the cost of the hall, but had realised a surplus. The executive of the U.I.L. had demanded that this surplus should be handed over to the central body, a demand that Wheatley successfully withstood. This was branch money, he maintained, and would remain in the branch.[45] It was not to be long before Wheatley and the U.I.L. would be at odds on much greater principles.

Throughout 1902 and the major part of 1903 Wheatley was heavily involved in local Irish affairs. He had played a leading role in the work of the Friendly Society, the Irish National Foresters, which catered for the needs of the Irish in sickness and in death. He held the position of Chief Ranger and had also acted as Auditor in the Father Terken branch of the Foresters.[46] It came as something of a surprise when, in October 1903, he resigned the Presidency of the Daniel O'Connell branch of the U.I.L. which by then had grown to be the largest branch of the U.I.L. in Scotland outside of Glasgow.[47] He offered no reason for his resignation although it seems likely that he was then re-examining his political beliefs. Part of the reason could have been a greater commitment to business.

Two years earlier Wheatley had left the retail grocery trade in Shettleston and joined the staff of the *Glasgow Observer* as a reporter-cum-salesman.[48] The *Glasgow Observer* was one of several weekly newspapers at that time which served the needs of the Catholic community in Scotland. Its owner was a Mr. Charles Diamond who was also chairman of the English Sewing Machine Company. Diamond used the paper subsequently to combat the spread of Socialism. Wheatley quickly established himself with his new employer. His capacity for hard work allied to his ability as a salesman earned him promotion to head of the advertising department.[49]

For two years after resigning as President of the Daniel O'Connell branch Wheatley appeared to be politically inactive. Early in

1904 he took a prominent part in a debate within the branch. The debate was on the current controversy between Free Trade and Protection and Wheatley argued on the side of Protection.[50] His arguments indicated not only how far he had moved from Liberalism, indeed he was to remain something of a protectionist for the rest of his life, but his concern for the working class. He based his argument against Free Trade on the bounties being given by some European Governments to their sugar manufacturers which he claimed were being used to undercut prices in this country. This, he said, was the logical outcome of Free Trade and would mean a further erosion of the living standards of the workers in this country. In the course of his argument he warned of the folly of making judgements on the basis of personalities. Throughout his political career Wheatley carried with him a dislike of the cult of the individual.

The debate took place shortly before a by-election in Lanark North East where the Irish were advised by the U.I.L. executive to vote for the Liberal candidate.[51] In 1901 with the backing of the U.I.L. the Labour candidate had polled 2,900 votes, at this election the Labour vote was increased to 3,884 an indication that many Irish had rejected the advice of their leaders. The registered Irish vote in this constituency was 2,500.

It was late in 1905 before there was clear evidence of a definite change in Wheatley's political allegiance. The Tory Government under Balfour was hopelessly divided on the issue of Imperial Preference. Balfour resigned the Premiership and his successor, Campbell Bannerman, went to the country on that issue with elections to take place in the first week of January 1906. In Lanark North West Joseph Sullivan, a Socialist and a miner, was adopted as the Labour candidate.[52] Wheatley was active in his support of Sullivan[53] who, like himself, had grown up in Irish politics. In an election that was fought mainly on the issue of Free Trade versus Imperialism Sullivan kept his campaign to matters such as unemployment, Workmen's Compensation, Pensions and the Land question.*[54] On the eve of the election the executive of the U.I.L. recommended that the Irish should vote Labour where the candidate was sound on Home Rule unless he was standing against an old and trusted friend of the Irish cause or where support for the Labour candidate would ensure the return of a

*Some Socialists of this period were advocating the theories of Henry George, an American, whose doctrine of Single Tax was based on the premise that all human life and effort is based primarily on the land, that the land belongs inalienably to all equally and that private ownership of land deprives some men of their equal right to life. Michael Davitt was, for a time, editor of George's periodical *Labour World*.

Tory.[55] The Liberal candidate, Dr. Douglas, was not a trusted friend, but Irish support for the Labour candidate in this constituency would certainly mean the return of a Tory yet the executive recommended that Sullivan be given the Irish vote.[56] Home Rule was not a burning question at this election nevertheless the Grand Orange Lodge of Scotland came out with a manifesto calling on its adherents to ignore the arguments within the Tory Party over tariff reforms and to ensure that their votes went against the Liberals and anything else that smelled of Popery.[57]

Sullivan polled 3,291 votes against Liberal's 4,931 and the Tories 5,588, but with an estimated Irish vote of 2,600[58] neither he nor Wheatley could have been terribly happy at the outcome. Labour returned 29 of its candidates to Parliament at this election. In Hutchestown, a Glasgow constituency with a huge Irish presence, George Barnes the Labour candidate was returned, but he also had U.I.L. support. To change the voting habits of the people of the West of Scotland would be a mammoth task.

References

1. *Dictionary of National Biographies* (1922–30)
2. *Decie* published by Old Waterford Society, 1980
3. *Glasgow Herald* – 6/7/27
4. *John Wheatley* – John Scanlon (The Book of the Labour Party, vol. 3), 1925, H. Tracy
   P. J. Dollan – unpublished *Memoirs* – Glasgow Mitchell Library
   J. Sullivan – debate on Scottish estimates, *Hansard* 27/6/23
5. P. J. Dollan – *Memoirs*
   County of Lanark, Third Statistical Account – George Thomson
6. Wheatley states on one occasion that he was 12 years of age and on another 13 years. The latter is more probable – see *Glasgow Observer* 3/8/07 and *Glasgow Herald* 6/7/27
7. *Scotsman* – 13/8/1886
8. *Lanarkshire Miners* – Alan B. Campbell, 1979
9. *Glasgow Herald* – 10/7/28
10. *John Wheatley* – John Scanlon (The Book of the Labour Party, vol. 3)
11. *Glasgow Evening Times* – 15/5/30
12. *Glasgow Herald* – 6/7/27
13. Extract from marriage register.
14. *Glasgow Observer* – 3/3/88
    P. J. Dollan – *Memoirs*
15. Ibid.
16. *Glasgow Observer* – 21/9/01 (letter in support of Smillie)
17. *Glasgow Herald* – 6/7/27
18. *Neither Fear Nor Favour* – John McGovern – 1960
19. See Irish notices in *Glasgow Observer* before and after 1898
20. *Glasgow Examiner* – 21/3/1896

21. *Glasgow Examiner* – 11/3/1899
22. *Labour Leader* – 11/2/1899
23. Ibid.
24. *Labour Leader* – 18/2/1899
25. *Labour Leader* – 25/2/1899
26. *Labour Leader* – 19/8/1898
27. *Glasgow Examiner* – 11/3/1900
28. *Glasgow Examiner* – 9/6/1900
29. *Glasgow Examiner* – 30/6/1900
30. *Glasgow Examiner* – 14/7/1900
31. *Glasgow Examiner* – 25/8/1900
32. *Glasgow Observer* – 21/9/01
33. *Glasgow Observer* – 15/3/02
34. *Glasgow Observer* – 20/7/01
35. *Glasgow Observer* – 27/7/01
36. *Forward* – 4/2/11
37. *Glasgow Observer* – 15/3/02
38. Ibid.
    Glasgow Examiner – 7/11/01
39. *Glasgow Observer* – 21/9/01
40. *Glasgow Examiner* – 3/11/1900
41. *Glasgow Observer* – 3/5/02
42. *Neither Fear Nor Favour* – John McGovern – 1960
43. *Glasgow Observer* – 5/4/02
44. *Glasgow Observer* – Letters to Editor April–May, 1902
45. *Glasgow Observer* – 3/5/02
46. *Glasgow Examiner* – January 1908
    Glasgow Observer – 30/1/1904
47. *Glasgow Observer* – 28/10/03
48. *Glasgow Herald* – 6/7/27
49. *Glasgow Observer* – 17/5/30
50. *Glasgow Observer* 6/2/04
51. *Labour Leader* – February 1904
52. *Scotsman* – 9/12/05
53. *Glasgow Observer* – 3/2/06
54. *Scotsman* – 6/1/06
55. *Glasgow Observer* – 6/1/06
56. Ibid.
57. *Scotsman* – 4/1/06
58. *Scotsman* – 6/1/06.

Chapter Two
1906–1910

At 36 years of age, when most people were settled in their political opinions, Wheatley had been converted to Socialism. What were the factors which led to this conversion? There were some who claimed that he had been influenced by the economic theories of Marx while rejecting his Materialist Conception of History. This is most unlikely. The Malthusian theory of effective demand which Wheatley later developed and expounded had been dismissed by Marx as pure tautology. The manner in which he dismissed the theory of the Materialist Conception of History when defending himself against a group of Marxists[1] demonstrated his complete ignorance of that theory. It seems doubtful that he ever read Marx. Dollan brings us closer to the truth when he wrote of the great influence that Robert Blatchford had on him.[2] Blatchford's *Merry England* was a book on practical Socialism and Wheatley was without doubt a practical Socialist. Years later Wheatley referred to Blatchford[3] as one of the great pioneers of Socialism in this country. Having accepted Socialism as the only force with which to combat the evils of Capitalism, Wheatley set out immediately and courageously to convert those within his own church to his new found beliefs.

On the 24th February, 1906, a letter written by Wheatley appeared in the columns of the *Glasgow Observer*.[4] It was headed 'A Catholic defence of Socialism' and it was a condemnation of the Capitalist system which he said made it impossible for Catholics to practice their religion and therefore it was incumbent on them to fight against it 'living in a society which is one of the swindler versus the swindled, how can there be brotherly love?'

This letter brought criticism from all sections of the Catholic church. The contents of a lecture given by Charles Devas[5] was published in pamphlet form and sold at church doors. In this lecture, as well as condemning Socialism, Devas recommended that the Catholic Church prohibit its members from joining Socialist organisations. In his reply[6] Wheatley challenged those who were anxious to impose such a ban to point out one item in the programmes of either the Social Democratic Federation,* the Independent Labour Party† or the Fabian Society‡ which is inconsistent with Catholicism. These reactionaries, he wrote, have wakened up in the wrong year. He condemned the clergy[7] who, he said, had consistently failed to fight against poverty. 'Step aside and let the workers, have a go,' he told them and he warned them of the danger of taking the side of the Capitalist against the workers, 'Do not keep the company of the oppressor for, in the smoke of battle, you may well be mistaken for one of them.' Wheatley's statements seemed to lack coherence. The S.D.F. was a Marxist body whose teachings, leading Catholic apologists would claim, was opposed to the Church. Considering too, the course of action Wheatley planned, his frenetic attacks on the clergy seemed likely to rebound on him.

Towards the end of that year an advertisement appeared in the *Glasgow Observer* inviting Catholics, interested in Socialism, to attend a meeting in the College St. Halls in Glasgow.[8] Catholics from every walk of life[9] responded to this call from Wheatley which must have been a major disappointment to those who were anxious to protect Catholics from the dangers of Socialism. The meeting with George Hardie, brother of Keir Hardie, as guest speaker was so successful that it was agreed to form an organisation which was named the Catholic Socialist Society. Wheatley was appointed President of the Society with Stephen Pullman as its Secretary.[10] *Forward* was quick to praise the emergence of this new Society which it hoped would attract Catholic workers to Socialism.[11]

Wheatley's conversion to Socialism had coincided with the arrival of *Forward*, a weekly Socialist newspaper under the editorship of Thomas Johnston.§ It was to become the unofficial organ of the I.L.P. in Scotland. Johnston opened the columns of *Forward* to every shade of Socialist opinion. John McLean, a Glasgow Schoolteacher and leading propagandist of the S.D.F. in Glasgow, was a regular contributor. Wheatley recognised

*The Party had its origins in the London Democratic Federation, Britain's first Socialist Party. Its founder was H. M. Hyndman whose 'England for All', a treatise on Marxism, led to the formation of the Party.

†The Party was formed in 1893. By 1906 it had 10 Branches in Glasgow with branches in the neighbouring Burghs of Partick, Govan and Rutherglen. First Chairman of the Party was Keir Hardie who also edited its organ *Labour Leader* published in Glasgow until 1905 when it moved to London.

‡Formed in 1884, it preached evolutionary Socialism. Its leading members included G. B. Shaw and Sydney Webb.

§Johnston, a future Secretary of State for Scotland wrote a book *Our Noble Families*, an exposition of how the Scottish aristocracy had attained and exploited the land. It made an impact with the dispossessed Highlanders living in the West of Scotland.

McLean as one of the greatest rebel leaders of his time because of his ability and fearlessness. McLean took his Marxist economics to the streets where his vibrant personality attracted huge crowds. James Connolly, a visitor to the Wheatley household and one of the leaders of the ill-fated Easter Rebellion in Ireland, had a regular weekly column for many years. A brilliant man who was years ahead of his time Connolly was that unique type – a Christian Marxist.

Patrick Dollan, who was encouraged by Wheatley to leave the coal mines in Baillieston to work in his publishing business prior to taking up journalism, was the paper's authority on mining affairs. He wrote under the pseudonym of Myner Collier and he combined his writings with useful outdoor propaganda work for the I.L.P.

Martin Haddow was the paper's expert on Education. Haddow was one of the earliest and most tireless workers for the I.L.P. in Glasgow. His work in the Parish Council for the poor children of Glasgow has not received the recognition it deserved.

One of the most popular contributors was Frank McCabe, a grave digger at Lambhill Cemetery. Until he emigrated to Australia shortly before World War I McCabe wrote a witty and satirical feature under the title 'Outside the Chapel Door'. Based on the habit of Irish Catholics of discussing the weekly topics outside church after Mass on Sundays, the feature portrayed Durkin and Doolan, pseudo Irishmen, debating subjects through which Irishmen's ignorance of real events was exposed. McCabe's feature must have given some Irishmen food for thought and could have only been helpful to Wheatley in his campaign to attract these Irish to Socialism.

Wheatley's decision to start a Catholic Socialist Society not only angered some Socialists of the time, but to this day has puzzled students of the Labour movement in Scotland. John Scanlon[12] said that it was an attempt by Wheatley to wean the Irish in Scotland from Liberalism, that Home Rule for Ireland would do nothing to alleviate their impoverished state in this country, for the Irish who were here were likely to remain here. Yet, at a time when sectarianism in the West of Scotland was already deep rooted, there was every justification for those who charged Wheatley with bringing sectarianism[13] into the Labour movement itself.

Irish immigration into Scotland, which had been a trickle in the first half of the nineteenth century became a flood in the second half. There were two reasons for this: the famine in Ireland and the new industries that had opened up to meet the needs of the industrial revolution. The vast majority of these immigrants were Catholics from the south of Ireland who were forced by circumstances to occupy the lowest paid and worst jobs. Congregated in the worst housing conditions there was much drunkenness and fighting amongst themselves. They did not endear themselves to the indigent Scot and in the circumstances separate schooling did nothing to improve the image that was being created of them. Helen Crawford[14] said, that as a young girl she looked upon the Catholic Irish as being sub-human. The smaller, but vociferous number of Irishmen who came to Scotland from that part of Ireland commonly called Ulster played no mean part in widening the gulf between the two races. They were Protestant and for the most part skilled workers. They brought with them, not only their skills, but their hatred of Catholics and, sharing the same places of worship and education as the Presbyterian Scot, they quickly transmitted this hatred to them. By the turn of the century the Catholic and Protestant communities in the West of Scotland were polarised.

Another charge levelled at Wheatley was that he was attempting to capture the Labour movement for the Catholic Church.[15] Protestants were uneasy over the rapid growth of the Catholic community. From a few thousand at the middle of the nineteenth century there were more than 350,000[16] registered baptised Catholics in the Archdiocese of Glasgow by the time Wheatley started his Society. Protestants were led to believe that Catholics were encouraged by their clergy to have large families as a means to the church attaining political power by virtue of numbers and, to many, Wheatley's Society looked to be the thin end of the wedge. Whatever the number of Catholics Wheatley was likely to attract to Socialism by means of his Society there would be many Protestants whose attitude to it would harden, looking on it as synonymous with Catholicism. Why he did not join Shettleston branch of the I.L.P.* and make that his base for attracting the Irish to Socialism is difficult to fathom, for when he did join the branch the following year, it looked suspiciously like the C.S.S. was for him but a ladder to climb to power in the Labour movement.

Wheatley soon made it clear that the C.S.S. was principally a Socialist organisation. In hailing Labour's astonishing by-election victory at Jarrow he attacked the leaders of the U.I.L. for their opposition to the Labour candidate.[17] 'They forget that in asking the Irish to fight Labour they are asking them to beat themselves.' He criticised Catholic representatives on public bodies for their

*The Shettleston branch of the I.L.P. was formed at a meeting in the Shettleston Cooperative Halls on the 21st August 1905. Its first chairman was T. G. Simpson.

reactionary conduct. There were some Catholic clergymen who had been reported as having adopted high-handed attitudes when interviewing the poor who had applied for Parish Relief. He made it clear to the members of the C.S.S. that it was their duty to enter the arena of local politics at the next elections and work for the return of Labour candidates even if that implied opposition to Catholics.[18] At a local by-election at Blackfriars in the summer of 1907 he wrote to the *Glasgow Observer*[19] and urged Catholic and Irish working men to vote for John Stewart the non-Catholic Labour candidate. This ward had a high percentage of Irish voters and sectarianism had crept into the election.

'Do not be used or sacrificed by men coming forward to avenge imaginary grievances. Your interests and those of your fellow Protestant worker are identical. Your enemies are their enemies. Workers of every creed unite.'

Wheatley had signed this appeal as chairman of the Catholic Socialist Society, the appellation led to his engaging a priest of the Jesuit Order in a debate which a more mature politician might have judged to be fruitless.

Immediately following on Wheatley's letter Father Puissant, a Jesuit living in semi-retirement at Ayrshire, wrote to the *Observer*[20] and slated Wheatley for the use of the term Catholic Socialist. An insult, he said, to the good sense of Catholic voters. By using this term Wheatley is as forward as he is backward. Fr. Puissant, basing his argument on Pope Leo XIII's encyclical *Rerum Novarum*, then went on to claim that Christianity and Socialism were irreconcilable so therefore, by using the term Catholic Socialist, Wheatley was guilty of demagogy or of ignorance. He advised him to read the Catholic catechism through which he might become more humble and more Catholic.

In replying to Fr. Puissant's attack[21] Wheatley dismissed his accusations as being typical of the class that sent him down the pits with his father at an early age. Socialism, he said, was purely an economic question and had nothing at all to do with religion. 'If Fr. Puissant wishes to discuss the soundness of my economic or political doctrines then he must do so as a politician whose views I may accept or reject. I am also willing to discuss the question of Catholic Socialists having the right to form themselves into a separate body.'

This of course brought a reply from Fr. Puissant which was merely a restatement of his previous arguments, but couched in paternalistic language. He ignored Wheatley's deceptive call to discuss the right of Catholic Socialists to combine and instead challenged[22] him to debate a Catholic's right to be a Socialist. The challenge was accepted by Wheatley.

A Catholic taking on one of the secular clergy in debate could provoke, perhaps, some mild hysteria among the faithful. To take on a Jesuit was an entirely different matter for he would be seen by the ordinary Catholic layman as questioning the highest authority of the Church. To the average Catholic a Jesuit, by virtue of his lengthy training and the commonly held belief that only men of the highest intelligence were accepted by that order, was a kind of dragoman. Such a debate, no matter the outcome, could only result in a hardening of attitudes and consequently it would seem that Wheatley had nothing to gain and much to lose.

The debate provided some excitement and much correspondence in the Catholic press and *Forward* during the four months it lasted,[23] but little intellectual stimulus. Wheatley began by outlining the policy which the C.S.S. advocated, public ownership of land and the basic industries. This policy did not mean the complete abolition of private property and while he recognised the Pope's authority on matters of faith and morals he asked Fr. Puissant to point to one item in this policy which the Catholic Church could condemn as being contrary to Catholic dogma.

Fr. Puissant answered Wheatley's challenging question with a question as to how his Socialism would come about. He condemned Marxism because it was anti-God, and evolutionary Socialism as being contrary to Providence and the Natural Law. He gave quotes from the Bible as proof that private property existed from the time of Cain and Abel and thereafter his whole argument against Socialism evolved around the inherent right of man to own, quoting extensively from Pope Leo's encyclicals, without being explicit on Wheatley's question.

Wheatley persisted in his argument that economics was no part of Catholic dogma and that the main question was, could or could not Socialism work? He answered Fr. Puissant's question by stating that his Socialism would be achieved honestly, legally and gradually. He kept insisting on the right of his Society to be called Catholic as he recalled no objections being made by the clergy to the *Glasgow Observer*'s use of Catholic to describe a millionaire who was a member of the church.

The debate stuttered to a close with Fr. Puissant, while refusing to concede Wheatley's Society the right to be called Catholic, conceding that there was a case for the socialising of certain undertakings, but only if these came under the administration of Catholics.

There is no way of gauging what effect this debate had on the membership of the C.S.S. What it did lead to was a greater intensity of anti-Socialist propaganda in the pages of the *Glasgow*

Observer.[24] A speech,[25] sympathetic to Labour's cause, by Archbishop Maguire the Roman Catholic Archbishop of Glasgow did nothing to lessen this propaganda. He, more than his priests, had an understanding of the workers' struggle and the need for working class unity. A dozen years earlier[26] he had exhorted the young Catholic men to get out of their ghetto and work with their Protestant neighbours. He may not have publicly subscribed to Wheatley's Society, but he displayed no antagonism towards it. There was opposition to the C.S.S. from other quarters. The Irish made attempts to disrupt meetings by using strong arm tactics and were successful on at least one occasion.[27] Emmanuel Shinwell, for different reasons, tried unsuccessfully to disrupt meetings.[28] Shinwell, a future Government colleague of Wheatley's, had no doubt that Wheatley's Society was divisive to the Labour movement. He would attempt to break up meetings with continual shouts of 'there is no such a person as a Catholic Socialist'.

Jim Larkin, leader of the Irish Transport Workers Union, had misgivings as to the role of the C.S.S. possibly because of the problems he was facing in attempting to unite Catholic and Protestant workers in Belfast. He had achieved the almost impossible there by persuading not only the dockers and carters to come out on strike, but also a section of the police. In August he had come to Glasgow to address[29] a huge crowd who had turned up at Glasgow Green to demonstrate its solidarity with the Belfast strikers. Larkin had magnetic appeal and became a big favourite with the Glasgow workers. Not long after this demonstration he came back to Glasgow and addressed the C.S.S.[30] when he told his audience that after his earlier misgivings he now had nothing but praise for the work of the Society. He enrolled as a member at the close of this meeting. His joining could only have attracted more members to the Society.

Not long after Larkin gave his address, the Society began to report a quite rapid increase in membership.[31] By the summer of 1908 branches had been opened in Hamilton, Motherwell, Dundee and Leeds with prospects of branches being formed in Liverpool and Manchester. Coincident with the growth in membership was the more left wing variety of speakers that were invited to address the members. William Gallacher, later Communist M.P. for Fife, was to speak on more than one occasion.[32] His appearance at these meetings led to an association with Wheatley that was to last for many years. Helen Crawford, another founder member of the British Communist Party, addressed the Society on 'votes for women'.[33] She was at that time a leading figure in the Suffragette movement. With the Society's growth in numbers so apparently did Wheatley's influence grow in the Labour movement.

Just when it seemed that Wheatley was settling to the role of Socialist propagandist within his own community there was an unexpected turn in events. In October 1907[34] Wheatley was invited by the Shettleston branch of the I.L.P. to stand as their candidate for the Lower Shettleston Ward in the Lanarkshire Municipal elections to be held at the end of November. The branch decision to nominate Wheatley seems puzzling. He had given a lecture to the branch the previous year on 'the influence of the Irish movement in British politics'[35] but there is no record of his participating in the work of the branch prior to his nomination. Given Wheatley's method of working, could the invitation have been extended after he had made the initial approaches? Was it because of the predominant Irish vote in the Ward? If he accepted the nomination on this basis it would have been at odds with a later stated objection to this method of choosing candidates.[36] No matter, it was the beginning of a relationship with the I.L.P. that was to change the shape of politics in the West of Scotland.

There was so much stacked against Wheatley in this contest that the outcome looked predictable. It was not only his first incursion into the political arena but also that of a young branch with sixty on its roll, but whose effective membership was probably about ten.[37] There was little time to organise any kind of campaign and his opponent was the sitting Councillor Walter Grant, a Catholic and local businessman. Grant had the support of the U.I.L., the Catholic press and more important, Fr. Andrew O'Brien. Fr. O'Brien had never forgiven Wheatley for building the U.I.L. Hall and often his Sunday sermons were diatribes on Wheatley's politics and personality. John McGovern,[38] describing these sermons, recalled that in those days Wheatley often sported a straw hat and a white waistcoat and he said that Fr. O'Brien would introduce his sermon by sarcastically referring to those politicians with the white waistcoats. No doubt Wheatley's debate with Fr. Puissant would rate some caustic comments.

Wheatley fought a brave and enthusiastic campaign. 'Wheatley is putting up a great fight in Shettleston', *Forward* reported.[39] 'He talks nothing but Socialism and is having crowded meetings of men who have never heard Socialism taught before. His advice to the electors is, If you vote for Wheatley you vote for Socialism. If you don't want Socialism vote for Grant.' 1,006 voters didn't want Socialism as against the 581 who did. In the circumstances it was a creditable performance by Wheatley and it showed that he could be as effective on the public platform as he was with small cliques.

After this election Wheatley began to operate more in the mainstream of Socialist politics. At a branch meeting[40] in the month following the election he stressed the need to organise the working class vote in the area. He suggested that the branch circularise all those, who at the election, had given a verbal promise to vote Labour. These circulars should then be followed up with a personal visit to encourage them to join the Party. He emphasised the importance of personal contact in any recruitment campaign. At the A.G.M. the following March[41] the branch elected Wheatley as its Chairman and almost immediately a propaganda campaign was launched with a series of outdoor meetings throughout the area which were to last right through the summer. Coinciding with a period of widespread unemployment* these meetings attracted large crowds.[42]

Pat Dollan[43] gives us an amusing anecdote concerning one of these meetings. The meeting had been organised to help the newly formed Baillieston branch of the I.L.P. of which Dollan was Secretary. Wheatley was the principal speaker and he had brought Manus McGettigan along as his devil's advocate. The subject of his speech was the need for houses with modern conveniences in mining areas and he also mentioned the need for baths at the pithead. Unfortunately for Wheatley the crowd was won over by McGettigan who questioned the need for pit baths if houses with baths were going to be provided. The outcome of the meeting was that Wheatley and Dollan were chased by a turf throwing mob. This, despite the fact that Wheatley was well known locally. Indeed, he was now well known in most of Scotland's mining districts through his pamphlet 'Mines, Miners and Misery or How the Miners Were Robbed'.[44] This pamphlet, which was serialised in *Forward*, was a satirical attack on Mining Royalties and did much to increase Wheatley's stature in the Labour movement.

McGettigan was not only a political partner of Wheatley, but also a partner in a business venture which they had started that year.[45] While working with the *Glasgow Observer* Wheatley had conceived the idea of producing 'Tear Books' for use in Catholic parishes. With McGettigan he had started a publishing firm to put this idea into practice. They named the company Hoxton and Walsh,[46] the names were chosen from a telephone directory to

*In January 1908 the Lord Provost of Glasgow opened a fund to help alleviate the hardship of the widespread distress. Within 3 months there were more than 5,500 applicants to the fund. One of the worst hit areas was Parkhead, which was adjacent to Shettleston.

offset any bias that was expected from the clergy. This partnership, together with their political association, was to end with acrimony. The business was also to add to the suspicions of those who doubted the sincerity of Wheatley's Socialism.

Wheatley's C.S.S. added its weight to the propaganda campaign that summer with a number of open-air meetings. Jim Larkin addressed one of these meetings.[47] A significant change in the organisation of the C.S.S. was the appointment of William Regan[48] as Secretary. Regan, who was to remain close to Wheatley, played a prominent part in the growth and organisation of the I.L.P. in Glasgow. Towards the end of the year the Society and Labour in general received a boost with a remarkable speech by Archbishop Maguire.[49] In it he hailed the workers as the 'rulers of the future' and he advised the church 'not to enter into a life and death struggle with this rising democracy. Instead, it should keep firmly in touch with the Labour movement and temper it with the Christian spirit.' As before his words were ignored by the Catholic press and many of his clergy.

The adverse economic climate brought with it a surge of interest in Socialism. Thirty thousand people, a more than usual attendance, paraded at the May Day rally at Glasgow Green in 1909 where Wheatley's Society had its own platform.[50] The political Party which was the greatest beneficiary of this new interest was the I.L.P., the number of whose branches throughout the country had increased in April from 545 to 765.[51] Besides its propaganda work on the streets the Party gained much publicity with its practical efforts to help the distressed. Its representatives on the School Boards fought bitterly for the provision of free food and footwear for needy children. For the large numbers of women and children who had been made homeless in Glasgow the I.L.P. set up a night shelter at Gibson St. where food was also provided for the children.[52]

Unemployment, of course, brought with it angry demonstrations and spontaneous rioting where the only injured were the workers themselves.* Wheatley would have much preferred the action of the I.L.P. rather than see defenceless workers seek confrontation with an authority that was prepared to use the full force at its disposal. It may have been such demonstrations that provoked him to write a near seditious article[53] for *Forward*. Entitled 'Will There Yet Be Bloodshed' it was an attack on evolutionary Socialism and demonstrated how far to the left Wheatley had travelled in less than two years. The skill by which he introduced his article showed the legal aptitude that enabled

*On the Sunday following the visit of Prince Arthur to Glasgow when he was hissed and booed demonstrators were bludgeoned to the ground by the police.

him to avoid the restraint of the authorities during the revolutionary war years on the Clyde. He was merely putting forward arguments debated by three Socialists and himself on whether it would be wise to arm the young idealists of the Socialist movement, he said, and the arguments went thus:

'Those in favour reasoned that the Capitalist class are brainy people imbued with their fair share of love of self preservation. They have power and desire to maintain it. For this purpose the army is kept, paid and controlled by them. The mightiest will always rule and neither a Socialist red flag, a hymn book or a bible is proof against the bullet. While this destructive force of the bullet increases, the resisting power of the others does not. The men who control the bullet will become or remain top dogs. The question is, who shall control the bullet?

At this stage the evolutionary Socialist interrupted to work off his theory that Socialism would come gradually, almost imperceptibly, like grey hairs or Socialist organisation so that man would not know, or woman detect, the moment of change from earth to paradise. We squashed him as easily as if he had been a Featherstone miner before Asquith's rifles. This is how we did it. This is how Socialism would come if there were no Socialists or Capitalists. The weak man asks, the strong man takes or tries to take. Today the working classes are disorganised and economically ignorant, therefore weak beggars. Tomorrow they shall be organised and Socialist and intent on seizing. You seldom see the patience of sixty in a man of thirty and those who promise the Socialist movement, which will embrace the majority or almost the majority of the people, that the trick will be done quietly if they wait but fifty years will hear remarks something like those hurled by some at the heads of those who preach contentment in time for the glories of eternity. An enlightened working class will wish to do their evolution in a 50 horse-powered car. And then there is the Capitalist. Will he be evoluted out of existence? Not if he knows it and you will have some trouble keeping it secret. He will make it Evolution Ltd. old age pensions, clearer beer and cheaper tea, all those things you may have, but he will draw the line at evolutionising the National purse to your possession. That is the price of power which he will only yield to a stronger force.

This is where the political power man entered with his enlightened proletariat controlling Parliament with a class-conscious majority, who with the army behind him will tell the Capitalists to stand and deliver. We declined to admit the majority on the following grounds. A minority in the country is often represented by a majority in Parliament. Such was the case in 1905. It is probably the same at the moment.

Let us assume that the Capitalist party is in power with a majority of 100 obtained at a General Election which took place five years ago. Meanwhile a wave of Socialist enthusiasm has swept the country and there is no reasonable doubt that an election would result in the return of the Socialists to power for the first time. The Capitalists would know that this could only mean their destruction forever as a governing class. They must play their last card. Rule by the majority presupposes power to enforce their decision, but this being in the hands of the minority they rule. The Socialist movement is declared seditious and meetings are proclaimed as dangerous to the safety of the State. A 100,000 men meet on Glasgow Green and hold up their right hands in the usual manner to signify their favour to the establishment of a Socialist Commonwealth. A 1,000 trained troops are called from Maryhill Barracks and the chairman's speech is suspended to allow for the extraction of two bullets from his lungs. At this point the 'won't shoot his brother' Socialist broke in with flesh of our flesh, blood of our blood and class of our class story. He was reasoned out of his position thus. Generally speaking, the army is recruited from the least intelligent section of the workers. These will be among the last converts to Socialism. Their early life and training make them as obedient as performing dogs. It is possible they might refuse to shoot their own fathers, but certain they will shoot each others. By nature cowardly, they display no mercy where it is safe to be brutal. In front or behind a horde of coloured or defenceless workers they earn Royalist Capitalist gratitude. Faced by armed men as in the Boer war they will turn their trousers. A 1,000 of them will make a 100,000 trade unionists such a sight as will gladden the hearts of funeral undertakers. Arm 200 trade unionists and the troops will arrive safely in camp after being hotly pursued by the enemy for 40 miles. As there was no further evidence against we came to the following decision. Ruling power depends on force. All people desire power. The Capitalists control the force and while they do so they will prevent you obtaining power. To combat this force you must create an equal one or to overcome it, a superior one. Rifle clubs should be formed in connection with every branch of the Socialist movement. Members should be taught that prevention of bloodshed is their object. That plus propaganda will realise a bloodless revolution.'

What Wheatley was advocating was a citizen's army, a theme he was to return to much later in his political career. For an aspiring politician it was self-damaging and had he been considered a person of any consequence in the Labour movement the Tory press would have punished him. Fortunately it went unnoticed. Both the content and style of the article showed immaturity for a man who had reached his fortieth birthday.

He was also politically naive when he challenged Hilaire Belloc to a public debate, that took place later that year in the Metropole Theatre in Glasgow. Belloc, essayist and at that time Liberal M.P. for Salford, was considered one of Britain's leading exponents of Catholic social teaching. He had written a pamphlet 'Socialism is a Political Theory and therefore not practicable' and which was published by the Catholic Truth Society. Its publication had resulted in an exchange of views between Wheatley and Belloc in the *Tablet*,[54] the leading English Catholic journal. These exchanges had culminated in Wheatley challenging Belloc to a debate. Politically it seemed senseless, for the average Catholic worker did not read the *Tablet* nor is it likely that he had even heard of Belloc. Those Catholics who did admire Belloc possibly included some who hoped that here at last Wheatley would get his come-uppance. The subject chosen for the debate was 'Should Catholics support Socialism'[55] and it became obvious when Belloc spoke that he hadn't come to Glasgow to debate the subject matter. He quickly conceded that Catholicism was not dogmatically opposed to Socialism, but that Socialism could lead to slavery and thereafter advanced the cause of Distributism, an economic theory that espoused a more wide distribution of property.* Wheatley kept his arguments to the hard facts of life and, although he was judged by the audience to be the winner, it was a disappointing debate. The only real winner was the C.S.S. whose funds were swelled by the profits of the evening.

It was also apparent before this debate that there was a diminution in the enthusiasm of the Irish for Nationalist politics. The number of U.I.L. meetings being advertised in the *Glasgow Observer* had greatly decreased. A Municipal by-election in Hutchestown, a ward with a huge Irish population, had resulted in the return of the Labour candidate with a big majority. Following the election,[56] Peter Stewart had toured the district with a loudhailer thanking the Irish for giving him their support. Wheatley had published a pamphlet about then which must have been much more effective in attracting the Irish to Socialism than was his debate with Belloc. 'The Catholic Working Man[57]' with illustrations by Willie Regan was an emotional and satirical appeal to the Irish in this country to fight towards the destruction of Capitalism before Capitalism destroyed the Irish race.

Literature was also playing an important part in the affairs of the I.L.P. The Library was now an integral part of each branch with all kinds of Socialist literature made available to the members. In 1909, as part of the Glasgow Federation's propaganda campaign, the Shettleston branch organised a canvassing scheme[58] by which it planned to make contact with three to four thousand electors. Auxiliary membership was to be offered for the cost of one penny per month and for this sum a pamphlet could be obtained from the branch library. Wheatley's younger brother Patrick was by this time Literary Secretary of the Shettleston branch.[59] The campaign was to last right through to the Municipal elections of November 1910 where Wheatley was again to contest South Shettleston for the I.L.P. The money that Wheatley made from lectures helped largely to finance the whole

*An Essay on the Restoration of Property by Belloc was published by the Distributist League in 1936.

Glasgow campaign.[60] Wheatley never at any time made personal gain from either his writings or his lectures. It was an ambitious and strenuous campaign for Shettleston, though no doubt the previous influx of new and younger members of the calibre of John Scanlon[61] helped to make it possible. David Kirkwood, who first met Wheatley about this time, described[62] him as the great persuader and he recalled how Wheatley had gathered around him a number of young men from the East End of Glasgow whom he had converted to Socialism. Dollan could also tell of the weekly meetings[63] with these young men that were held in the Wheatley home where all kinds of reforms were discussed and he also added that 'no one could have had a better tutor for a Franciscan political life, for he taught them to work hard and sacrifice everything for the cause.' That some of these young men were later to have important roles in the Executive of the Glasgow Federation of the I.L.P. bears witness to the effect of Wheatley's teaching. However, it is also laid him open to the charge that he had begun early to build an organisation within an organisation and that he was indeed the great intriguer. In Wheatley's defence one can point to the very close relationship that later existed between him and James Maxton. Maxton hated intrigue and would not have been happy in the company of an intriguer.

The campaign met with the opprobrium of the clergy. In the nearby Carntyne Fr. Paterson denounced[64] Socialism from the pulpit and the methods being used by the I.L.P. to propagate it. Wheatley himself did nothing to reduce the friction between himself and the Catholic clergy. In 1910 he invited such anti-clerics as Larkin and James Connolly to lecture the C.S.S.[65] Larkin had only just been released from prison in Ireland for preaching sedition and Connolly and his Marxism had been the subject for a series of Lenten sermons given by a Jesuit Priest in a Dublin church.* John McLean had also addressed the Society on two occasions.[66] What was more damaging to the relationship between Wheatley and his church was an article he had written in the Autumn edition of the *Catholic Socialist*,[67] a short lived periodical published by the C.S.S. In this article he claimed that the reason for the Catholic Church's inability to win new adherents was its failure to carry out the social work which had been a mark of the pre-reformation church and consequently it was now played out. It was a simplistic Cobbett like view of the pre-reformation church yet it took some courage, perhaps foolhardiness, to express such a view with an election closely approaching.

*Connolly sat through these sermons which he answered in his book *Labour, Nationality and Religion*. It was a brilliant exposition of the Economic Determinism of Marx.

1906–1910

Events seemed to conspire to harm Wheatley's election prospects. The General Election of 1910 had brought sectarianism once again out into the open in Lanarkshire with the Liberals being the biggest offenders. They had handbills distributed which called on Catholics to support their priests by voting Liberal.[68] The Liberals had been returned to power but with a much reduced majority and were dependant on the support in Parliament of the eighty odd Irish Nationalists. Many of their reforms had been blocked by the House of Lords and eleven months later they returned to the country again looking for a mandate to curb the power of the Lords. The Nationalists took advantage of the situation to make Home Rule a live issue at this election and again sectarianism crept into the Lanarkshire campaigns. In Lanark N.E. Captain Boyd Carpenter, the Tory candidate, required to be escorted from an angry meeting for offensive remarks he had made about Catholics.[69] With these elections being held on the 13th December they completely overshadowed the Municipal elections of the previous week. Wheatley was further handicapped in that there was no Labour voice to be heard in Lanarkshire at the General Election. The Osborne judgement had so weakened Labour's finances that they were unable to contest many of the seats of previous years. In the event, the Liberals took both Lanark N.W. and Lanark N.E.

When the polls opened for the Municipal Elections it seemed that even the weather had joined in the conspiracy against Wheatley.[70] It was a cold, miserably wet day and the Shettleston branch did not have one single conveyance with which to help its supporters to the polling booth. Wheatley had to meet the same opposition, Walter Grant, the U.I.L. and the pulpit. Despite the odds Wheatley triumphed. It could not have been closer, 760 votes to 758 after four recounts.[71] It was a victory for the organisation and propaganda work of the previous three years. The recent propaganda campaign had its successes in Glasgow too, Labour gained four seats on the Council, increasing their representation to eleven.

An aftermath of Wheatley's victory was an attempt to set up an Independent Catholic Co-operative Society.[72] The move was initiated by Walter Grant and supported by the clergy and the reasons put forward for this move were that Catholic charities were being ignored by the Shettleston Co-op Society and that it was impossible for Catholics to be elected to the Board of Directors of the Society. 'The real inspiration behind this move,' wrote *Forward*, 'was that Wheatley had received the support of Shettleston Co-op at the election.'[73]

References

1. *Forward* – 6/4/18
2. *Glasgow Evening Times* – 15/5/30
3. *New Leader* – 7/11/24
   Eastern Standard – 8/11/24
4. *Glasgow Observer* – 24/2/06
5. *Forward* – 20/10/06
6. *Glasgow Observer* – 10/3/06
7. *Glasgow Observer* – 10/3/06
8. *Clydesiders* – R. K. Middlemass – 1965
9. *Neither Fear Nor Favour* – John McGovern – 1960
10. *Forward* – 2/12/06
11. Ibid.
12. John Wheatley – John Scanlon – (The book of the Labour, Party, Vol 3), 1925, H. Tracy
13. Ibid.
14. *Memoirs* – *Helen Crawford* (unpublished in the care of the Marx Memorial library)
15. John Wheatley – John Scanlon (The book of the Labour Party etc.)
16. *Glasgow Observer* – 3/12/07
17. *Forward* – 13/7/07
18. *Forward* 24/2/07
19. *Glasgow Observer* – 6/7/07
20. *Glasgow Observer* – 20/7/07
21. *Glasgow Observer* – 3/8/07
22. *Glasgow Observer* – 10/8/07
23. See *Glasgow Observer & Forward* for Correspondence on Debate
24. *Glasgow Observer* through 1908
25. *Forward* – 20/10/06
26. *Glasgow Examiner* – 12/5/1895
27. *Forward* – 14/3/08
28. *Neither Fear Nor Favour* – John McGovern – 1960
29. *Forward* – 3/8/07
30. *Forward* – 9/2/08
31. *Forward* – 5/9/08
32. *Forward* – 8/3/08 & 14/3/08
33. *Forward* – 23/2/08
34. Minutes of Shettleston Branch I.L.P. 30/10/07
35. Minutes of Shettleston Branch I.L.P. 21/3/06
36. *New Leader* – 29/6/23
37. Minutes of Shettleston Branch I.L.P. 25/8/07
38. *Neither Fear Nor Favour* – John McGovern 1960
39. *Forward* – 26/10/07
40. Minutes of Shettleston Branch I.L.P. 4/12/07
41. Minutes of Shettleston Branch I.L.P. 11/3/08
42. P. J. Dollan (unpublished *Memoirs*)
43. P. J. Dollan (unpublished *Memoirs*)
44. *Mines, Miners & Misery Or How The Miners Were Robbed* 1908
45. *Glasgow Herald* – 6/7/27
46. J. P. Wheatley – Correspondence
47. *Forward* – 10/6/08
48. *Forward* – 5/8/08

1906–1910

49. *Forward* – 4/10/08
50. *Forward* – 8/5/09
51. *Glasgow Evening Citizen* – 10/4/08
52. *Forward* – 14/3/09
53. *Forward* – 29/5/09
54. *Tablet* – October – 1909
55. *Forward* – 26/11/09
    John Wheatley – John Scanlon (The book of the Labour Party etc.)
56. *Forward* – 14/3/09
57. *Forward* – 8/5/09 (32 page pamphlet published by C.S.S.)
58. *Forward* – 16/10/09
59. Minutes of the Shettleston Branch of I.L.P. 25/3/09
60. *Forward* – 23/10/09
61. Minutes of the Shettleston Branch of I.L.P. 15/10/09
62. *My Life of Revolt* – D. Kirkwood – 1935
63. P. J. Dollan – *Memoirs*
64. *Forward* – 6/11/09
65. *Forward* – 9/10/10 & 23/10/10
66. *Forward* – 23/10/10
    Glasgow Observer – 12/12/09
67. *Catholic Socialist* – August 1910
68. *Forward* – 29/1/10
69. *Glasgow Evening Citizen* – 15/12/10
70. *Forward* – 11/12/10
71. *Neither Fear Nor Favour* – John McGovern – 1960
72. *Forward* – 18/2/11
73. Ibid.

Chapter Three
Council Politics

Wheatley attended his first meeting as an elected representative of the people at the County Buildings, Ingram St. Glasgow, on the 10th December, 1910.[1] Lanarkshire was divided into three administrative wards, the upper ward which was the southern part of the county, the middle ward with its centre in Hamilton, and the lower ward, that part adjacent to Glasgow which included Shettleston and Tollcross. Council meetings were held every three months and of the 48 representatives the most prominent were J. P. Baird of the Coal and Iron Company, Sir Nathaniel Dunlop, Sir Simon McDonald Lockhart and Colonel King Stewart who was elected Chairman at the first meeting.[2] These men represented the industrial, commercial and property interests of the county and were the powerful voices in the making of decisions. Those on the Council who shared Wheatley's convictions were lamentably few: David Hardie, brother of Keir Hardie, and James Tonner from the mining village of Blantyre were his strongest supporters.

Wheatley quickly adapted to the work of Municipal politics and for the two years he served on this Council he was to prove a hard working and relatively successful Councillor. He seemed to mature politically with the added responsibility, for he was able to separate, with the proper emphasis, the special needs of his constituents from the broader issues and he also recognised the value of the Council as a political forum. Significantly, health and housing were his major concern. His first act was to call for an immediate, and thereafter regular, inspection of the storage tanks from which the people of Shettleston drew their water supplies. The initial inspection revealed that the tanks were a serious health hazard, many of them being without covers with some of these having drowned rats and mice in them.[3] He was successful in initiating a survey being carried out in Shettleston as a preliminary to a Town Planning Scheme and within two years he could report that the wheels had been set in motion for such a scheme for Shettleston and Tollcross.[4]

On the wider field he fought stubbornly to help the sufferers, and prevent the spread, of tuberculosis. He refused to support a proposal by the Council for a Memorial to King Edward VII unless it took the tangible form of provision of treatment for consumptive persons.[5] Insanitary housing he saw as being the chief contributory factor to the spread of T.B. and he condemned the Council for its lack of effort in seeking to improve the standards of miners' houses and he proposed that 'single room back-to-back houses be declared uninhabitable.'[6] The 1909 Housing Act had given Local Authorities powers to issue closing orders on properties which they considered to be sub-standard. While the Council ignored this proposal a similar proposal by Wheatley to the Scottish Conference on T.B. at Edinburgh was unanimously approved.[7] Wheatley was afterwards responsible for the issue of a Closing Order[8] on properties in Cleland which were owned by the Coalmaster, John Agnew. This was not a popular order with the tenants of these properties who seemed quite content with their surroundings. A motion calling on the Council 'to petition the Government to give financial aid to Local Authorities to provide healthy dwellings on terms that would bring them within reach of every family in the community'[9] had an apocalyptic ring.

One of the promises that he had made when campaigning for this seat was that he would press for an improvement in the wages and conditions of Council employees[10] and here he had mixed results. He was successful at the first attempt to secure an increase of 3/- per week for Lamplighters bringing their wages up to 26/- per week.[11] He fought hard to get a similar increase for Scavenging workers whose job he described as being equal only in its service to the community to that of the medical service.[12] He failed in his first attempt, but at the second attempt he managed to have their pay increased from 20/- per week to 22/-.[13] He was also responsible for having these workers provided with oilskins. With the support of David Hardie he eventually was able to get the council to agree to have a Fair Wage clause on all contracts for Council work,[14] but his plea for a reduction in the long hours worked by nurses fell on deaf ears.[15] On the face of things, these wage increases that Wheatley was able to obtain for Council employees looked good, but one has to compare them with neighbouring Glasgow which had a minimum scale of 25/- per week and where Labour Councillors faced similar weighty opposition. To be fair though, it was only when Wheatley joined the Glasgow Council that the same minimum scale was built into contracts for all Council work.

Outside the Council, Wheatley found an opportunity to bring his campaign for higher wages to a much wider public. In August

1911 the railway workers had gone on strike for more pay. It was a strike that led to demonstrators clashing with the troops and the fatal shooting of two of the demonstrators. In the middle of the strike Wheatley wrote in defence of the strikers claim and putting forth his views on the fundamental cause of the strike.[16]

'The root cause of the trouble was that £47 million was taken out of the railways by their shareholders who gave no service to the creation of this surplus. Whatever they do as directors or managers is paid for in addition. Less than £30 million is paid in wages to the railway employees. By raising rates and reducing the number of workers the profits of the master class are increased. By every improvement whereby men are discharged the value of the servant is decreased. The ever improving organisation of those who control our food supplies raises the cost of living. The stationary wages of the worker purchases less and less. In the midst of abundant and ever increasing wealth the producer struggles and sometimes starves while idlers take so much in one year that would maintain them in luxury for a thousand years. The mere fact of some claiming more than they can use in itself adds to the evil. Workers obtain wages and consequently food in proportion as their services are required. If the rich could spend as they receive there would be more work, more wages and more food for the workers. Or, if the surplus wealth was divided among those who had unsatisfied wants and would be used immediately the same result would be achieved.'

It was the embryo of his theory of the lack of effective demand which over the next twelve years he was to develop and expound.

Wheatley did not shed any of his other commitments when he took up his Council work. He lectured, he was still deeply involved with the C.S.S., his business demanded much of his time and his family had suffered a bereavement. He was still very much in charge of the local branch of the I.L.P. where his brother Pat was now vice-chairman[17] and to which John McGovern had by this time been introduced.[18] He had arranged the purchase of the branch's own premises in William St. where Saturday evening socials were being held.[19] It was ironic that these premises were bought from the U.I.L. (Fr. O'Brien would have had mixed feelings over the change of ownership). One cause from which Wheatley had completely severed all connection was the U.I.L. It was strange that he maintained a connection with this organisation for so long, he was still a member up to as late as 1909. Even so, his work load was to increase still further.

While Wheatley was settling in to his work as a Councillor in Lanarkshire talks between that County and Glasgow had been going on which were to lead eventually to a radical change in circumstances, not only for Wheatley but for Glasgow itself. For some years Glasgow had been seeking to extend its boundaries in a bid to reduce the density of its population. Parliament had been petitioned and negotiations had been taking place between representatives of Glasgow and the areas which it had hoped to annexe. Shettleston was one of the areas and Wheatley had himself been involved in the negotiations. He had been personally opposed to Shettleston's annexation, but eventually agreed on the condition that Shettleston and Tollcross be considered as an entity in any proposed administration change.[20] These negotiations reached a satisfactory conclusion early in 1912 and a Boundaries Bill was quickly processed through Parliament. The Bill received the Royal Assent in August the same year to become effective on the first Tuesday of the November following. Along with other suburban areas, Shettleston and Tollcross together with the burghs of Partick, Govan and Polockshaws came under the administration of Glasgow. Wheatley now had to resign his seat in the Lanarkshire Council and contest it again in the elections for the Greater Glasgow Council.

Events leading up to this election looked certain to destroy any hopes Wheatley had of a seat in Glasgow's City Chambers. Basically these events had similar origins to those which threatened him at the previous election, the Catholic Church and the Home Rule movement.

In the June preceding the new elections Father Andrew O'Brien had given a sermon that was not merely abusive to Wheatley, but an attack on his character. In it he accused Wheatley of being a hired slanderer and a professional propagandist for Socialism. This time Wheatley did not sit quietly back. He replied to these allegations through the pages of *Forward*.[21] He denied that he had ever received nor would he ever take a penny for his writings. 'Father O'Brien would go to any lengths to find a Socialist who had deprived a worker of a shilling, but would ignore the wholesale exploitation of workers. Why did he not denounce pawnbrokers and moneylenders?' Wheatley was alluding to members of Fr. O'Brien's family who were engaged in these enterprises. He concluded his defence by stressing that he did not confuse clericalism with Christianity which, like anything else of value in the world, was created by a member of the working class. *Forward* printed extra copies of this edition for sale in Shettleston.

There was immediate reaction[22] to Wheatley's published statement. Incited by Fr. Morrissey, a curate in the parish, a number of young girls attacked a Mr. Fleming who had been Wheatley's election agent and who was also a member of the local School

Board. In lauding this action from the pulpit Fr. Morrissey added the wish that the men had half the courage of their sisters. As a result, a Parish meeting was held on the Sunday afternoon to decide what action should be taken against Wheatley for his slur on the Parish Priest. It was decided that a protest should be made at an I.L.P. meeting which had been scheduled to take place at Shettleston Cross on the following evening. Fortunately this meeting was called off at the last minute because of the unavailability of the invited speaker. However, some of the younger members of the branch decided foolhardily to hold a meeting and brought out the soap box. There were only a few people present when more than a thousand parishioners arrived at the Cross carrying with them an effigy of Wheatley. Disappointed at not confronting Wheatley they attacked one of the young speakers. Not content with this they then turned on Mr. Fleming whom they proceeded to kick unmercifully with the result that he sustained a broken leg. The crowd then marched to Wheatley's home which was occupied at the time by Wheatley's two children who were being tended by friends, Mr. and Mrs. McAleer, while waiting on Wheatley and his wife to return from an evening stroll. When Wheatley arrived home, via the back entrance, he and Mr. McAleer went to the front doorstep and confronted the howling mob for more than an hour, all the while Wheatley calmly stood puffing his pipe. This show of courage no doubt prevented any damage to persons or property and the vigil ended with the mob singing 'Faith of our Fathers' and the burning of Wheatley's effigy in his garden.

There was no mention of this in the *Glasgow Observer* – space was reserved for reports of Catholics being persecuted in Belfast – and it was left to *Forward* to report the incident. Alongside this report Wheatley made an appeal to the mob in what was headlined 'Shettleston Special'.[23]

'Fellow workers, on Monday night you gathered in your hundreds or thousands to prove that you hated me. You cursed and swore and you prayed. You proved that you are still a force to be reckoned with, but you grieved me by your cowardly and unjustified assault on innocent people. I would prefer a thousand times that you punished me alone. Why do you demonstrate so seldom and why is it always on behalf of somebody else?

The earth and materials on it have been given to you by God so that you could develop for yourselves a cultured lifestyle. They have been stolen from you so that you have to beg and crawl for an existence. You are the people who build everything for which you receive scant reward. The mansions you have built for the rich are owned by them and you do not even own the miserable hovels in which you live. Instead, you are insultingly told that you choose to live there so that you may have enough for booze. You stand by and see your children murdered by the conditions in which you live. I have never murdered any of your children, it is poverty that kills them. In order to change this system and be independent of the rich you must be rich in body, stand shoulder to shoulder, unite in your workshops and be unanimous at the polling booth.

I did not attack your priest, I merely defended my character. My reputation is all I have and while I have strength to strike, no-one will attack me with impunity.'

One cannot say whether Wheatley expected such a reaction to this public defence of his character. It may not have been the wisest course to take with an election looming, but he displayed an honesty and courage that was to be characteristic of his political life. The incident would take some time to be erased from local memory and, added to the bitter controversy that was raging over Home Rule in the months that led up to the Municipal elections, even Wheatley's most fervent supporters gave little for his prospects.

Home Rule was being debated in Parliament and the old sectarian wounds had begun again to fester. In the West of Scotland the debate spilled over to the local press, the streets and the Municipal elections. Large public meetings were being addressed by prominent members of both the Orange[24] and Nationalist[25] factions and in some wards[26] the Irish were putting forward their own candidates for election. In this situation Wheatley looked like the pig in the middle. He was a Catholic disowned by his own and representing a Party which supported Home Rule. He was also handicapped in that he did not have the support of the powerful Ward Committee.*

The new Greater Glasgow was now composed of 37 electoral wards each having three representatives on the Council. Labour, who held 11 seats in the old Council, had candidates in only 20 of these wards.[27] The creation of the Glasgow Labour Party the previous year,[28] the brain-child of the I.L.P., had boosted Labour's confidence for this election. It had been established principally to unify and control all working class organisations in the city. Candidates approved by it could expect help in organising and publicising their election campaigns. For this election the G.L.P. had issued an 8 page manifesto[29] in support of a policy on

*These Committees had their origin in the Citizens' Union which had been formed in 1898, whose aim it was to assist in securing the election of suitable persons to the Town Council and to further the good government of Glasgow. It was described in its constitution as being non-political and non-sectarian and membership was open to those in favour of these aims. By 1912, while yet claiming to be non-political it had a programme which was opposed to Municipal Socialism and Municipal Trading. The support of this body was normally looked on as essential to anyone with an ambition to be a City Councillor.

Workmen's Cottages which had been pursued by the Labour members on the old Council. In Shettleston, the I.L.P. put forward only the one candidate and advised its supporters to use only one of the three votes allowed them. The elections were scheduled for the 4th November and Wheatley opened his campaign in the second to last week of October[30] with support from the most unlikely quarter, the Syndicalist Socialist Labour Party. It is possible that his friendship with James Connelly played some part in this.

Wheatley's election address signposted the way in which he intended to lead the Socialist movement in Glasgow. He began by promising to confine his work on the Town Council to the practical application of Socialist policy. He then went on to condemn the shocking high rates of T.B. and infant mortality and he compared disparately the death rate of children under 12 months in working class areas to those in middle class areas, 178 per thousand in Blackfriars as against 45 per thousand in Kelvinside.

"Everyone argues that there is a need for radical change in housing policy, but no-one has dared to put forward a scheme. If there was financial profit to be made in solving the housing problem there would be 100 competitors offering plans to show how it could be done."

The housing problem would not be solved until the working classes produced their own scheme and controlled the council to bring the scheme into operation. He had no great faith in the Council's proposed 400 cottages which in any case would be too little. He favoured not only working class cottages, but the purchase and improvement of tenements. In his address he also advocated a Municipal Bank which would free Glasgow of heavy interest charges, it was a theme he was to return to again and again.

The 'Wheatley Wins' posters displayed[31] at the polling booths reflected his own confidence, but it is doubtful if even he expected to get such a large slice of the vote. With 2,129 votes he was returned top of the poll, a truly remarkable performance. The two other successful candidates were Vass Graham and George Dott, both of whom had the support of the Ward Committee.[32] They received 1,751 and 1,655 votes respectively. How, in the face of such odds did Wheatley manage to win such a decisive victory? John Scanlon said[33] that 'the Fr. O'Brien affair had an opposite effect. Protestants indifferent to Wheatley's politics, but angry at the treatment he had received from his own church, turned out in their hundreds to support him.' This explanation is rather naive and perhaps insulting to the intelligence of the working class voter. Wheatley had gained a considerable reputation for what he had achieved for the people as a Lanarkshire Councillor and had made a practice of reporting back regularly to his constituents. He

Council Politics

kept his promises and was respected for that more than his religion. In so far as the Fr. O'Brien incident was concerned, it would have brought nothing but amusement to many Protestants.

In Glasgow as a whole Labour's results did not match their expectations. They entered the new Council with a mere 14 representatives. At a post mortem carried out by the Glasgow Trades Council the blame was laid on Labour's poor organisation and in some cases the lack of the Irish vote. Obviously the G.L.P. needed more time to build an effective organisation. The Trades Council was, however, fulsome in its praise of Wheatley's success in Shettleston.[34]

References

1. Lanarkshire County Council Minutes 12/12/10
2. Ibid.
3. *Forward* – 28/9/12
4. Ibid.
5. Lanarkshire County Council Minutes – 1/3/11
6. Lanarkshire County Council Minutes – 13/12/11
7. Lanarkshire County Council Minutes – 19/7/11
8. *Forward* – 6/1/12
9. Lanarkshire County Council Minutes – 13/12/11
10. *Neither Fear Nor Favour* – John McGovern – 1960
11. *Forward* – 28/9/12
12. Ibid.
13. Ibid.
14. Ibid.
15. *Forward* – 28/9/12
16. *Glasgow Evening Times* – 25/8/11
17. Minutes of Shettleston Branch I.L.P. – 27/3/11
18. *Neither Fear Nor Favour* – John McGovern
19. Minutes of Shettleston branch I.L.P. – April 1910
20. *Forward* – 28/9/12
21. *Forward* – 29/6/12
22. *Forward* – 6/7/12
23. Ibid.
24. *Glasgow Evening Times* – 19/10/12
25. Ibid.
26. *Glasgow Evening Times* – 7/11/12
27. *Glasgow Evening Times* – 5/11/12
28. Glasgow Labour Party Minutes – 18/5/11
29. *Forward* – 26/10/12
30. Ibid.
31. *Glasgow Evening Times* – 5/11/12
32. Ibid.
33. *John Wheatley* – John Scanlon (Book of the Labour Party)
34. *Glasgow Evening Times* – 7/11/12

Chapter Four
£8 Cottages

With the boundary changes Glasgow's population had increased from 784,000 to 1,010,000. More than two thirds of this increase came with the annexation of the burghs of Govan and Partick which stood respectively on the south and north banks of the upper reaches of the river Clyde. These burghs had witnessed remarkable growth in a short period of time with the rise of the shipbuilding industries. Govan, which half a century earlier had been a mere village with 9,000 inhabitants, was by now the largest Police Burgh in Scotland with a population of close on 100,000.[1] During approximately the same period Partick's population had increased from 11,000 to almost 60,000.[2] The inhabitants of both these burghs were housed mainly in four storey tenement buildings of one and two apartments. If the boundary changes had reduced the density of Glasgow's population it also added to a housing problem that had previously been described as one of the worst in Europe. 62% of the City's population were residing in one and two apartment houses*[3] where the death rate for children under 12 months was 165 per 1,000.[4] With the steady influx of new labour to meet the demands of the Government's re-armament programme, overcrowding was a major concern to the health authorities. Some Labour leaders were also concerned that landlords were taking advantage of the serious shortage of accommodation by increasing rents.

Before Wheatley entered into Glasgow's politics, different bodies had been making efforts to alleviate the worst excesses of the housing problem. The Sanitary Department under Peter Fyfe worked night and day in trying to prevent overcrowding reaching disastrous levels.[5] The Royal Society of Physicians and Surgeons had put forward a resolution to the Council which called for the closing of slum properties and for the building of specially structured housing to cater for T.B. patients.[6] There were 2,340 notified cases of T.B. in Glasgow in 1912.[7] The fight against increased rents had been taken up by John McLean's Defence of the Tenants Association[8] and in the Council John Stewart led the small Labour Group's bid to have workmen's cottages erected.

*Of the City's housing stock of approximately 200,000, 23.1% were one apartment and 46.3% were two apartment.

36

£8 Cottages

The 1890 Housing Act had given the Corporation power to erect workmen's cottages and although Glasgow was not lacking in Municipal enterprises – Gas, Water, Electricity and a most efficient Tramway service were managed by the City – its efforts to house the poorer classes were inept. The Council did have a committee for the Erection of Workmen's Cottages and proposals had already been considered, and tenders received, for the erection of 240 cottages at a site in Riddrie[9] and the Labour group had envisaged these as being the first of 1,000 such houses.[10]

In a Council where the new Lord Provost, Daniel Stevenson, and nearly a third of the Councillors had vested interests in Glasgow's private housing,[11] Wheatley had every reason to be sceptical of this scheme ever being approved. He himself had been preparing a housing scheme which he had submitted to the Glasgow Labour Party[12] even before he joined the Glasgow Council. It was a scheme which was instrumental in changing the whole complexion of politics in Glasgow yet, at the time, it looked as if he were trying to undermine the policy of the Labour group in the Council, a policy which had the support of the Trade Unions, Co-operative Society and other Friendly Societies[13]

'The scheme, which was to be published in pamphlet form the following year under the title of "£8 cottages", was for the building of 1,000 cottages by the Corporation at Riddrie, each costing £260 and to be let at an annual rent of £8. The cottages were to be of the exact type proposed in the Corporation scheme where prices quoted by the contractor were £199 per house and where rents had been fixed at £15–15s for three apartments and £18 for four apartments. Wheatley's cottages would cost an additional £26 to offset any increased costs in building and a further £35 to meet the cost of land, roads and sewage. Fifteen houses were to be built on each acre and, at £253 per acre, this represented a cost of £17 per house. The rent included £4–6s–8d towards repayment of capital over a 60 year period. The capital for this project was to be borrowed, interest free, from an estimated surplus from the Tramways. Wheatley considered this surplus as being a conservative estimate based on figures and reports provided by the Corporation itself.'[14]

If there was scepticism over the proposals before the Corporation being accepted then surely no-one, not even Wheatley, could believe that this scheme would be greeted with any greater fervour from a Tory dominated Council. Surprisingly, one month after the elections the G.L.P., at a special meeting, agreed to adopt Wheatley's scheme and make it a major policy issue.[15] This decision, which virtually installed Wheatley as leader of the Labour movement in Glasgow, was taken as John Stewart was putting forward the Corporation scheme to the C.S.S. as Labour's solution to Glasgow's housing problem.[16]

Despite the G.L.P.'s decision, the Labour group continued its fight in the Council for the Riddrie scheme. Its hopes were raised when the Special Committee on Workmen's Cottages passed the scheme to the full Council for approval.[17] The Tory majority, or Progressives as they were named in Glasgow, had however, already signalled their intention not to support the scheme. They now saw the solution to the housing problem as lying in the very heart of the city. The slums could be demolished and new tenements built on the same site or old tenements bought over and improved. They were strengthened in this by the claims of the chairman of the Liverpool Housing Committee that it had proved the best policy in that city, for it had meant that the workers were still living in houses adjacent to their places of work.[18] It was this argument that was used to defeat the Riddrie proposal when it came before the full Council on the 3rd April. The Progressive's amendment described the scheme as an insult to the poor people of Glasgow and one which would only aggravate the housing problem. There was uproar in the Council when the result of the voting was announced, which led to the expulsion of John Stewart from the Chambers.[19]

The Corporation's decision gave free rein to Wheatley's scheme. The housing problem was now to be taken directly to the people themselves. Towards the end of that year the Glasgow Labour Housing Committee was formed[20] and it brought to the forefront another of Wheatley's East End protégés. Andrew McBride was a member of the C.S.S. and also of the Bridgeton branch of the I.L.P.[21] The aim of this committee was to publicise Wheatley's cottage scheme and organise the fight against increased rents.[22] Thousands of handbills were printed and distributed.[23] Public meetings were called in every part of the City where resolutions were passed and deputations appointed to petition the Council.[24] At the Municipal elections in November the cottage scheme was the central issue in Labour's campaign with Wheatley's pamphlet being widely distributed.[25] Opposition to the scheme in this campaign only served to heighten the interest. The inordinate amount spent by the Citizens Union in campaigning against the scheme intensified the debate at the Ward Committees.[26] Wheatley's defence of his scheme in a public debate with James Miller,[27] Chairman of the Shettleston branch of the Unionist Party, could only have benefited James Walker, the Labour candidate in that area. In this election, Labour gained six seats and lost two. In addition to Walker, the Labour group on the council would have been happy to welcome James Welsh from Dalmarnock in the East End and Dollan, representing Govan.

£8 Cottages

Obviously Labour's Housing scheme contributed greatly to Labour's successes in this election, for in the two seats that were lost, Maryhill and Cowcaddens, housing did not figure prominently in the Labour candidates' campaigns. Following on this Wheatley attempted to block the selection by the G.L.P. of Municipal candidates who were unwilling to give 100% support to his scheme. In the case of George Smith, nominated for a by-election by the Woodside Ward, the G.L.P. refused to bow to Wheatley's objections.[28] Smith's refusal to endorse the £8 cottage scheme was singled out by his opponent in the election as a split in the Labour ranks. However, Smith did subsequently give a promise to Wheatley that, in the event of the cottage scheme coming before the council, he could count on his support.[29]

At the beginning of 1914 Wheatley took steps to widen the area of support. With McBride and John S. Taylor, secretary of the G.L.P., he addressed a meeting of the Trades Council in the City Halls in support of the following resolution:[30]

(1) That this meeting of householders protest against the action of houseowners in seeking to increase the burden on tenants by compelling them to pay excess rates* and by adding to the already high rents.
(2) Being of the opinion that no Act of Parliament can prevent the houseowners from increasing rents or passing their share of the rates on to the tenant and we believe that the time has now arrived when the Corporation should proceed to erect and acquire houses for the citizens of Glasgow and for that purpose we press for an annual loan, free of interest, from the Tramways surplus or any other source from which Capital can be obtained on similar terms.
(3) This meeting pledges itself to support the policy outlined in previous resolutions by forming a committee to prepare a petition in support of same and herewith appoint a deputation to wait on the Town Council in support of this resolution.

Speaking in support of the resolution Wheatley made reference to the recent annual meeting of the Houseowners Association at which he said 'it had been boldly and impertinently stated that rents would be increased from between five and ten per cent. If the Labour Party scheme was adopted they, the Trades Council, would find that competition would force down the rents of tenement houses.' The resolution was carried unanimously and Shinwell and Cairns were voted to carry it to the Town Council. This was but the beginning of Wheatley's bid to involve all elements of the working class in a common cause. Almost immediately after

*The House Letting (Scotland) Act of 1911 allowed for the compounding of rents and rates and landlords were taking advantage of this to pass on an unequal amount of rates to the tenants.

this meeting, the Glasgow Housing Association came into being. Sponsored by the Labour Housing Association it was representative of the G.L.P., Labour members of the Council, Women's Labour League and the Trades Council. Its purpose was to (1) Establish branches in each of the City's Wards, (2) Organise the tenants to fight against increased rents and (3) Support Wheatley's cottage scheme.[31] Shortly afterwards an appeal was made through *Forward* for persons who would be willing to be trained as speakers to carry the message of £8 Cottages to every part of the City. Speakers Conferences would be arranged. The appeal was signed by Wheatley, Johnston, John Stewart and J. S. Taylor.[32]

All this activity took place during a period when there was widespread industrial unrest. J. R. Clynes, then leader of the General Municipal Workers, stated that the nation had been terrorised by more than a thousand strikes in the eighteen months preceding the First World War. He maintained that it was only the outbreak of war that prevented a bloody revolution.[33] The failure of wages to meet the rising cost of living was the cause of these strikes. Wheatley's fight on behalf of the low paid workers both inside and outside the Council Chambers would have gone a long way towards winning the confidence and support of the local workers' leaders, many of whom were members of the S.L.P.

In taking up the cudgels on behalf of the lowly paid, Wheatley, in what was to be characteristic of him, used the facts and figures provided by his opponents in support of his arguments. One month after his election a proposal came before the Council to increase the close sweepers pay by 1/– per week. This class of workman was being paid 22/– per week and previous attempts to have their wages brought up to the Corporation minimum had been treated almost with contempt. A close sweeper's job was considered suitable only for the elderly or physically handicapped and the prevailing attitude was that these people were fortunate that the Corporation could provide them with such work. Wheatley put forward an Amendment for a 3/– increase and he supported this by pointing out that, when the Council had agreed to the 25/– miminum, they had done so only after it had been proved that a man could not sustain himself and his family for less. Therefore, it remained for those who supported the proposal to prove that 23/– was a sufficient rate for subsistence.[34] His Amendment was defeated, but he was instrumental in having the sweepers' hours reduced from 54 to 48.[35] He was supported in his amendment by Rosslyn Mitchell, a Liberal -

lawyer. Mitchell was later to come under the influence of Wheatley and convert to the I.L.P. where his legal training was to prove invaluable.

Shortly after this Wheatley again made full use of official figures to publicise the plight of the poorly paid. The results of a survey carried out by the Corporation on whether the working classes had a diet sufficient for them to do a hard day's work were seized on by him. He claimed[36] that, on the basis of these results, the working classes were being slowly starved to death. Seven groups had been interviewed for this survey whose incomes ranged from 20/- to 30/- per week. From the figures provided, Wheatley stated that in the top income group three of the seven families were slowly starving to death and those in the lowest income groups would starve to death even without doing a day's work. While Labour representatives in Parliament and elsewhere were debating about below-minimum wage levels Wheatley preferred to speak in terms of starvation levels, language that was readily understood by the workers fighting, often using violence,* for decent standards.

It was not only poverty that the workers fought against in 1913 and the first part of 1914. The war drums had been beating throughout Europe during this period and the Socialist movement, not only in Britain, but on the continent had been demonstrating for peace. The International Socialist Bureau had issued a manifesto condemning war, Keir Hardie and Arthur Henderson were the British signatories. The most outspoken of Glasgow's opposition were Maxton, John McLean and the Reverend James Barr whose anti-war sermons were acclaimed in the Socialist press. Wheatley, while his opposition to the war was well known, took no prominent part in any of the demonstrations. Perhaps, on this occasion, he guessed the fickleness of the mood in Glasgow for, right up until the eve of the outbreak of war, there was strong opposition to the threatened hostilities, but immediately war was declared it evaporated in a wave of jingoistic fervour.[37]

References

1. *History of Govan* – T. C. F. Brotchie – 1905
2. *Partick Past and Present* – C. Taylor – 1902
3. *The Making of a City* – Andrew Gibb – 1983

*The Employers Parliamentary Committee met in London in February, 1914, to inquire into the workings and effects of the Trades Disputes Act 'in view of the growing menace to personal freedom, public order and industrial peace.' They were seeking amendments to the law regarding picketing.

4. Ibid.
5. Ibid.
6. Glasgow Corporation Minutes – 13/1/13
7. *M.O.H. Report* – 1912
8. *John McLean* – Nan Milton
9. Glasgow Corporation Minutes – 13/1/13
10. *Forward* – 22/11/12
11. *Forward* – 30/1/15
12. Glasgow Labour Party Minutes – 12/9/12
13. *Forward* – 19/10/12
14. *£8 Cottages* – Civic Press
15. Glasgow Labour Party Minutes – 12/12/12
16. *Forward* – 23/11/12
17. *Glasgow Evening Times* – 4/4/13
18. *Daily Record and Mail* – 1/2/13
19. Glasgow Corporation Minutes – 3/4/13
    Glasgow Evening Times – 4/4/13
20. *Forward* – 4/12/15
21. Glasgow Corporation Minutes – 3/4/13
    Forward – 18/11/11
22. *Forward* – 4/12/15
23. Glasgow Labour Party Minutes – January 1924
24. Glasgow Corporation Minutes – 23/12/13
    Partick and Maryhill Express – January – 1914
25. *Glasgow Evening Times* – 4/11/13
26. *Glasgow Evening Times* – 31/10/13
27. *Forward* – 19/10/13
28. Glasgow Labour Party Minutes – 12/6/14
29. *Forward* – 27/6/14
30. *Glasgow Evening Times* – 22/1/14
31. *Forward* – 4/3/16
32. *Forward* – 29/3/14
33. *Memoirs* – J. R. Clynes – Vols 1 – 2 – 1937
34. *Forward* – 4/1/13
35. Glasgow Corporation Minutes – 11/9/13
36. *Forward* – 8/3/13
37. *No Mean Fighter* – Harry McShane – 1976

Chapter Five
The Rent Strike

The war had split the Labour movement in Europe. Many of its leaders who preached international brotherhood had now become decidedly nationalistic. In Britain, Trade Union leaders, amongst whom were Henderson and Clynes, were fully behind the Government in waging war against Germany. There was one notable exception, Bob Smillie the miners leader. In Glasgow, only two of Labour's Councillors were known for their opposition to the war, Wheatley and John S. Taylor.[1] It was not until after conscription was introduced that Dollan and others joined in the opposition. Nevertheless, Wheatley seemed content to let the more charismatic figures such as McLean and Maxton preach the gospel of peace. Maxton, with whom Wheatley was now beginning to forge close ties, gave the outward expression to Wheatley's sentiments when he delivered a violent anti-war speech to the C.S.S. shortly after its outbreak.[2] It was not that Wheatley lacked the courage to express his own convictions, he would never have commanded the respect he was to gain later. His opposition was to be of a different nature.

As the war got under way it soon became evident that Wheatley's policy was to focus attention on its harmful social and economic effects. Panic buying at the start of the war had caused a sharp increase in the prices of bread and sugar and within four months the cost of living had increased by 19%.[3] Those most affected by this rise in the cost of living were the dependants of servicemen causing a high increase in applications for Poor Relief. Wheatley pressed the Council to open a Glasgow Relief Fund to aid those either directly or indirectly affected by war and particularly those necessitous families not covered by the Prince of Wales War Relief Fund.[4] Wheatley later exposed to the press the high administrative costs of this fund[5] which had been set up at the beginning of the war to help only those directly affected by the war. Following his exposure the Glasgow War Emergency Workers committee advised the workers to stop contributing to the fund.[6]

There were some who believed that the distress caused to some was self inflicted, particularly by the abuse of alcohol. One Poor

Law official described the applicants for relief as being 'women of a very low class, living in slums and drinking whenever they could get it thus dissipating their separation allowances'.[7] Alcohol was also being blamed for poor performance in industry and a prominent poster of the time was 'THE DRUNK WORKER FIGHTS FOR GERMANY'.[8] However, when the President of the Abstainers Union openly accused the workers and dependant wives for excess spending on drink Wheatley quickly sprang to their defence. 'He is indulging in the popular pastime of insulting the workers. This practice, which cannot be justified, is rapidly becoming mischievous and if persisted in could cause incalculable injury.' Wheatley invited the accuser to visit Shettleston where he would find that there was less money spent per head on drink than there was in the West End of the City.[9] Wheatley was ever vigilant in protecting the character and interests of the workers.

In fighting causes, which for many at the time would seem trivial, he made use of events. One example was his fight to win a decent burial for the very poor. It had been the practice in Glasgow since 1833 for the Sanitary Inspector to hand over the remains of those whose relatives could not afford a decent burial to a man in College St. who, in turn, sold them for scientific experiments. Wheatley's exposure of this practice, coming at a time when Glasgow was beginning to count its losses on the Western Front, caused so much outcry that the practice was discontinued, the Sanitary Department agreeing to take responsibility for the burial of such poor unfortunates.[10]

Inside the Council Chambers the Labour group fought to protect the people from the worst effects of the war. Through the influence of Wheatley the group was becoming a more cohesive opposition[11] and exercising an influence out of all proportion to its relatively small numbers. Shortly before the outbreak of the war the Council had agreed to Wheatley's proposal to introduce Municipal tailoring and a small beginning was made with the Corporation taking responsibility for the repair of all its workers' uniforms.[12] The Council was also persuaded to agree in principle to the idea of Municipal printing.[13] It reacted negatively to Wheatley's proposal for a Municipal Bread Supply.[14] Aware of the effect the war could have on prices of materials required to be purchased by the Corporation and the subsequent cost to the ratepayer, Wheatley forced the Council to set up a Committee to monitor these prices. He was appointed to lead this Committee.[15] Labour's gain at the by-election at Kinning Park in February 1915 was generally attributed to this aggressive policy and to the £8 Cottage scheme.[16]

The Rent Strike

'The prime aim of Labour's housing policy is not to rescue people from the slums, but to prevent them getting there,' said Wheatley in his Chairman's address to the Glasgow Labour Party Housing Conference at the beginning of that year. There were 420 delegates at this Conference representing the Trade Unions, Co-operative Movement, Ward Committee and 13 Women's organisations. The purpose of this conference was to put pressure on the Council to adopt this policy.[17] The campaign for the Cottage scheme met with a setback some weeks after this conference. The Tramway surplus was being diverted to help the war effort and Labour had turned its attention to the Common Good Fund to provide the capital, but when the scheme came before the Council the Town Clerk ruled it illegal to use this Fund for housing.[18] However, it was becoming evident that the G.L.H.A. was now putting greater emphasis on the issue of rents.

While re-stating the case for Interest Free Housing McBride warned of the houseowners stated intention to raise rents yet again.[19] According to Archibald Speirs, President of the Houseowner's Association, previous increases had come purely as a result of market conditions.[20] Wheatley voiced his concern at a Council meeting and he moved 'that Parliament be petitioned to take the necessary steps to prevent the rents of dwelling houses being increased during the continuance of hostilities.'[21] The motion was defeated and it was to be left to the people to uphold it. Speaking from the Glasgow Housing Association's own platform in Glasgow Green at the May Day Rally Wheatley gave a stern warning to the property owners not to increase rents.[22] Indifferent to, or underestimating the mood of the people, this warning was ignored and the scene was set for a bitter struggle between tenants and landlords, the intensity of which Glasgow had never before experienced. A few days after the May Day Rally Thomas Neilson and Sons of Buchanan St., one of the largest House Factors in Govan, intimated that rents in their properties would be increased by amounts ranging from 13 shillings to 24 shillings per annum. This was the second increase for these tenants since the beginning of the war.[23] Almost immediately the Women's Housing Association organised a protest meeting in Cressy Halls.[24] This Association had been formed at the instigation of the G.L.H.A.[25] and had as its President Mary Laird of the Women's Labour League. At this meeting it was agreed to strike against these increases and a strike committee was formed from representatives of the W.H.A., the G.L.H.A. and the Govan Labour Representation Committee.[26] Behind the scenes advising on the campaign were Wheatley and McBride.[27] Close Committees were organised and lookouts were appointed whose function it was to ring handbells to warn of approaching bailiffs. Posters proclaiming 'WE ARE NOT REMOVING' were displayed in the windows of those tenants who had opted to join in the strike.[28] Foremost among the women of Govan involved was Mary Barbour[29] who later became a City Councillor for the district.

In the second week of June just when the Govan women most needed a stimulus to strengthen their resolve Wheatley seized on what he called a 'Terrible Story'.[30] Mrs Michael McHugh, wife of a serviceman who was lying wounded in a hospital in France and who had two other sons in the army, was five weeks behind with her rent. Notwithstanding that the local branch of the Miners Union had promised to meet these arrears given a few weeks to make all the necessary arrangements, Mrs McHugh and her five children were given 48 hours to quit her house at 30 William St. in Shettleston. The evening before the eviction was due to take place Wheatley called a protest meeting outside the McHugh home.[31]

'This is pre-eminently a fight for a poor woman and poor women should undertake it.' Wheatley told the crowd of between three and four thousand. He urged the women to get organised for this fight against evictions, but he warned them of the folly in taking their wrath on particular persons with a reminder of how he had once been such a victim.

Seeming to take heed of this warning 500 women marched to the local branch headquarters of the I.L.P. and volunteered for picket duty. The following day the people of Shettleston were out in their thousands armed with all types of weapons. They not only stood watch over the McHugh household, but demonstrated outside the Factor's office which was guarded by the police. Angry and unmindful of Wheatley's warning the crowd burned an effigy of the Factor, stoned his property and broke several of the windows.[32] The eviction warrant was never executed.

Addressing a large crowd the following day at William St., Wheatley praised the women for defending the McHugh home and said that they had brought a glory to the Ward, the memory of which would take a long time to fade but, he added, the disturbances of the previous day would bring no praise from him. They were there to defend homes, not to destroy them. The sole object of the agitation was to make it illegal for any soldier's dependant to be evicted during the course of the war and in this connection he had taken the liberty of sending a telegram to Lord Kitchener in the following terms, 'Numerous cases of soldier's dependants here threatened with eviction for non-payment of rent. Appeal for and await your suggestions of protective measures.' He had no doubt, he said, that he would receive a sympathetic reply. He also suggested to the crowd that they picket the West of Scotland Armaments Committee headquarters with the same object.[33]

Wheatley's part in this affair became the subject of criticism from various quarters. The Factor himself said that he found it difficult to understand how anyone could defend the McHughs, a family notorious in the city for being consistently in arrears with rent.[34] The Soldiers and Sailors Families Association came to the Factor's defence, quoting occasions when it had come to the family's rescue not only in meeting rent arrears, but also with medical expenses. The Association was of the opinion that Mrs. McHugh's separation allowance of £1-8-9d for herself and the five children plus allotments of 3/6d from each son was perfectly adequate to meet the needs of the family.[35] Wheatley challenged the Association on the adequacy of the separation allowance by contrasting the amount to the £2-1-7d it took to keep, in food alone, a similar size family in Belvedere Hospital. In any case, he argued, there never was any justification for the eviction of five children.[36] Wheatley's real motives in this case could be questioned for, in an undefended action on the 1st July, an eviction order was issued against the McHugh family.[37]

Resistance to rent increases was now spreading to other parts of Glasgow and it was becoming more and more noticeable that it was not only the poorer sections of the working classes that were involved in the strike. Cathcart could in no way be described as a slum area.[38] John McLean was addressing large meetings in many areas, but he was particularly active in the Ibrox district where he had the support of Dollan and Harry Hopkins the District Chairman of the Amalgamated Society of Engineers.[39]

In September the strike took what was to prove a decisive turn when the women of Partick turned their wrath on the House Factors. The trouble began there when Daniel Nicholson of Neilson and Sons notified rent increases of 1/- per month to tenants whose annual rental was £15 or more. Led by Mary Ferguson and Mrs. Nixon 150 tenants immediately joined the strike and within two weeks this number had increased to 500.[40] The Partick women were supported in their struggle by two leading members of the I.L.P., Neil McLean* and Andrew Hood the editor of the local *Gazette*.[41] Partick was the scene of some angry exchanges between the strikers and the Factor's deputies. These

*He was at one time Secretary of the S.L.P. and was expelled from that Party in 1909 when it was discovered that his name was also on the register of the Portobello branch of the I.L.P. He was physically assaulted by members of the S.L.P. when the discovery was made, *Socialist Monthly*, April, 1909.

deputies who came to return the pre-increase rents were bombarded by flour and other missiles.[42] The women refused to let houses be occupied where the previous tenant had been evicted for non-payment of rent. The strike took on a nationalistic flavour in Partick with Union Jacks being displayed in the windows alongside the 'We Are Not Removing' posters. The Factors were being branded as Huns and slogans such as 'WE ARE DEFYING THE PRUSSIANS OF PARTICK'[43] were paraded. Dollan was particularly guilty in the use of these slogans, slogans that Wheatley would have been careful not to use.

By October, there were an estimated 20,000 tenants on strike with huge meetings being held simultaneously in different areas of the City.[44] Resolutions were carried from these meetings to Parliament and Scottish Members were being pressured to ask questions in the House.[45] Lloyd George, Minister for Munitions, appeared to have sympathy with the strikers and he even went as far as declaring that much of the Labour unrest in the areas where munitions were produced was the result of the unpatriotic action of Houseowners in raising rents.[46] The slogans may have had their effect, but Lloyd George must have been aware of the threatening noises coming from the Clydeside workers.[47]

Kirkwood, Convenor of Shop Stewards in the giant Beardmores, wrote to Glasgow's Town Clerk pledging the workers solidarity and warning that evictions would be seen as an attack on the working class.[48] Kirkwood was by this time completely under the spell of Wheatley who had just recently written a very complimentary profile of him in *Forward*.[49] The threat of industrial action and the large number of cases coming before the Small Debt Court for arrears of rent brought a response from the Government. On the 11th October, McKinnon Wood the Scottish Secretary came to Glasgow and had talks with McBride and Baillie James Stewart.[50] The outcome was that the Government promised an official inquiry into the whole question of rents in Glasgow. The Inquiry, at which McBride put forward the tenants case, began on the 27th October[51] and published its report in the second week of November.[52] It called on House Factors to give a public guarantee (a) that rents of servicemen's dependants would not be raised and (b) that eviction warrants against strikers would not be carried out. The inquiry Committee also promised a full Government investigation into the question of rents.[53]

Before the Government investigation got under way the strike took a dramatic turn. Eighteen Partick tenants were issued with summonses to appear before the Court on the 17th November for refusing to pay increases of 2/- per month on rents of £2 per

The Rent Strike

month.[54] The Women's Housing Association called a protest meeting and, while Helen Crawford reiterated Wheatley's plea that the fight was essentially a women's fight,[55] the men were solidly behind them. On the day the tenants were due to appear in Court the workers of five major shipyards and one large engineering factory stayed out and joined the women in procession to the Court. Glasgow was then experiencing its worst fog in living memory[56] and it was an eerie spectacle with thousands of men and women marching to the accompaniment of the music from tin whistles through a thick fog.[57]

Long before the proceedings got under way the court was filled. Outside, makeshift platforms were erected from which John McLean and Gallacher raised the temperature of the crowd still higher.[58] Inside, there was much confusion before Sheriff Lee, aware that some kind of legislation on rents was about to be introduced, decided not to proceed with the case.[59] Eight days later the Government passed a Rent Act which restricted rents to pre-war levels in areas where munitions were being produced.[60] The Act was described by Daniel Nicholson as being iniquitous.[61]

In any epic of working class history the heroes are sketched from the pen of the writer and the Glasgow Rent Strike is no exception. In many of the recent accounts we have of this struggle John Wheatley is seen to play a less than significant role and from all the available evidence this seems unfair. It has been written in turn that

'the strike was organised by the housewives, who fought it until, attracted by their courage, the workers ultimately joined forces,' or
'It was started by the housewives and then sustained by the organisational skill of Andrew McBride and the evangelism and courage of John McLean and lesser men.'

What seems to have been ignored is that it was Wheatley who formatted Labour's Housing plan, at first despised as one Glasgow poet put it, and then becoming a vote catcher. Wheatley's leadership of the Scottish Labour Housing Committee was attained, not by words, but by deeds. What other Glasgow Labour leader then, or since, has demonstrated his or her ability to organise a campaign on a wide front over a lengthy period and bring it to a successful conclusion? The campaign which took 11 Glasgow Labour men to Parliament was of his making.[62] No other Labour leader has shown the same skill in using events and none at that time had the confidence and respect of all elements of the working class to be able to co-ordinate them in a rent war. Dollan, himself involved in the struggle, maintained that Wheatley was the brains behind all left wing opposition on the Clyde throughout the war years.[63] Another contemporary, John McNair, a biographer of Maxton, had no doubt that Wheatley was the organiser of all rent resistance during the war.[64] Helen Crawford, one of the leading women activists in the strike, said that throughout the strike Wheatley and McBride were ever in the background giving advice.[65] This in no way detracts from the deeds of the others involved in the strike. Without McBride, McLean, Helen Crawford, Agnes Dollan and the three Mary's, Barbour, Laird and Ferguson, it would have been impossible to win such a fight.

Further evidence of the predominance of Wheatley in the Glasgow Labour movement came in the six months that followed the conclusion of the Rent Strike. The hysteria which had accompanied Britain's entry into the war had resulted in many skilled tradesmen volunteering for the armed forces. By the end of 1915 the replacement of these men was becoming a matter of priority for the Government and they saw the solution in dilution of Labour. The union leaders had reached agreement with Lloyd George on this principle,[66] but the rank and file, especially in the North of England and the Clydeside, saw it as yet another attempt to reduce their living standards and were unwilling to accept it. Determined to break down this resistance Lloyd George came to Glasgow on the 23rd December, hoping that his personal charm would win over the workers and their new leaders. Following on the Amendments to the Munitions Act earlier in the year which had resulted in their freedom being restrained, the Clyde workers had lost confidence in the official leadership of the Union. To defend themselves against this restraint the workers' Shop Stewards had organised a separate body known as the Clyde Workers Committee.[67] Prominent among the leaders of this body were Kirkwood, Gallacher, James Messer and John Muir.[68] There had already been open conflict between the C.W.C. and the official Union and there had been serious industrial unrest on the Clyde before Lloyd George planned his visit. On the day after his arrival in Glasgow he met the leaders of the C.W.C. and failed in an attempt to win their backing.[69] On Christmas day he addressed a packed meeting in St. Andrews Hall where he met with a very noisy reception. The meeting ended in uproar with the Shop Stewards taking over the platform.[70] As a direct result of this meeting *Forward* was banned for six weeks. It had refused to print the Government's authorised text of the meeting, instead giving a verbatim report of the proceedings.[71]

Several weeks after this calamitous meeting the Government sent a Commission to the Clyde in an attempt to get the workers to agree to some form of dilution. After visiting several shipyards

The Rent Strike

and factories the Commission, led by Lynden Macassey, eventually came to Beardmores where it engaged in joint discussion with workers and management. Following hours of fruitless talks Macassey turned to the Shop Stewards and asked if they themselves would be prepared to come up with a scheme that would satisfy both workers and management. Kirkwood promised to produce such a scheme within twenty four hours. Immediately he and the Stewards left the meeting and went straight to Wheatley. According to Kirkwood it took Wheatley just thirty minutes to prepare his scheme which, he said, was accepted by the Commission without alteration and became the basis for all dilution schemes throughout the country. The scheme was contained in five clauses;[72]

(1) That the income of the new class of labour be fixed, not on the previous training or experience of the worker, but on the amount of work performed based on the rates presently obtaining for the particular operation.
(2) That a Committee, appointed by the workers, be accepted by the employers with power to see this arrangement be loyally carried out. Failing agreement between employers and committee the matter be finally referred to a tribunal, mutually agreed.
(3) That a record of all past and present changes in practice be handed to the Convenor of Shop Stewards and by him remitted to the District Office to be retained for future reference.
(4) That all skilled and semi-skilled men who were engaged in the engineering trade in the services of the firm immediately prior to the war be granted a certificate to that effect.
(5) No alteration shall take place in this scheme unless and until due notice is given to the workmen concerned and the procedure is followed as described by Clause 7 of Schedule 11 of the Munitions of War Act.

For the workers in this situation to seek the aid of a man who had never worked in a shipyard or a factory is testimony alone to Wheatley's wide influence over the working class movement on the Clyde. 'Few decisions were made by the Clyde workers of which Wheatley was not aware and on which his advice was not accepted,'[73] wrote John Scanlon who was himself involved in the Clyde workers movement. Gallacher later claimed that Wheatley's action broke the front of the Clyde worker's opposition to dilution,[74] but this is contrary to a statement issued at the time by the Clyde Workers Committee apropos the Beardmore's strike which sections of the press had alleged was a deliberate plot to sabotage production. The statement, signed by Gallacher and Messer, was a rebuttal of this charge and it concluded by saying 'nor is the C.W.C. opposed to dilution of labour if the shop in which the President and other officials of committees are employed find that dilution is working smoothly and without a hitch.'[75]

Before Macassey came to the Clyde it was in a state of industrial and political ferment. Concurrent with the opposition to dilution and the restraints of the Munitions Act was the agitation against Conscription. The War Cabinet placed the responsibility for all this unrest on the shoulders of 'a small, by comparison, number of men with revolutionary aims who were deluding the vast majority of loyal and patriotic Trade Unionists by a misrepresentation of the facts.'[76]

On the day that Macassey arrived in Glasgow the Conscription Bill was passed by Parliament. Six days later, demonstrations against dilution and conscription were held simultaneously at Glasgow Green.[77] John McLean moved the opposition to conscription and was arrested several days later and charged with sedition. During this period the C.W.C. was campaigning against conscription in its own newspaper. *The Worker*, of which Muir was editor, had been introduced following the banning of *Forward* and John McLean's *Vanguard*. On the fourth issue of *The Worker* an article appeared entitled 'Should the Workers Arm'.[78] The article itself was innocuous, but the authorities saw fit to arrest Muir, Gallacher and Walter Bell also on charges of sedition.[79] At the end of March Kirkwood, contrary to established procedure, was refused permission to enter one of the departments in Beardmores to conduct Union business. He resigned his Convenorship in protest and the shop stewards brought the men out on strike. The shipyards and other factories came out in sympathy and the Government reacted by deporting Kirkwood, Arthur McManus and four other C.W.C. leaders from Glasgow.[80] The Government completed its job of clearing the Clyde of the men with 'revolutionary aims' when Maxton and John McLean's disciple, James McDougall, were charged with sedition[81] some days later.

In the period leading up to the trials of those charged, Wheatley was ever on hand with help and advice for the accused. Indeed, Gallacher stated that his co-accused, with the exception of McLean, would do nothing without first consulting Wheatley.[82] At the trials McLean was sentenced to three years imprisonment with Gallacher, Maxton, Muir and McDougall each receiving a twelve month sentence. Immediately a Defence Fund was launched, designed to provide aid to the prisoners and deportees and of which Wheatley was Treasurer.[83] Years later Gallacher strongly criticised Wheatley for his arbitrary disbursement of the fund claiming that Kirkwood was the greater beneficiary. He also maintained that Wheatley had been determined to make capital from Kirkwood's popularity with the Parkhead workers to further his own political ambitions.[84] No one within the Labour movement at that period has questioned Wheatley's integrity and in any case, Wheatley's standing with the Parkhead workers at that time was high. Camlachie constituency, which embraced the Parkhead works, had lost its prospective Labour Party candidate the previous November with the death of Baillie James Alston. Wheatley was the choice of the local branch of the I.L.P. and his selection was confirmed with a petition on his behalf put forward by the Parkhead workers.[85] There can be no doubt that Wheatley was determined to exploit Kirkwood's popularity, but for the benefit of the Labour movement.

Recognition of Wheatley's work came from other sections of the Labour movement during this period. At the first Conference of the Scottish Labour Housing Association in January 1916 Wheatley was elected President,[86] but perhaps the greatest tribute paid to him was at the end of the previous year when, departing from precedent, the Labour group in the Council voted him as leader. Hitherto this position had been decided on the basis of seniority.[87] All this made nonsense of later judgements that he was a Tammany Hall type politician whose rise to power in Labour politics came as a consequence of a city of Irish electors.[88] The Irish at that time were not prepared to give a commitment to Socialism and the people who turned to Wheatley for leadership would only give recognition to someone prepared to work hard and honestly on their behalf.

References

1. *No Mean Fighter* – Harry McShane – 1978
   Forward – 15/8/14
2. *Forward* – 18/10/14
3. *Glasgow Evening Times* – 1/8/14, 6/1/15, 22/1/15
4. Glasgow Corporation Minutes – 4/3/15
5. *Forward* – 10/4/15
6. Ibid.
7. *Glasgow Evening Times* – 31/12/14
8. *Glasgow Evening Times* – 5/5/15
9. *Glasgow Evening Times* – 13/5/15
10. *Forward* – 16/1/15, 20/3/15
11. *No Mean Fighter* – Harry McShane 1978
12. *Forward* – 28/2/14
13. *Forward* – 20/6/14
14. *Forward* – 12/7/13
15. Glasgow Corporation Minutes – 9/2/15

16. *Forward* – 13/2/15
17. *Glasgow Evening Times* – 4/1/15
18. Glasgow Corporation Minutes – 28/11/15
19. *Forward* –23/1/15
20. *Glasgow Evening Times* – 12/1/15
21. Glasgow Corporation Minutes – 4/3/15
22. *Partick & Maryhill Express* – 7/5/15
23. *Forward* – 6/5/15
24. Ibid.
25. *Forward* – 11/8/14
26. *Forward* – 28/5/15
27. *Memoirs* – H. Crawford
28. Ibid.
29. *Revolt on the Clyde* – William Gallacher – 1935
30. *Forward* – 12/6/15
31. *Glasgow Evening Times* – 12/6/15
32. *Glasgow Herald* – 14/6/15 & *Forward* – 12/6/15
33. *Glasgow Evening Times* – 12/6/15
34. *Glasgow Evening Times* – 19/6/15
35. *Glasgow Evening Times* – 18/6/15
36. *Glasgow Evening Times* – 19/6/16
37. *Glasgow Evening Times* – 1/7/15
38. *Glasgow Evening Times* – 30/8/15, 7/9/15, 29/9/15, 30/9/15
39. *Rent Strikes* – J. Melling – 1983
40. *Partick & Maryhill Express* – 1/10/15
    Glasgow Evening Times – 27/9/15, *Bulletin* – 19/10/15
41. *Rent Strikes* – J. Melling – 1983
42. *Partick & Maryhill Express* – 5/11/15
    Memoirs – H. Crawford
43. *Glasgow Evening Times* – 7/10/15
44. Ibid.
45. *Glasgow Evening Times* – 15/9/15
46. *Glasgow Evening Times* – 14/10/15
47. *Revolt On The Clyde* – W. Gallacher – 1935
48. *Forward* – 3/10/15
49. *Forward* – 21/7/15
50. *Forward* – 17/10/15
51. *Glasgow Evening Times* – 27/10/15
52. *Glasgow Evening Times* – 16/11/15
53. Ibid.
54. *Glasgow Evening Times* – 17/11/15
55. *Glasgow Herald* – 15/11/15
56. *Glasgow Evening Times* – 17/11/15, 19/11/15
57. *Glasgow Evening Times* – 17/11/15, 19/11/15
58. *Revolt On The Clyde* – W. Gallacher – 1935
    Glasgow Evening Times – 17/11/15
59. *No Mean Fighter* – H. McShane – 1978
60. *Glasgow Herald* – 26/11/15
61. *Glasgow Evening Times* – 26/11/15
62. *Maxton 'Beloved Rebel'* – John McNair – John Wheatley – John Scanlon

63. *Glasgow Evening Times* – 15/5/30
64. *Maxton 'Beloved Rebel'* – John McNair
65. *Memoirs* – H. Crawford
66. *Glasgow Evening Times* – 3/1/16
67. *Glasgow Evening Times* – 13/8/15
    Revolt On The Clyde – W. Gallacher
68. *My Life Of Revolt* – D. Kirkwood – 1935
    Revolutionary Movement in Britain – W. Kendall – 1969
    Revolt On The Clyde – W. Gallacher
69. *Revolt On The Clyde* – W. Gallacher
    Revolutionary Movement in Britain – W. Kendall
70. *My Life of Revolt* – D. Kirkwood
    Revolt On The Clyde – W. Gallacher
71. *Forward* – 5/2/16
72. *My Life Of Revolt* – D. Kirkwood
73. *John Wheatley* – John Scanlon
74. *Revolt On The Clyde* – W. Gallacher
75. *Glasgow Evening Times* – 30/3/16
76. Cabinet Minutes – R276 – 30/3/16
77. *Glasgow Evening Times* – 31/1/16
78. *Revolt On The Clyde* – W. Gallacher
79. Ibid.
80. *Glasgow Evening Times* – 29/3/16
81. *Glasgow Evening Times* – 31/3/16
82. *Revolt On The Clyde* – W. Gallacher
83. *Forward* – 25/3/16
84. *Revolt On The Clyde* – W. Gallacher
85. *Glasgow Evening Times* – 26/1/16
86. *Glasgow Evening Times* – 3/1/16
87. *Glasgow Evening Times* – 9/12/15
88. *Memoirs Of A Fighting Life* – Josiah C. Wedgwood – 1941

Chapter Six
The War Years

The Glasgow journalist who referred to Wheatley as 'the merry glutton for work'[1] had no idea how much of an understatement that was. In a single week there were two days when he often worked the full twenty four hours.[2] It was this capacity that helped him achieve so much on the Council during the war years which in turn inspired the Labour group to exert an influence in areas which were causing the greatest hardship to the community.

Even before coal had become scarce Wheatley had forced the Council to keep a watching brief on supplies.[3] A Committee had been set up for this purpose to which Dollan was appointed Chairman. James Welsh became the leader of another Committee responsible for ensuring the cheap transit of small parcels to the troops serving abroad.[4] As the war progressed and the scarcity of food became a serious problem Wheatley prevailed on the Council to adopt a scheme that would enable the people to produce their own food and raise their own livestock from existing parklands.[5] He was himself given the task of developing this scheme. Parks ranging in size from 6 to 15 acres were taken over and divided into allotments of 200 and 300 square yards and let at rents of up to 6/3d per annum. Public meetings were called to explain the scheme and model allotments were laid out by Corporation gardeners for the benefit of those without gardening experience. Grants could be had for the purchase of tools and Wheatley encouraged allotment holders in the different areas to form themselves into associations, not only so that the purchase of seed and fertiliser could be done in bulk, but also that ideas may be pooled. This scheme was greeted with scepticism and derisory cries of 'Socialism'[6] from the Progressives when it was first proposed, but within 18 months there were 4,500 allotments under cultivation. These were Glasgow's first Collectives.

Wheatley[7] also had a practical idea for the saving of food. He called on the Council to set up Municipal Cookery Depots that would provide the people with pure, well-cooked food ready for consumption in their own homes at economic prices. Much saving, he said, could be effected if 1,000 meals were cooked in

The War Years

one establishment instead of 1,000 separate homes. The saving would not only be on food, but in coal, gas and domestic labour. These Depots would be of great benefit to women in munitions and other work and he was certain that hundreds of well-trained women would freely give of their services to these Depots. Wheatley also added that a page could be written on the health benefits of such a scheme.[8] Unfortunately his proposal was declared by the Council to be incompetent.[9] A year later a similar scheme was put forward by the London Savings Committee.[10] While others, such as Dr. Chalmers, the City's M.O.H., and the Education Dept., were putting forward their own ideas on food economy[11] it was noticeable that the Progressives on the Council had little of any value to contribute on this subject. The Lord Provost, Sir Thomas Dunlop, had the bright idea of posting his daily lunch menu on the Tramcars in the hope that it would encourage others to economise with their food. The result of displaying this menu, which consisted of soup, half a potato, 2 ozs of meat, 2 ozs of vegetables, coffee and a biscuit,[12] thereafter earned for him the soubriquet of half-spud Tommy[13] among the workers, many of whom had much less to eat at their main meal.

After more than two years of war Glasgow became like a city under siege. Prices had risen by 65% in that period and there was a grave shortage of food, particularly of potatoes and sugar.[14] Wheatley and the Labour group in the council fought unsuccessfully to set up depots that would perhaps have ensured a more equal distribution of food.[15] In this fight they had the support of the G.H.A. and the Glasgow Food Protection Association who were persistent in their lobbying of the Council.[16] The group did manage to ease the burden on mothers with an 'Experimental Creche in Parks scheme'[17] which gave the mothers some time away from their children and which provided milk and milk puddings for the children. The shortages and high prices could only have added to the already high risk of infectious disease and it was perhaps in the struggle to minimise this risk that Wheatley did his greatest service to Glasgow.

In 1915, the year before Wheatley took over the chairmanship of the Sub-committee for the prevention of Tuberculosis, the death rate for this illness was 137 per 100,000[18] of Glasgow's population and the facilities for its treatment were grossly inadequate. The year before the outbreak of war the number of cases under observation was 3,574 of which 1,093 were receiving institutional treatment. Dispensaries had then been set up in six of the worst affected areas i.e. Exchange, Calton, Gorbals, Cowcaddens, Kinning Park and Mile End. An extension to Ruchill hospital had been built to provide eight new pavilions and these were in use before the beginning of the war. Negotiations had begun then for the purchase of Bellfield Sanatorium in Lanark and the building of a sanatorium at Southfield.[19] By 1916 the number of notified cases of T.B. had risen because of scarcity of food, greater overcrowding and the number of men who had contracted the disease in the trenches.

Wheatley's committee immediately began to investigate the circumstances of the dependants of T.B. sufferers. The plight of a dependant is often a psychological barrier to the recovery of the patient. It put pressure on the Scottish Insurance Commissioners to increase the rate towards the cost of the treatment of discharged soldiers. X-Ray equipment was installed in Ruchill hospital and the committee encouraged General Practitioners to send their doubtful patients there. Extra beds were provided at Bridge of Weir, Ochil Hills and Bellfield sanataria. The Corporation was persuaded to grant £1,000 to the Directors of Ochil Hills and an extra grant to East Park to help support the treatment of children. The whole of Knightswood hospital was turned over for the treatment of T.B. and plans prepared for an extension to be built there. Southfield was pushed forward for completion and in March 1917, through the efforts of Wheatley and Baillie James Steel, a Progressive who had sat on the Council since 1891, the Ministry of Munitions was persuaded to grant the necessary certificate to allow for the completion of Robroyston Hospital. Building work on this hospital, intended for the treatment of smallpox, had begun before the war and was then postponed.[20] Under the most adverse conditions the achievement of Wheatley's committee was quite remarkable. At the beginning of 1918 only 216 notified T.B. cases were waiting for admission to hospital and of these only one third were children. In 1919 the Medical Officer of Health was able to report the lowest death rate ever recorded in Glasgow for this disease, 107 per 100,000 of the population.[21]

During this time Wheatley was fighting old hates and creating new enemies. The ill-fated Easter Rebellion in Ireland and the subsequent execution of Connolly met with mixed reception in Scotland. *Forward*, while it condemned the rebellion, attacked the British Government for the stupidity in its treatment of the leaders.[22] The U.I.L., following the lead of Redmond, condemned the rising and called on Irishmen to support the Allies more especially because of the atrocities being committed by the Germans on Catholic Priests.[23] Wheatley's reaction was typical in that he was quick to make political capital from the tragedy.

'Connolly's death has removed a mountain of prejudice against Socialism. "He was a socialist and he died for Ireland" is a common remark of the people in Ireland. They are now more interested in Connolly and Connolly's views. Prejudice removed, the whole tragedy of Irish working class life will reveal itself to the Celtic mind.'[24] Sinn Fein was later to come under attack from Wheatley for its failure to recognise the class war and for its support of Irish Capitalism.[25]

Many of Wheatley's opponents would have considered this criticism of Sinn Fein as being somewhat hypocritical when he was himself engaged in private enterprise. His business at this time was in danger of complete collapse. The problems were such that his partner had pressed for the firm to be put into the hands of the liquidator. Convinced that the business still had a future, Wheatley resisted this pressure, bought the goodwill from his partner and came to an arrangement with the firm's creditors.[26] Whatever happened during the dissolution of the partnership turned McGettigan against Wheatley and he later tried to damage him politically.

An article written by Wheatley in *Forward* in the spring of 1916[27] brought a new host of enemies which seemed to reveal a prejudice foreign to his Socialist beliefs. Wheatley had attacked the rise of interest rates at the onset of the war which he looked on as a burden to be met by the working class. These rates had now risen from $3^1/_2$ to 5% and using a pseudo question and answer column he tried to explain what these rates were costing the average family in terms of fighting the war. The explanation in this instance was in reply to the fictitious Michael Mulligan.

'As you know Micky, the war is costing us, that is you, Rothschild and the rest £5 million a day. Rothschild could pay his share cash down, but as a partner it is necessary for you to borrow your share from Rothschild. Since you are poor Rothschild won't lend you the money so therefore the Government has to borrow it for you and Rothschild insists on this method of carrying out the transaction. Because, with all the shrewdness of Abie, Isaac and Moses on his head, he knows that the Government is in a better position than he to make the regulations as will enforce you to pay the Jew his pound of flesh. So Micky, with a population of 50 million it means that the cost works out at 2/- per day. That means that you, Mary and the five weans are spending 14/- per day i.e. £4-18/- per week. Interest at 5% per annum over 20 years adds another £4-18/- per week. Please note Micky, of the £9-16/- that is debited against you, £4-18/- goes to smash the Germans and £4-18/ goes to square the Jew.'

There was a flood of angry protests to the editor following on this article. There was a half-hearted apology from the editor,[28] but Wheatley's apology was less than convincing. 'There was no disrespect meant for the Jews', he had been writing only in general terms, he said.[29] Even if he was not an anti-semite he could not have been ignorant of the harm it could cause to the Jewish community in Glasgow. One wonders if the long lasting enmity between Shinwell and Wheatley[30] had its origins in this article. However, it is the enigma of Wheatley that as one is ready to judge him on his response to a particular issue then one has to reverse that judgement with his response to another. It was on Wheatley's motion that Shinwell* was co-opted to the Council to fill the vacancy caused by the death of John S. Taylor even though Shinwell did not have the support of the local Ward committee.[31]

Wheatley looked on interest charges as unearned income, an evil which was the keystone of the Capitalist system and he never missed an opportunity to attack it.[32] He condemned the interest charges the Corporation was paying on money borrowed to invest in War Bonds.[33] The Corporation had invested £2 million in these bonds and the money borrowed was to be repaid over a period of eight years from the Tramway surplus. It was this that prompted him to ask the finance Committee to consider and report on the following:[34]

(1) The extent of the increases in recent years in the amount of interest being paid on borrowed money and the effect of this burden of interest on the operations of the Corporation.
(2) The advisability of approaching the Government with a view to obtaining power for the Corporation to issue at their own hand, notes of such value or values, as may be fixed bearing no interest, to the amount of the free assets of the Corporation having regard to the rating powers of the Corporation, such notes to be recognised as legal tender.
(3) The condition of issue of such notes and the provision to be made for the withdrawal, retiral and redemption of same.

The council refused to follow up this proposal on the grounds that it would be impossible to start a Bank without liquid assets.[35] Nevertheless Wheatley was to return with a more prepared scheme which was to become an election issue. He blamed interest rates as being the reason for the failure of the City to solve its housing problem and he expressed this view to McKinnon Wood when he met with him as leader of a delegation from the S.L.H.A. to discuss Glasgow's housing shortage, a shortage which he claimed would require 4,000 new houses per annum to meet.[36] McKinnon Wood could not agree that interest rates had any bearing on the matter but argued that land famine was the cause of house famine.[37]

*Within weeks of being co-opted, Shinwell's aggressive tactics were to bring him into disfavour with Wheatley and the Labour group.

The War Years

Wheatley tried in vain to get the Council to put pressure on the Government to fix a maximum amount for money as it was doing with other commodities.[38] The Government's response to the growing agitation on food shortages and price levels was to appoint Lord Devonport as Food Controller. He was negative in his response to the call for rationing, but he did try to limit prices to the levels of those at the 15th November, 1916. By this time the 4lb loaf, which had cost 6d at the beginning of the war, was now costing 10d. It wasn't until the following year when the loaf had risen to 1/- that a subsidy was given.[39]

The class of people finding it most difficult to cope with rising prices was the dependants of servicemen. The dependants allowance of 25/- for a wife and four children had been fixed in March 1915. Evictions of these dependants were still taking place, a fact that was brought to the attention of the press by the Progressive Councillor, Dick Williamson.[40] Williamson had concerned himself from the beginning of the war with the lack of compassion being shown to these dependants, particularly with the haphazard manner in which their allowances were being paid. Women often had to stand in queues for hours for this money, often to find that the allowance had not come through. Mainly because of Williamson's efforts the women were spared this inconvenience.[41] It was however, the amount of this allowance that provided Wheatley with another opportunity to organise the women. With the end of the Rent Strike many of the women who had been involved in that struggle had disappeared from the political scene.[42]

Wheatley opened his campaign for the dependants of servicemen with an article in *Forward* [43] in which he condemned an allowance that was well below the subsistence level set by the Parish Council. Almost immediately a National Association for the Protection of Soldiers and Sailors Dependants came into being with Wheatley as President.[44] Meetings were arranged in all working class areas of the City for the dependants and other interested parties. 'Enrol the Women' was the slogan that dominated these meetings.[45] Branches were formed at the conclusion of each meeting and the campaign was climaxed with a huge rally in the City Halls. Five thousand women attended this rally which passed a resolution demanding increases in allowances commensurate with the 30% increase in the cost of living since the present rates had been set.[46] The Association had the support of the trade unions, Scottish Labour Party and surprisingly from the Glasgow Pensions Committee.[47] In January 1917, just a little more than two months after the rally, the allowances were increased so that a woman with four children was now being paid the level of subsistence set by the Parish Council.[48]

1917 witnessed a change in the Clydesiders' attitude to the war. Depressing news from the battlefront allied to shortages brought more and more people onto the streets to demonstrate for peace. Casualties, which were given as 8,000 per week killed, wounded or missing at the beginning of the year, had risen to 20,000 per week in May.[49] The Government's Manpower Bill, which brought the age for conscription down to 18 years, had the women up in arms. Helen Crawford and Agnes Dollan organised a 'Peace Crusade' in which thousands of women converged on George Square.[50] These demonstrations often led to violent clashes with extreme right wing organisations like the British Workers' League and the Patriotic Federation.[51] Wheatley had earlier called for the establishment of a European Council to consider terms that would bring the war to an immediate conclusion. He suggested that this council be composed of belligerent and non-belligerent nations. It was his first direct reference to the war.[52]

The release from prison of Gallacher, Maxton and Muir at the beginning of the year added to the voices clamouring for peace. Wheatley was on hand to meet them, arranging for them a short holiday before their return to Glasgow.[53] Their release was celebrated by a huge rally in St. Mungo Halls which demanded the return of McLean and the other internees.[54] Kirkwood had caused a sensation in January when he breached the terms of his deportment by arriving at the Labour Party Conference in the guise of a Presbyterian Minister. In a well prepared speech, which some ascribed to Wheatley, Kirkwood roundly condemned the Government's policy on deportment.[55] According to Gallacher this was all part of a Wheatley plan.[56] By the end of June, McLean was released and the deportees were allowed to return to Glasgow.

Another event which helped to spread resistance to the war was the February revolution in Russia. It had a tremendous influence on the May Day Rally with the attendance variously estimated as between 70,000 and 100,000.[57] A resolution was unanimously passed which called for 'the overthrow of the Capitalist system of production for profit and the establishment of a Co-operative Commonwealth based on production for use.'[58] It saw the setting up in Glasgow of Workers and Soldiers Councils and a Russian Committee.[59] A demonstration was organised in St. Andrews Halls to celebrate the revolution at which the principal speaker was Ramsay McDonald.[60] McDonald was a popular

The War Years

figure in Glasgow at that time because of his opposition to the war which he had expressed through his regular column in *Forward*. While Wheatley was loud in his praise of the new free Russia[61] he was content to stay in the background of this movement. Unlike some members of his Party he was not convinced that the British worker was prepared to follow the example of the Russians.[62] All his actions hitherto suggested that his use of events was aimed at increasing the strength of the I.L.P. as a political force within the democratic framework.

There is no doubt that Wheatley's policies and his use of events more so than the conventional propaganda was responsible for the spectacular growth of the I.L.P. during the war years. Ten new branches had been formed in the City by 1917 and in 1916 alone the Party had gained 500 new members.[63] Helen Crawford had joined the Party and Rosslyn Mitchell, no doubt through Wheatley's example on the Council, had also become a member. Kirkwood and Muir had deserted the S.L.P. to join up with Wheatley. These policies were based, of course, on sound organisation and it was possibly through the lack of organisation that the other two left wing parties in the City did not experience anything like the growth of the I.L.P. If propaganda alone could have built a Party, then the S.D.F. with men of the calibre of McLean and Gallacher would have outdistanced the others. John McLean, who had been appointed Soviet Consul for Scotland by the new Bolshevik Government, had by the beginning of 1918 became something of a hero with the working class of Glasgow. The S.L.P. had a strong association with the workers through its close links with the Shop Stewards movement and yet it failed to make any great impact. In any case, it is doubtful if the British worker, nurtured in democratic trade unionism, would have been prepared to accept the Syndicalist policies of this Party. Lacking any worthwhile organisation the propaganda work of these two Parties could only have been an unwitting aid to the I.L.P.

Throughout his political career Wheatley was conscious of the necessity for a strong power base. This was evident in his early days with the U.I.L. and in the formation of the C.S.S. from which he launched his career in working class politics. It was the strength of his organisation in Shettleston that helped him overcome the opposition of the various sections. The G.L.P. was the inspiration of the I.L.P. and, although there is no direct evidence, it had some of the handiwork of Wheatley. What was different in its formation was that he did not occupy the Chair, but there is sufficient evidence to show that his influence on this body was considerable. However, there were growing signs that he was becoming less inclined to occupy the front position and more prepared to work through others, others that he could trust. He had handed over the Chairmanship of the C.S.S. to Regan.[64] He never at any time had a place on the executive of the Glasgow Federation of the I.L.P. although by the end of the war his brother Pat, John Scanlon, Regan and Dollan were all members of the executive, Dollan was President.[65] While John McLean attracted firebrands like himself, so Wheatley attracted good organisers and administrators, for all of these men excelled in those functions. Only once did Wheatley ever occupy a position of power in the I.L.P. outside of his own branch. His first appearance at an annual conference of the Party was at Leeds in the Easter of 1917.

The strength of the I.L.P. in Glasgow in 1917 was reflected in the unusually large delegation of 14 that represented the Federation at the Annual Easter Conference. This Conference was noticeable in that Snowden was elected Chairman in succession to Fred Jowett. Peace was the dominant theme of the Conference and Snowden had a couple of months earlier endeared himself to the rank and file by his strong advocacy for peace in a Parliamentary debate. It was also noticeable in that Wheatley and Maxton were beginning to make themselves heard. Wheatley moved the vote of thanks to Jowett's opening address and Maxton narrowly failed to win a place on the N.A.C.[66] He was to be successful the following year.

As the war dragged to an end the I.L.P. in Glasgow made propaganda from the ever increasing casualties at the Front. Posters, with the bold heading 'RIVERS OF BLOOD', giving details of these casualties were displayed in the windows of Branch Offices.[67] These posters led to branch offices being raided by the police and officials being interrogated.[68] More and more open-air meetings were being held and in areas never before considered as fertile for recruitment. Attempts to disrupt these meetings came from the British Workers' League at times aided by the police. One successful attempt was at Anniesland,[69] but the I.L.P. retaliated by holding a Free-Speech Rally shortly afterwards on the same site. That this meeting passed off without incident can be explained by Wheatley's presence on the platform as chairman.[70] He had been appointed as a magistrate at the end of 1917 and it would have been foolhardy of the police to encourage lawlessness with a member of the Bench as witness. These meetings coincided with a membership drive by the Scottish Division of the I.L.P. which was proving successful in many parts of Scotland.[71] Simultaneously to this a Fighting Fund had been

The War Years

launched in preparation for the elections that Lloyd George had promised would be held immediately the war ended, Lloyd George having replaced Asquith as head of the War Government at the end of 1916. The I.L.P. in Glasgow seemed reasonably confident as to the outcome of these elections with none more confident than Wheatley.[72]

References

1. *Glasgow Evening Times* – 20/10/16
2. *Glasgow Evening Times* – 15/5/30
3. Glasgow Corporation Minutes – 23/10/15
4. Glasgow Corporation Minutes – 11/2/16
5. *Glasgow Evening Times* – 5/10/15, 3/12/15, 7/2/16
   Glasgow Corporation Minutes – 8/12/16
6. *Glasgow Evening Times* – 7/10/15
7. *Glasgow Evening Times* – 2/5/17
8. *Glasgow Evening Times* – 30/5/16
9. *Glasgow Evening Times* – 29/3/17
10. *Glasgow Evening Times* – 25/3/17
11. *Glasgow Herald* – 4/9/15, 16/9/15
12. *Neither Fear Nor Favour* – John McGovern
13. Ibid.
14. *Glasgow Evening Times* – 3/3/17, 28/2/17, 16/9/16
15. *Glasgow Evening Times* – 2/3/17
16. Glasgow Corporation Minutes – 15/3/17
17. Glasgow Corporation Minutes – 8/12/16
18. M.O.H. Report – 1914–19
19. M.O.H. Report – 1913 & 1914–19
20. Glasgow Corporation Minutes – 8/6/16 thro' 21/8/18
21. M.O.H. Report – 1919
22. *Forward* – 20/5/16
23. *Glasgow Evening Times* – 7/3/16
24. *Forward* – 17/6/16
25. *Forward* – 16/9/16
26. *Glasgow Herald* – 6/7/27
27. *Forward* – 26/2/16
28. *Forward* – 12/3/16
29. Ibid.
30. *Memoirs of a Fighting Life* – J. C. Wedgwood. 1941
31. Glasgow Corporation Minutes – 18/8/16
32. *Forward* – 18/10/14
33. *Labour Leader* – 15/2/17
34. Glasgow Corporation Minutes – 10/1/18
35. Ibid.
36. *Forward* – 24/6/16
    Labour Leader – 4/1/17
    Glasgow Evening Times – 20/6/16

37. *Glasgow Evening Times* – 20/6/16, 24/8/17
38. *Glasgow Evening Times* – 21/11/16, 7/11/16
39. *Glasgow Evening Times* – 1/9/17
40. Glasgow Corporation Minutes – 24/8/16
41. *Glasgow Evening Times* – 7/11/16
42. *Forward* – 4/3/16
43. *Forward* – 26/8/16
44. Ibid.
45. *Glasgow Evening Times* – 18/10/16
46. Ibid.
47. *Glasgow Evening Times* – 29/11/16
48. *London Times* – 8/1/17
49. *Labour Leader* – July 1917 issues
50. *Glasgow Evening Times* – 13/12/17, 9/1/18
    Revolt On The Clyde – W. Gallacher
51. Ibid.
52. *Forward* – 18/3/16
53. *Revolt On The Clyde* – W. Gallacher
54. Ibid.
55. *Labour Leader* – 25/1/17
    My Life of Revolt – D. Kirkwood
56. *Revolt On The Clyde* – W. Gallacher
57. *Forward* – 12/5/17
    Glasgow Evening Times – 13/5/17
58. *Forward* – 12/5/17
59. Minutes of The Glasgow Federation of the I.L.P. – 15/10/17
60. *Glasgow Evening Times* – 30/4/17
61. *Revolt On The Clyde* – W. Gallacher
62. *Forward* – 24/1/20
63. *Labour Leader* – 11/1/17
64. *Forward* – 17/2/17
65. Minutes of the Glasgow Federation of the I.L.P. – 5/10/17, 19/10/17
66. *Labour Leader* – 22/3/17, 12/4/17
67. Minutes of the Glasgow Federation of the I.L.P. – 25/1/18
68. Ibid.
69. *Forward* – 6/4/18
70. Ibid.
71. Ibid.
72. *Neither Fear Nor Favour* – John McGovern

Chapter Seven
The 1918 Election

Peace has come and we rejoice.
To our tear-stained widows,
Whose share of the victory is a bitter memory,
We offer sympathy.
C.S.S. Notes, *Forward*, 16th November, 1918.

In the election that immediately followed the signing of the armistice, the Coalition Government was unscrupulous in its bid to retain power. 'No other Government would be better able to negotiate the terms of peace and maintain national and imperial unity.' It blackmailed the candidates by offering a letter of endorsement [The Coupon] to those who supported the Coalition and its programme. This programme promised living conditions to secure plenty of opportunity for all, better and more houses and wages which would be maintained at a point that would ensure efficiency and better working conditions. The programme also called for development of the empire, imperial preference, but no tax on food. It also promised Home Rule for Ireland when that country settled down, but there would be no coercion of Ulster. It evoked hysteria by reducing these aims to slogans such as 'MAKE GERMANY PAY' and 'HOMES FIT FOR HEROES'. Nowhere was the Government campaign so aptly illustrated as in Shettleston.

In 1917 the Government had passed a new Boundaries Bill which in effect increased the number of constituencies in Glasgow from seven to fifteen. One of these new constituencies was Shettleston, and Wheatley had been adopted by the I.L.P. to contest that constituency. Before nomination day Wheatley faced the prospect of a four-legged contest. The Tory choice was a Rear-Admiral Adair and the Liberals and British Workers' League had also named candidates. Adair was given the Government Coupon and the other two withdrew pledging their support to Adair. Adair was a Director of Beardmores and despite the fact that he had retired from active naval service in 1908 his title was neatly tagged to the war and its hysterical aftermath. 'We must not let the whines of the Germans influence us at the forthcoming peace negotiations,'[1] he told the electorate. On the question of Ireland, Adair was more forthright than the Government. He was in favour of Home Rule for Ulster as well as Nationalist Ireland. Ireland, he said, was the most pampered of the British family of nations and he asked what freedom that country did not have that England and Scotland had.[2] Much rowdiness attended Adair's meetings and one meeting had to be abandoned because of disturbances.[3] Adair received the support of the Orange Lodge which had issued a circular advising its members to vote for the Coalition candidates. Indeed, at this election Wheatley met with opposition from quarters both conceivable and inconceivable.

In the *Glasgow Observer* at the beginning of November the editor, Mitchell Quinn, wrote of the widespread, strong, deep and bitter opposition to Wheatley's candidature in Shettleston, not on political grounds, but on personal grounds and that in the circumstances Wheatley did not have the ghost of a chance of being elected.[4] Quinn was referring to a letter purported to have been written by Wheatley, copies of which were being distributed all over Britain. The letter, whose contents have never come to light, was supposed to have been written as a consequence of a circular issued by the I.L.P. When the letter was brought to the attention of Wheatley he immediately raised an action for slander against the distributor, Manus McGettigan his ex-business partner. The outcome of this action was a public apology from McGettigan. He admitted to being responsible for the widespread distribution of copies of the letter unaware that the original was a forgery.[5]

Previously Wheatley had come under attack from a group of Marxist theorists in the constituency because of what they claimed was his failure to understand the true conception of Socialism and in not recognising the strength of the industrial Unions. He replied to these criticisms by condemning Marx's Materialistic Conception of History in terms not dissimilar to those used by Fr. Puissant. He also dismissed their arguments that workers' power could only be gained by industrial action. While he did not underestimate the value of the Trade Unions he pointed to the fact that the Union had been unable, over the past 30 years, to gain for the miners any significant increase in their living standards. He wanted to impress on the minds of the workers the tremendous importance in this country of political power.[6]

Following on Quinn's article a letter signed by 'A Catholic' appeared in the *Glasgow Evening Times*.[7] Referring to this article the writer was at pains to assure Baillie Wheatley that he had the

The 1918 Election

support of all thinking Catholics in the district. 'Since he, Wheatley, had entered the Council he had been assiduous in looking after Catholic affairs and it was only proper that these affairs should be looked after by one of their own. We know that he has opposition from the I.L.P. and the S.L.P., but he can be assured of the support of four large Catholic congregations in the constituency.' This letter was quickly followed by one from another Catholic denouncing Wheatley's support of the Class War, John McLean and other Marxists, and challenging him to justify the company he kept in the I.L.P. while he remained a Catholic.[8]

Wheatley was quick to respond to his detractors and so-called admirers.

'I am doomed as a candidate especially suited to Catholics and at the same time in the Catholic press my candidature is condemned.'[9]

He warned the public that these statements emanated from the same source and were intended to arouse the prejudice of Catholics against his Socialist beliefs and of others to his religious beliefs. He insisted that he had always stood as a Socialist and hoped that he always would.

It can be said of the *Glasgow Observer* that it was the first of the Capitalist newspapers to recognise the influence that Wheatley had over the Labour movement on the Clydeside. It was to take the others another five years almost to awaken to this fact.

The charge that Wheatley supported Marxists was based on the G.L.P.'s endorsement of the candidatures of McLean and McDougall in Hutchestown and Tradeston respectively.[19] Both were representing the new British Socialist Party, a breakaway from the S.D.F. and definitely Marxist. McLean was opposing George Barnes the Labour incumbent. Unlike Henderson and Clynes, Barnes had refused to accept the ruling of a specially convened Labour Party Conference which called on Labour members to leave the Coalition Government. Despite this and the local Party's refusal to back Barnes the Labour Executive, dominated by Trade Unionists, refused to go along with the G.L.P. in endorsing McLean.[11] Of the remaining twelve City constituencies the I.L.P. was contesting eleven. In this election Wheatley did have the official support of the U.I.L. as did most of the other Labour Candidates in Glasgow including John McLean. The exceptions were Muir in Maryhill, George Hardie in Springburn and Jimmy Stewart in St. Rollox.[12] The support of the U.I.L. in these constituencies went to the Liberals. There were a number of Liberals, under the leadership of Asquith, who could not accept the policies of Lloyd George. This small group stood as Independent Liberals with little constructive to offer the electorate. The decision of the U.I.L. to give its support to these Liberals in view of the fact that the Labour Manifesto was unequivocal in its call for a free Ireland merely confirmed Wheatley's view that the Irish leaders had no real sympathy with the working class.

The Labour Party Manifesto was brief. In addition to a free Ireland it advocated the Nationalisation of the Land, a comprehensive Public Health Act, a million new houses and the democratic control of mines, railways, shipping, armaments and electricity. It also called for the withdrawl of all Allied troops from Russia. Labour's appeal lacked the aggression to combat the jingoistic flavour of the Coalition's campaign and also little was done to attract the new women voters. The Representation of the Peoples Act of that year had given the franchise to all males over 21 years and women over 30 years. Neither was there enough emphasis given to the likely economic chaos which would follow the return of 5 million servicemen to the labour market. It was an issue that Wheatley did not ignore. In a well-organised and aggressive campaign Wheatley skilfully tied the war to its aftermath to bring to the electorate the real issue which was facing them.

'We must not go back to the old conditions, we are on the march to industrial, social, political and international liberty.' The course and colour of reconstruction would be determined by which class controlled Parliament. The issue lay between Capital and Organised Labour, he told the electorate. He forecast that full-scale unemployment and high house rents would come in the wake of the war. Even now, he said, there are thousands of men and women being laid off and we are rapidly approaching one of those periods of unemployment and poverty with which we are all too familiar. He attacked the Government's proposals for a 30/– per week minimum wage and an unemployment allowance of 24/– as being ridiculous in terms of present day food prices, and when it cost more than three times as much to keep a family of six in the Poor House. He reminded them that the dependants of Soldiers and Sailors had been allowed to subsist on a starvation allowance and warned that it was the Government's intention to reduce the entire community to a similar level. A Labour Government, he assured them, would create a state of society in which every willing worker would be certain of a decent and comfortable standard of living.[13] In contrast to Adair's purely negative campaign Wheatley's appeal was such that the press was confidently predicting Shettleston as a Labour gain.

The outcome was a bitter disappointment to Wheatley who was himself extremely confident of victory, Adair captured the seat with a majority of 74 votes. The Glasgow results were disappointing to the I.L.P. whose hopes had also run high. Only one seat was gained and that was Govan where Neil Mclean had a majority of 815 in a three cornered contest. Nevertheless, there

The 1918 Election

were a number of pluses for the I.L.P. in this its first major election campaign. Its share of the City's vote was over 35%. Bridgeton and Rutherglen, contested by Maxton and Regan respectively, had been lost by less than 4,000 votes and in the nearby Dumbarton Kirkwood had lost by only 1,000. Considering the patriotic fervour which surrounded this election the I.L.P. in Glasgow could be proud of its performance. Wheatley could have taken personal satisfaction from the results of those Liberal candidates to whom the U.I.L. had given its support. In each constituency they were returned bottom of the poll and in Springburn and St. Rollox their share of the votes was less than 2,000, constituencies in which the estimated Irish vote was in each case 12,000.

Nationally the Labour Party returned 59 members to the new Parliament. Opposition to the war cost both McDonald and Jowett their seats and oddly enough Henderson, who supported the war, also lost his. Wm. Adamson was elected leader of the Parliamentary Labour Party in place of McDonald and the former Irish Nationalist Clynes became his deputy. Asquith's Liberals made even less impact on the electorate and with only 27 seats it left Labour as the official opposition.

References

1. *Glasgow Evening Times* – 20/11/18
2. *Scotsman* – 30/11/18
3. *Glasgow Evening Times* – 10/12/18
4. *Glasgow Observer* – 2/11/18
5. *Forward* – 23/11/18
6. *Forward* – 23/3/18, 30/3/18, 6/4/18
7. *Glasgow Evening Times* – 12/11/18
8. *Glasgow Evening Times* – 14/11/18
9. Ibid.
10. *Forward* – 9/11/18
    Glasgow Evening Times – 19/9/18
11. *Revolt on the Clyde* – W. Gallacher
12. *Scotsman* – 7/12/18
13. *Scotsman* – 3/12/18
    Glasgow Evening Times – 3/12/18

Chapter Eight
The Post-War Years

Disappointment at the election results only served to increase the intensity of the Glasgow I.L.P.'s propaganda campaign. This campaign had an early boost by the events that followed the Clyde workers' reaction to the growing unemployment problem. Wheatley's warning of large scale unemployment had not been premature. The beginning of 1919 saw thousands being laid off all over the country and, with the prospect of demobilisation swelling the ranks of the unemployed still further, the Unions became concerned. They saw the solution as being a shorter working week and the employers reacted by offering a 47 hour week without loss of pay. The employers' offer was put to the workers in a national ballot which they accepted on the recommendation of their leaders.[1] The Clyde Shop Stewards did not see this as going anywhere near to solving the problem of unemployment. They were looking for a 30 hour week, but after a conference which representatives of the C.W.C., Trades Council and local Union officials attended, their demand was reduced to a 40 hour week without loss of pay.[2] A strike, called to back this demand culminated in serious rioting in George Square and the take-over of the City by the military. The leaders of the strike were arrested and charged with inciting to riot. Gallacher and Shinwell were subsequently jailed for their part in leading the strike. The whole affair had the national press singling the Clyde out as an arena for Bolshevism,[3] the *Times* had it clearly established that there was a plot to seize the City Chambers and set up a Glasgow Soviet.[4]

What part, if any, Wheatley had in this affair would have stopped far short of Sovietising Glasgow. He certainly would not have approved of the workers engaging the authorities in what for them was unequal combat, yet he did not hesitate to make political capital from it. In the Council he bitterly attacked the Lord Provost's decision to read the Riot Act and call in the military.[5] At the I.L.P. Conference in Huddersfield he put forward an emergency resolution protesting against

'the unwarrantable and brutal attack by the police in George Square on the 31st January for the purpose of smashing the 40 hour strike and the iniquitous persecution of the leading members of the Labour movement. If law and order had to be respected then the head of the striker must be considered as sacred as the head that wears the crown.'[6]

He later opposed a Council notion to increase the policemen's wages in accordance with a new scale recommended by the Government. This increase would have meant an extra sixpence on the rates and, said Wheatley, it was not being awarded because of any enthusiasm for a higher standard of living for the police, but because it was a well-known fact that the workers were showing signs of giving trouble and it was necessary therefore to have a strong Praetorian Guard for Capitalism.[7] The Council Chamber was to prove a useful propaganda platform for Wheatley and the I.L.P. over the next three years when Glasgow was to be witness to some of the worst excesses of Capitalism.

The I.L.P. propaganda bore some fruit at the Municipal elections in November, 1919, the first local elections to be held for six years. By rotation, one seat in each of the 37 Glasgow Wards had to be contested and in Shettleston it was Wheatley's turn to seek re-election. His opponent Hugh Boyd, proprietor of the Dean Paper Works was no match against the Wheatley machine, gaining little more than half of Wheatley's 3,872 votes. Labour gained five seats at this election increasing their numbers on the Council to 24. The group had earlier been strengthened by Kirkwood's victory at Parkhead and the co-option of George Buchanan to represent the Hutchestown Ward. Big Geordie, a pattern maker, was to become one of Wheatley's staunchest supporters in later years. The electoral gains, poor as they were, could be ascribed in part to Labour's fight for work on the Council.

'The purpose of Local Authorities was to provide *useful work* for the unemployed'[8] said Wheatley when he was appointed Dean of Guild after the elections and was then in a much stronger position to put into practice some of the schemes for the workless he had earlier proposed. In March previously he had pressed the Council to set up a Sub-Committee to inquire into, and if possible put into operation, projects that had been suspended because of the war. Because of the now increased costs to these projects Wheatley also asked the Council to press the Government for aid in meeting these extra costs.[9] The Council agreed to set up a Committee and appointed Wheatley as Chairman. One of the first things that Wheatley did was to convene a special conference of all Scottish Local Authorities to consider the question of Government financial support to all L.A.s to cover the excess costs of Public Works undertaken to alleviate the plight of the unemployed. An Executive Committee was appointed from this conference with Wheatley as its Chairman.[10] This committee did meet with the Secretary of State, but received only sympathy.[11] As Dean of Guild Wheatley was able to sanction projects worth £6½ million which included the building of a bridge over the Clyde.[12] It was quite remarkable the influence that Wheatley had, not only over the Labour group, but on Council as a whole. One interesting proposal put forward by the Labour group, which the Council would not wear, was for the Health Dept. to provide temporary domestic help to women before and after childbirth.[13] However, given Labour's fight in the Council, the incessant propaganda coming from the I.L.P. and the economic climate, the election results were not entirely heart warming.

Disenchantment over the Government policies had early set in and this was reflected in the Labour Party's win over the Coalition candidate in the by-election at Bothwell in July. Judged against Labour's majority at this election of over 7,000 Glasgow's results were poor. The Labour candidate at Bothwell was John Robertson who was a Union sponsored candidate and a member of the newly constituted Labour Party. Previously membership of the Labour Party was through membership of affiliated bodies such as the I.L.P., Trade Unions, Fabian Society and the Co-operative Party, the new constitution now allowed for individual membership. It was a subtle change to the constitution, not unlike Martov's proposals at the second Russian Congress. Some members of the I.L.P. were rightly suspicious of this change and at the Scottish conference in January 1920 an amendment was put forward that sought to have the I.L.P. sever its association with the Labour Party. Wheatley argued strongly against this amendment which was defeated.[14] For a man who was said to have greatly admired Lenin one finds it difficult to reconcile Wheatley's stance on this question. In addition, Wheatley could not have been ignorant of the characters of those who controlled the Labour Party. It was a grave error for, within five years, Lenin's dictum that 'a broad, loosely organised Socialist Party would become an inert image of the working class instead of its inspiration' was to prove correct as far as the Socialist Movement in Britain was concerned.

A feature of the I.L.P.'s platform at the Municipal election was its call for a Municipal Bank[15] – it was Wheatley's brain-child. The Council had proposed to invest £1 million at 4% interest on a victory loan. Wheatley had described the proposal as farcical in view of the fact that the Corporation had already invested £3½ millions on War Loans from money borrowed and with only £276,000 having been repaid. He countered this proposal with a motion, backed by Rosslyn Mitchell, that the Corporation should summon a conference of all Scottish Local Authorities to consider the advisability of constituting a Joint-Stock Bank, the Shares of which would be held only by Local Authorities.[16] The motion was referred to a sub-committee where it received approval, but it was heavily defeated at the full Council meeting.[17] Nevertheless, Wheatley continued to propagate his scheme and he was invited to present a paper on it to representatives of Labour organisations in Glasgow. The paper, entitled 'How the City could save Millions'[18] was printed in pamphlet form. The idea of a Joint-Stock Bank, municipally owned, was not a new one. Several of the Federal Governments of the U.S. had operated their own banks in the early 19th century. What was different about Wheatley's paper was the simplicity with which the idea was explained and how he used house building to illustrate the cost to Glasgow of borrowing from private banks and also as a measure of wealth.

Beginning with a short history of banking, how assets replaced gold as a means of exchange and how eventually the credit of the State was placed at the disposal of the joint-stock banks in the form of Treasury notes, replacing the need for these banks to carry gold, the paper also detailed what the community was paying as a result of Glasgow's borrowing policies.

'This burden is best illustrated with housing. By 1922 the Corporation expect to build 7,000 new houses, each costing £1,000. The present interest rate is 6% so that, for every £1,000 borrowed, the Corporation would have to repay £3,712 or, in other words, before the community is able to produce one house it must guarantee to produce 2 & 3/4 houses or the equivalent in some other form of wealth. Credit is the basis of banking and Municipalities have credit. The free assets of the Scottish Municipalities are greater than the combined assets of the Scottish Joint-Stock Banks so there is no reason why the L.A. should not be allowed to issue its own notes backed by the Treasury like the other banks. 7,000 houses would require an issue of £7 million notes which would cost the City little or nothing while in circulation. To illustrate this let us suppose that, of 1,000 Municipal £1 notes in circulation, 100 are presented to the Bank for payment in cash. Demand would be met by cash deposited on Savings or Deposit receipts or by Treasury notes. [The paper had suggested the setting up of a Municipal Savings Bank as a means of supplying liquid assets for the bigger Bank.] If Treasury notes are required to meet the demand it would not mean that Municipal money would cost the 5% that was the Government's rate of interest for these notes. There would be £900 worth of notes free of interest in circulation so that the average rate of interest would be only $1/20\%$. The sum paid to the Government would go to the benefit of the nation. It is highly probable that, as this joint State and Municipal Banking developed, the Municipal Bank would become less inclined to accept investments from interest-seeking depositors and would incline to buying Treasury notes and so divert any profit or interest in Banking to the National Treasury. This course would rapidly destroy private interest altogether because manufacturers or merchants could not compete with Municipalities if their capital was burdened by a charge from which Municipal Capital was almost free.

The argument commonly used against this type of Bank is that any new notes issued in large numbers reduces the value of money already in circulation. The critics instanced what happened during the war when the Government issued new notes to pay for armaments. These notes added to the notes already in circulation and had a claim on a quantity of wealth which had not increased. If Glasgow uses its own 7 million notes to pay for its seven thousand houses then, it would not be using those of the private banks. The number of notes in circulation therefore, would not be increased, only the ownership would be different. There is all the difference in the world between issuing notes for war and issuing them for the production of wealth. When 7 million new pounds in circulation are balanced by more than 7 million pounds worth of new and cheap houses, the purchasing power of the pound is not depreciated but, on the contrary, the community is enriched.

It is argued that people would no longer save when the reward of interest was taken away and that the subsequent squandering would maintain a boom in prices, but when a man knows that his wealth will be reduced by every pound he spends, the incentive to save will be greater than it is now when he may spend freely if his capital is large without reducing the principal by a penny. He lives, not on his own money, but on the fruits of exploitation.'

While the paper showed that Wheatley understood the principles of banking, he failed to appreciate that, in a society geared to profit, interest was the only motive for saving. The system would have to be changed to provide the environment for men to change.

In his paper Wheatley had stated that Glasgow required 57,000 new houses to solve the problem of overcrowding. So serious was the problem that the M.O.H. had gone on record as saying that he would refuse to take the responsibility for the consequences should an epidemic attack the City.[19] In March 1919 Dr. Addison unveiled the Government's eagerly awaited housing plans which Wheatley saw as promising little for Glasgow. It was estimated that the plan would result in providing 3,000 new houses for the City in three years, an estimate that not even the most optimistic members of the Corporation could envisage, said Wheatley.[20] Nevertheless, the plan was significant in that, for the first time, it sought to grant subsidies to Local Authorities to build working class dwellings. However, it stipulated that the L.A. must first of all exhaust the proceeds of a penny rate before being entitled to any subsidy. There was to be a time limit of three years for the submission and carrying out of any scheme and seven years for completion. Within three months of the Act being passed the L.A. must forward their schemes to the Local Government Board for approval.

The Act went through Parliament in the June following and almost immediately there was speculation that the shortage of labour and materials would hamper the Government's programme. This was Glasgow's excuse for the delay in building and Wheatley demanded that the council ignore Government red tape and get on with the work of building houses. He knew of nothing essential to the building of houses that could not be produced in Britain with the possible exception of timber and of which he knew there were sufficient stocks at Tyneside. On the shortage of labour he pointed to the army of unemployed who were being paid £30 million in dole money. He also instanced the armies in Russia and Ireland, "bring them home to build houses,' he insisted.[21] By November, the Government, citing shortages of materials and labour, admitted failure of its policy and introduced a new scheme that would give subsidies to builders instead of L.A.s.[22] Before the Government withdrew its subsidy to L.A.s the Ministry of Health had warned that, if housing was to be restored to an economic footing, there would have to be heavy increases in house rents. Pressure had been mounting on the Government for some modification of the Rent Restrictions Act. Even before the war ended Scottish landlords had been lobbying the Secretary of State for a then immediate $12^1/_2\%$ increase in rents and for a further $12^1/_2\%$ increase at a later date.[23] The Government responded to pressure by appointing a Commission under Lord Salisbury to examine the whole structure of rents. At the annual conference of the S.L.H.A. in January 1920 Wheatley warned[24] of the Government's intention to amend the Rent Restrictions Act, an amendment which could mean tenants facing rent increases of 10%. In his Chairman's address he bitterly condemned the Government's housing policies.

'Not one house had been completed in Glasgow in 1919 under the Government's scheme despite the fact that the City required 5,000 houses per annum to maintain existing levels. The 92 houses being completed at Garngad were commenced while the Government was still trying to make up its mind on a policy and because of this all financial aid was being withheld on the grounds that the Corporation had acted too hurriedly. The City's M.O.H. had reported that 47,000 persons were occupying houses which were considered unfit for human habitation. Over 4,000 families, mostly homeless, were on the Corporation's waiting list to be housed and there must be thousands more who hadn't registered, considering it a worthless exercise. This state of affairs was reflected in an increase in the Infantile Mortality rate, 44 over the already high rate of 210 per thousand. Workers are accused sometimes of being unnecessarily noisy and troublesome, but in view of the wholesale slaughter of their children they display a disgraceful and discreditable patience. If the workers were mobilised to build houses as they had been to produce armaments, every family in Britain could have a new house in two years.'

He called for a unification of Labour's forces in the fight for decent homes at reasonable rents. United action by Trade Unions, Co-operative Movement, Socialist organisations and Labour representatives on the L.A. could, to a large extent, control matters now and, he said, in forming a new policy we should consider the following points:

(1) The Land must be captured for the people immediately by any and every means.
(2) The creation of a Scottish Municipal Banking system.
(3) The establishment of Public Works for the manufacture of building materials.
(4) The abolition of speculative building contracts and the substitution of Municipal Works Departments or direct contracting with Unions.
(5) The Trade Unions to boycott all luxury buildings until every family has a healthy home.

Before the Salisbury Commission had completed its report the Council met to decide on the rents of houses under construction at Coplawhill. Despite a warning from Wheatley[25] that it was settling the minimum rents at which housing accommodation would be obtained by the vast majority of the people in Glasgow for the next generation, the Council voted in favour of rents of £26 per annum for 3 apartments and £31 for 4 apartments. There was an uproar in the Chambers with this decision which led to Shinwell being suspended for refusing to accept the Council's ruling. 'Fixing rents at these prices,' said Wheatley, 'would only intensify the agitation for the relaxation of the Rent Restriction Act.'

When the Salisbury Report was published at the end of April its proposals were more drastic than Wheatley had predicted. The rents of houses, hitherto protected, were to be increased by 15%. The 1915 Act gave protection only to houses with an annual rental of £30 or less. This was extended in 1919 to rentals up to £60. In addition, landlords who were responsible for repairs could charge a further 25%. These increases were to be based on the standard rent and one of the qualifications of the 1919 Act was that where the actual rent of a house at August 1914 was less than the rateable value then the rateable value was to be taken as the standard rent. Many houses in Glasgow stood on the Valuation

The Post-War Years

Roll in August 1914 at a figure higher than the actual rent obtainable at the time, consequently the increase to many would be much greater than 40%. Immediately the Report was made public the G.L.H.A. organised a protest meeting at Glasgow Green where Wheatley described it as but a declaration of a rent war by Capitalists.[26] It was a war in which the I.L.P. was again in the vanguard.

Wheatley raised the standard when he presided over a specially convened conference of the S.H.A. on the 22nd May. One thousand delegates from all working class organisations listened to Wheatley's address.[27]

'Ever since the end of the war we have lived in a land of robbers. While we experience daily the painful results of their operations and have public records of the magnitude of their spoils, the complex system by which they operate and our relatively disorganised condition make us their powerless prey. Now we have an opportunity of defending ourselves in a square fight on equal terms and I hope we won't refuse it. For the Government to implement the Salisbury Report, or even a modified version of it, would be to go back on their election promises. It is absurd to argue that existing houses are intrinsically more valuable than they were in 1914 and I cannot understand anyone wanting to charge more for what is worth less. The tradesmen who built them would be as much entitled to come forward and claim the difference between the scale of wages then and now. One of the arguments for increasing rents is the rising cost of repairs. The only remedy for costly repairs is smashing the rings which control material and fighting those food combines which, by inflating prices, force up wages. An increase in rents is but another step in a vicious circle. Another of the arguments is that the owners' cost of living has risen. No mention is made of the fact that properties are now fully let, whereas in pre-war days almost one in every ten houses was unlet. We are familiar with workers' claims for increases on these grounds, but the workers' wages must be maintained above subsistence level or production stops. Production and distribution are the natural, and ought to be the normal, methods of obtaining a living. It is all very well for a society to encourage thrift so that people in their old age may enjoy the fruits of their industrious years, but it is utterly wrong to compel the community to pay more than the real value of property so that owners may enjoy idleness. When the owners' property becomes insufficient for his maintenance, he should return to the source of all wealth-work!'

At the close of the meeting Wheatley moved a No Rent Increase resolution which was carried by 940 votes to 8. The delegates then agreed to enter into a Covenant binding them not to pay any increases authorised by Parliament which did not have the sanction of the people.

On the 2nd of July the Rent Act, which adopted most of

Salisbury's report, was given the Royal Assent and by the close of the month 30,000 tenants had signed the No Rent Increase Covenant.[28] Wheatley's pamphlet 'THE NEW RENT ACT (A REPLY TO THE RENT RAISERS)' was selling in large numbers.[29]

'Fight now,' he called to the tenants. "Surely you have the courage. I know how much you detest strife and love peace but, on this cost of living question of which rents are but a part, you cannot avoid a bitter struggle. We are being carried rapidly towards financial and industrial chaos, starvation and worse. You alone can change the course. They can starve you into acceptance of their terms for food, but houses are in your own hands, if you fight here you cannot fail.'

The strike spread rapidly throughout Scotland and at the end of July the leaders organised a great demonstration at Bothwell Bridge, the scene of the great Covenanter battle of the 17th century.[30] Once again Wheatley involved the workers in the struggle. A one day General Strike was called for the 23rd August in protest at the Rent Act. Shipyards and factories were idle as were Scotland's coal fields. In Glasgow, the transport system was paralysed.[31] However, this show of strength and all the strong words coming from Wheatley, Kirkwood and McBride had little effect on the landlords. By November, 850 had appeared before the Courts for non-payment of rent with 445 decrees being issued.[32] Wheatley must have known at the outset that this was a battle that could not be won. The Glasgow Council's decision to raise the rents of its houses by 25% even before the Rent Act was passed only met with protests from the Labour Councillors.[33] With a high upward trend in unemployment Wheatley would have been naive to expect anything other than token support from the workers. His appeals to the people were more emotional than reasonable and it looked too obviously like a battle he had to engage in, and lose, in order to win the war. The casualties in this battle were those who had to pay the expenses of the Court and with the new rents, unemployment and food now 167% above 1914 prices it was a high price to ask anyone to pay. Perhaps this may explain John McLean's coolness towards Wheatley, he did not have to share in the suffering of the people. Yet Wheatley was only too aware of the emotive appeal of housing and with the Municipal elections due in November, all 117 seats were due to be contested in Glasgow, perhaps the propaganda to be gained from the Rent Act could not be ignored.

'Nowhere has the I.L.P. movement been more successful than in Glasgow. There is an incessant flow of propaganda which is maintained throughout winter and summer. Between them, the

City's 30 branches run 9 theatre meetings each Sunday.'[34] Thus wrote a political correspondent. What this correspondent did not mention was the I.L.P. Sunday Schools for young people. These schools, perhaps every bit as much as housing, involved the women. Glasgow Presbytery recognised the threat posed by these schools when it urged its Ministers to increase their home visitations to 'avert the people from suicidal Socialism'.[35] To convert Glasgow to Socialism the I.L.P. had to gain 60,000 more votes than the 89,000 they got at the General Election. It was a tall order, yet it launched a confident campaign. Regan, none was closer to Wheatley, was the organiser of the campaign.[36] Large posters proclaiming 'Great Labour Victory' were on display everywhere. Housing naturally played a prominent part in the campaign and there was a pledge to introduce direct labour into the housing department in an effort to reduce unemployment. Wheatley's scheme for a Municipal Bank was also a feature of the Campaign which Dollan highlighted in *Forward* in a series of articles that set out Labour policies. A statement by Sir Robert Graham, former City Treasurer, that 'the only people who gave serious consideration to Municipal problems was the Labour group' was used by *Forward* to give credibility to Labour's fitness to rule.

Councillor John Izett set the tone of the opposition when he withdrew his support from Labour. "I could give my support to decent Labour candidates, but not to these revolutionaries."[37] Izett had first been a Progressive, changed his allegiance to Labour and was now returning to the Progressives. The Orange Order issued a manifesto advising its adherents not to give their support to extreme Labour candidates.[38] The Citizens Union again put its weight behind the anti-Labour candidates,[39] but perhaps a greater threat was the decision to conduct a Veto Poll on liquor licences simultaneously with the election. The I.L.P.s well known opposition to alcohol would not have endeared it to many a Glaswegian.

'Nearly a red Glasgow' was how Regan described the results. Of the 87 candidates put forward by Labour 44 were returned and they had captured 120,000 votes. "On the basis of these results,' said Regan, 'five of the City's Parliamentary seats were for the taking'.[40] Wheatley was again top of the Poll in Shettleston with 5,397 votes. In nine Wards, including Shettleston, all three Labour candidates were returned. Having reduced the Progressive's majority from 65 to 25 Labour was now a powerful minority and had the audacity to challenge Thomas Paxton for the Provostship.

As Chairman of this powerful group Wheatley put forward its plans which he said were practical and it was their duty to develop them rapidly to reduce the numbers of unemployed. These policies he summarised:[41]

(1) To petition the Government to give the Corporation powers to impose a special tax on land, apart from improvements, to meet the cost of dealing with the unemployed.
(2) Urge the Government to pay the Corporation for every person employed under the special employment schemes the same amount that each person would receive from unemployment benefit.
(3) To remit to the Health Committee for the provisions of milk and other food for necessitous children under the age of five.
(4) To ask the Corporation to consider the establishment of a poultry farm at Robroyston to supply the demand for poultry and eggs at the hospital.
(5) To establish, on an experimental scale, a scheme of Municipal Domestic Service, e.g. laundry work.
(6) That the District Committee promote schemes of Market Gardening in and near the City and that all road-making schemes and improvements that the Corporation had in prospect be accelerated, beginning with Western, Govan and Renfrew Boulevards.
(7) That the Health Committee seek complete control and probable distribution of all milk coming into the City.
(8) That coal be purchased, not only for Corporation Departments, but for the needs of the City.

Surprisingly, the Council agreed to most of these proposals and also agreed to setting up a Special Committee on Unemployment, of which Wheatley was appointed Chairman.[42] This committee faced a mammoth task: at the end of the year there were 18,000 registered unemployed[43] with thousands more on short time. At the beginning of the following year the Government was proposing that all its industrial establishments should go on short time so that jobs could be made available for the greatest possible number and it appealed to Local Authorities and the private sector to do likewise.[44] The Minister for Labour appealed to the Building Trade Unions to accept dilution into its industry to enable ex-servicemen to find jobs. The Unions rejected this appeal on the grounds that there were many men in various trades unemployed. Instead, the Unions called for a better organised housing policy.[45] In 1920 Glasgow had completed building on 64 houses only, a situation which Wheatley's committee set out to remedy.

The Committee reported that construction would begin shortly on 2,287 houses at Mosspark, Craigton and Drumoyne. The latter scheme involved 318 houses which would be built by direct

The Post-War Years

labour – this project was completed in 1923 well below the estimated cost. The committee also announced that ex-servicemen would be employed in the making of bricks and concrete slabs and that this work was expected to begin in March. It also reported that the Corporation had purchased a Brick Works at Dalry which had a capacity to make 11,000 bricks per day. Work, such as road-widening and extensions to wash-houses had already begun. The M.O.H. had been instructed to provide free milk vouchers for children under five years of age, necessitous children of school age were being provided with food and clothing by the Education Dept. Females were being offered cleaning jobs.[46]

By March, the special schemes introduced by Wheatley and his committee had created only 2,665 new jobs while unemployment had soared to 44,000.[47] Many were dissatisfied with the efforts of Wheatley's committee, none more so than John McLean and his Committee for the Unemployed. McLean took the cause of the unemployed to the streets, organising large demonstrations and protest meetings. He had previously led a deputation to the City Chambers to demand that the Corporation make provision for the feeding and clothing of the unemployed and their dependants.[48] He went further than Wheatley by advocating that the Corporation establish farm colonies within a fifteen mile radius of the City, that those employed there be paid T.U. rates of pay and be provided with housing. He insisted that on any committee set up to deal with unemployment, the unemployed should be equally represented. He also demanded that, for those unable to find employment, the Corporation should provide free passages to Russia. Wheatley, who was Halls Convenor, did agree to McLean's request for the use of Corporation Halls in which the unemployed could hold afternoon meetings, but this gesture did nothing to lessen the workers' growing mistrust of Wheatley at this period.[49] A demonstration in the City Halls in February, 1921,[50] organised by the Trades Council to protest at the Corporation's failure to help the unemployed broke up in disorder. McLean and Wheatley, who was there to defend his Committee's work, were to be the principal speakers. McLean was received with wild applause, but when Wheatley rose to speak he was greeted with more catcalls than cheers and such was the feeling that Wheatley was not permitted to finish his address. These feelings were carried into the Municipal elections in the following November when the I.L.P. lost five seats. McLean and his aide, Harry McShane, beat the I.L.P. candidates into third place in Kingston and Kinning Park respectively. This election was notable too in that Andrew McBride lost his seat. However, this criticism of Wheatley was a bit unfair for, without substantial Government aid, little more could have been achieved.

Wheatley did attempt to put pressure on the Government for greater assistance when he convened, yet again, a meeting of representatives from Scotland's L.A.s.[51] High on the agenda for this meeting was the applicability of the residue of Scotland's National Relief Fund. Wheatley wanted this money to be used like the equivalent Lord St. David Fund south of the border for job creation schemes. The Scottish Office had previously refused to give its permission for the money to be used for this purpose. Other ideas put forward by Wheatley were for the setting up of a National Committee for Scotland to act in conjunction with the L.A.s and the Health Board to see that certain work was undertaken or speeded up during periods of exceptional unemployment. Work on the main arterial road between Glasgow and Edinburgh and the Forth and Clyde Canal were examples he quoted, schemes that would be elastic in character to provide thousands of jobs for years to come. He also mentioned that this Committee could also advise on schemes such as afforestation and he suggested that the Committee be given executive powers. These proposals were put forward to Munro, the Scottish Secretary, and Dr. McNamara, Minister of Labour, at a subsequent meeting in London.[52] One result of this meeting was that Glasgow received £3 million from the Lord St. David Fund to help with tramway extensions and the setting up of farm colonies. Towards the end of 1921 the Government did approve a system of grants designed to ease the burden on L.A. borrowing and which was intended to give employment to exservicemen, by that time Glasgow's unemployed totalled 84,000.[53] The Scottish Office issued a circular suggesting that wages paid to unskilled men on grant aided work should be considerably lower than the District rate.[54]

High unemployment coincided with savage wage cuts in every sector of industry. The unemployment benefit which had been increased in February from 15/- for men and 12/- for women to 20/- and 15/- and the period extended from 15 to 26 weeks was returned to the status quo in July. Worse was foreshadowed in August when the Government appointed a Committee under Sir Eric Geddes to enquire into National Expenditure. Glasgow's destitution, described by Wheatley as worse than that of Russia,[55] saw the appearance of soup kitchens in some parts of the City.[56] By the close of 1921, 5,000 cases for non-payment of rents had come before the Courts resulting in almost 2,000 eviction orders being granted.[57]

The Post-War Years

Shortly after the elections Wheatley had put pressure on the new Council to provide money to aid the distressed. He was supported in this by Mrs. Baird-Smith, a Progressive, and one of six women on the Council. £15,000 had been made available from the Common Good Fund and other sources.[58] Within two months 30,000 food vouchers had been issued and almost 200 had been given assistance towards payment of rent.[59] Wheatley and his Special Committee had enlisted the aid of the Ward Committees to distribute these monies. When this money was exhausted the Council refused to give any further funding – instead, Lord Provost Paxton opened his own Distress Fund. The arbitrary manner in which this fund was disbursed came in for strong criticism from the public and Wheatley in particular. Within a month £14,000 had been contributed to this Fund and out of almost 9,000 applications for relief just over 3,000 were given food vouchers to a total value of £3,443.[60] Wheatley condemned the administrators of the Fund for shifting the burden of Relief on to the rates, for many who had been refused had been advised to apply to the Parish for relief.[61] Officialdom's attitude to Poor Relief could be summed up in the report of one Glasgow journalist.[62] He dismissed many of the complaints against the administration of the Lord Provost's Fund as being negligible and he was of the opinion that much of the hardship could have been avoided if the workers had been more thrifty with the big wages they had been earning up until as recently as the previous year. He also considered those men naive who had returned from the war with the conviction that, having fought for their country, the country should now keep them. One of the negligible complaints that Wheatley had instanced was that of a married man who had been told that he had no right to get married if he was unable to support a wife and family.[63] The complaints did have some effect for, at the end of the year, when the Fund had reached £21,000 almost all of it had been disbursed.[64]

What was surprising during this period was the attitude of the workers on the Clyde and, for the most part, Glasgow's unemployed. While there were reports of serious rioting in places like Aberdeen and Dundee, Glasgow, with the exception of John McLean and his small army of unemployed, was strangely passive.[65] The McLean threat was dealt with when he was arrested and jailed for inciting the people to steal the food they were unable to obtain legally.[66] Despite Wheatley's appeal to the workers to fight the threatened destruction of family life by taking the necessary steps to prevent the occupation of a house which had become empty through an eviction,[67] it was the women of the

The Life of John Wheatley

G.L.H.A. who fought and demonstrated against these evictions at every turn. They organised a deputation to the Council to publicise the gravity of the situation. A motion by Wheatley that Standing Orders be suspended to allow the Council to meet and discuss with the women was defeated. Ignoring the ruling, Kirkwood went out and ushered in the deputation. The Lord Provost declared the meeting adjourned and quit the chair. Wheatley immediately took over the chair and invited the deputation to address the Council.[68] This was a typical Wheatley publicity stunt to bring housing once again to the forefront of Glasgow politics and with it the involvement of the women. Despite the continuous flow of propaganda the I.L.P. needed a cause which would be meaningful to the whole of Glasgow's working class and central to any campaign that would be launched to fight a General Election of which there were vague hints towards the close of 1921.

References

1. *Glasgow Evening Times* – 22/1/19
2. *Glasgow Evening Times* – 18/1/19
3. *Glasgow Evening Times* – 31/1/19
4. *London Times* – 31/1/19
   Glasgow Evening Times – 12/8/19
5. *Glasgow Evening Times* – 7/2/19
6. *Forward* – 3/5/19
7. *Forward* – 13/9/19
8. Glasgow Corporation Minutes – 16/5/19
9. Glasgow Corporation Minutes – 20/3/19
10. Glasgow Corporation Minutes – 16/5/19
11. Glasgow Corporation Minutes – 20/6/19
12. Glasgow Corporation Minutes – 20/3/19
13. Glasgow Corporation Minutes – 5/12/19
14. *Forward* – 3/1/20
15. *Glasgow Evening Times* – 4/11/19
16. Glasgow Corporation Minutes – 10/7/19
17. *Forward* – 17/7/20
18. *Municipal Banking* – John Wheatley – circa 1920
19. *Glasgow Evening Times* – 5/10/17
20. *Glasgow Evening Times* – 23/8/19
21. Ibid.
22. *Glasgow Evening Times* – 10/10/19, 20/11/19
23. *Glasgow Evening Times* – 5/1/18
24. *Forward* – 16/1/20
25. Glasgow Corporation Minutes – 18/3/20
    Glasgow Evening Times – 19/3/20, 25/3/20
26. *Glasgow Evening Times* – 3/5/20

27. *Forward* – 29/5/20
28. *Forward* – 17/7/20
29. *The New Rent Act (A reply to the rent raisers)* – National Library
30. *Forward* – 31/7/20
31. *Glasgow Evening Times* – 23/8/20
32. Glasgow Corporation Minutes – 3/12/20
33. *Forward* – 3/7/20, 10/7/20
34. *Glasgow Evening Times* – 23/1/20
35. *Glasgow Evening Times* – 26/1/21
36. *Forward* – 10/11/20
37. *Glasgow Evening Times* – 28/10/20
38. Ibid.
39. *Glasgow Evening Times* – 2/1/20
40. *Forward* – 10/11/20
41. *Forward* – 27/11/20
42. Glasgow Corporation Minutes – 3/12/20
43. Glasgow Corporation Minutes – 14/1/21
44. *Glasgow Evening Times* – 3/1/21
45. *Glasgow Evening Times* – 1/1/21
46. Glasgow Corporation Minutes – 19/11/20
    Glasgow Evening Times – 16/10/23
    Working Class Housing in Glasgow – John Butt
47. Glasgow Corporation Minutes – 24/3/21
48. Glasgow Corporation Minutes – 21/10/20
49. *John McLean* – Nan Milton
50. *Glasgow Evening Times* – 17/2/21
51. Minutes of Special Scottish Conference – 28/12/20, 7/1/21
52. *Glasgow Evening Times* – 27/1/21
53. *Glasgow Evening Times* – 21/12/21
54. Scottish Office Circulars – R1769– 22/9/21 & R1776 – 12/10/21
55. Glasgow Corporation Minutes – 8/9/21
56. *Glasgow Evening Times* – 3/5/21
57. *Forward* – 26/11/21, 7/1/22
58. *Glasgow Evening Times* – 12/1/21
    Glasgow Corporation Minutes – 13/1/21
59. Glasgow Corporation Minutes – 3/1/21, 3/2/21
60. *Glasgow Evening Times* – 31/3/21
61. *Glasgow Evening Times* – 25/8/21
62. *Glasgow Evening Times* – 28/3/21
63. *Glasgow Evening Times* – 25/8/21
64. *Glasgow Evening Times* – 22/12/21
65. *Glasgow Evening Times* – 8/9/21, 20/9/21
66. *Glasgow Evening Times* – 21/9/21
67. *Forward* – 7/1/22
68. Glasgow Corporation Minutes – 20/10/21

Chapter Nine
The 1922 Election

Before the Geddes Report was published in February 1922 the Tories had begun to distance themselves from Lloyd George and the Coalition. Writing to all Tories in the previous month, Sir George Younger warned them that in the event of being forced into an election they would stand not as Coalitionists, but as Independent Unionists.[1] It was a shrewd move, not only would Lloyd George be seen as being responsible for the heavy cuts in public expenditure that had been proposed by Geddes, but also for the general state of industry. To reduce the burden on taxation Geddes proposed, among other things, cuts in Health, Education and the sale of Council houses. The government adopted most of these proposals and then in May, reduced Income Tax. With unemployment around the 1½ million mark the engineers were forced, after a lock-out, to accept another cut in wages. However, the Tories were not the only ones able to make propaganda from the general economic situation.

The I.L.P. had begun its election campaign towards the end of the previous year with a series of Manifestos[2] drafted by Wheatley. These Manifestos, written in support of all the Labour candidates in the West of Scotland, were published in *Forward*[3] and local newspapers. Emphasis was placed on Scotland's needs and the policies of successive Governments which had resulted in vast areas of Scotland being used mainly for sport. One quoted a report of the Royal Scottish Agricultural Society which had stated that afforestation in Scotland with its subsidiary trades could provide profitable employment for 200,000 men. It contrasted an area in Germany where 13,000 acres under afforestation provided 300 jobs to a similar sized area in Scotland which employed 15 shepherds and gamekeepers. Home Rule for Scotland was now a part of the I.L.P. policy. Dollan, who was Chairman of the Glasgow Executive at this time, was to say later that Wheatley took no part in the organisation of these campaigns.[4] However, the evidence against Dollan's statement is rather weighty. John McNair, a contemporary, was adamant that Wheatley was the organiser. 'Seldom, if ever, in the Labour and Socialist movement has Wheatley's administrative ability and

The 1922 Election

political acumen been equalled.'[5] John Scanlon, also an activist at this time, wrote that the election was fought on manifestos and leaflets largely drafted by Wheatley.[6] Wheatley's own record in the U.I.L., the C.S.S. and his own campaigns in Shettleston cannot be ignored.

In the planning, Wheatley left nothing to chance. The I.L.P. candidates met each week in a Glasgow restaurant to discuss the campaign. On each occasion a different subject matter was chosen for discussion so that the risk of conflicting statements on public platforms would be minimal. The candidates, in addition to Wheatley, were Kirkwood, Maxton, Buchanan, Johnston, Neil McLean, Johnny Muir, James Stewart, George Hardie, James C. Welsh and the Rev. Campbell Stephen. All were total abstainers and "not a lum hat among them" said Kirkwood.[7] Wheatley had been determined to keep the I.L.P. Movement in the West of Scotland free of middle class infiltration.[8]

In August a special revival campaign was launched. Twenty eight branches were organised to take part in the campaign with 140 meetings held throughout the City. A special feature of these meetings was the large turn out of women.[9] The campaign received a further boost with the M.O.H.'s Report[10] that there were 58,000 people living in 13,195 houses which were not fit for human habitation. Wheatley seized on this disclosure by demanding that the Director of Housing submit plans for the speedy erection of 13,000 houses on sites held by the Corporation. He followed this up with the distribution of a leaflet. Headed 'GLASGOW'S HUMAN SLAUGHTER HOUSES'[11] the leaflet contained a list of the City's dangerous streets i.e. streets which contained houses which were unfit for human habitation. A couple of weeks after the distribution of this leaflet Lloyd George resigned as Premier. The rank and file of the Tory Party had become less enamoured with the Coalition when their spokesman in that Government, Bonar Law, resigned because of ill health. It came as no surprise when, at a meeting in the Carlton Club on the 19th October, these back benchers overwhelmingly approved a motion that 'the Party fight an election with its own leader and its own programme'.[12] It was a motion that Lloyd George did not ignore and almost immediately he tendered his resignation to the King. Bonar Law, by this time sufficiently recovered, was invited to form a new Government. He decided to appeal to the country on the single issue of expansion of world trade as the only cure for unemployment and towards this end he stated his intention to promote a conference of all the Dominion countries. The date set for the election was the 15th November.

The Liberals were again divided going into this election. Those Liberals who supported Lloyd George contracted an alliance with the Tories, some called it an immoral alliance, and stood as National Liberals. Their policy was little different from the Tories, in addition to fostering Empire trade, it called for stern economy and greater co-operation between Capital and Labour.

The Independent Liberals had more radical policies. They proposed to tax Land Values. They would seek to defend the Social Services and secure the worker against the widespread hardship of unemployment. They would invoke an International Economic Conference and work for the revision of the Versailles Treaty. They also promised to legislate for Proportional Representation. Free Trade was to remain an integral part of their policy.

The National Council of the I.L.P. failed to interpret the early mutterings of the Tories and were not quite prepared for the election when it was called. Propaganda campaigns had been scheduled for November and December which were preceded by a public meeting on the 12th October at which the Party policies were unveiled. These advocated the nationalisation of land, the organisation of industry, transport and finance to the service of the nation, but not bureaucratic State control. The Party called on the Trade Unions to broaden the scope of their membership to include all workers. It also promised to work towards total disarmament. On the platform at this meeting, together with McDonald and Snowden, were Colonel Wedgwood and C. P. Trevelyn.[13] These two were among a group of Liberals who had recently converted to the I.L.P. because of its pacifist policies, a group that included such figures as Hobson, Wise, Brailsford and Clifford Allen. Wheatley did not take kindly to many of these converts, believing that they would compromise the Party's Socialism.[14]

The Labour Party, equally unprepared, issued a short policy statement which called for a more equitable distribution of the nation's wealth by constitutional means.

In Glasgow, the I.L.P. was contesting eleven of the fifteen seats. The decision to contest Central Division was a last minute one. The incumbent here was Bonar Law and it had earlier been considered pointless to oppose such a personality. When the decision was taken to contest the seat, Rosslyn Mitchell was selected to oppose Law. In the final two weeks of the campaign in the West of Scotland the I.L.P. increased the level of its intensity. They had powerful advocates in Maxton and Buchanan. Maxton, with the long flowing hair and cadaverous features, could raise an audience to fury and, just as quickly, reduce it to tears. Though not a candidate, the Rev. James Barr was tireless in his efforts for the cause of Socialism.[15] Barr had come into conflict with his superiors because of his sermons on the 'Spiritual Foundations of Socialism' which condemned landlordism. There were also the hundreds of anonymous helpers who made use of every spare piece of ground in the City on which to paint their graffitti.[16] Wheatley's speeches reflected the aggressiveness and substance of the campaign.

The Central Halls was the venue for the official launching of the I.L.P. bid to capture Glasgow. Presiding over a packed audience and a platform which included all the Scottish Labour candidates, Wheatley's address[17] was a scathing attack on a Capitalist system in which he claimed there was nothing to distinguish Tory from Liberal.

'The political bankruptcy of the Capitalist politician has been reflected in the speeches of the old and new Prime Ministers. These people have ruined the trade and industry of the country. They have denied to 1½ million people the chance to earn a livelihood for millions of their dependants. They have reduced the working class to a state of panic lest, by word or deed, they give offence to the foreman. They have increased rents by 50%. They have stopped the building of new homes. They have passively allowed the finances of the country to go into the hands of a cosmopolitan gang who were able to state the nation's policies. The people have been beaten to their knees and stripped of everything but their votes. The Carlton Club rupture led people to expect a deadly struggle between rival policies and opposite principles. The truth is, the fight is a farce. It resembles a trumped up contest between professional pugilists where the blows fall softly on smiling faces and the proceeds are afterwards amicably shared. Neither Lloyd George nor Bonar Law can give substantial reason why the government of a country so beaten and oppressed should be placed in their hands.'

In Shettleston, Wheatley had two opponents: Wilson Ramsay, National Liberal, and Guy Aldred, Communist. Admiral Adair's late decision not to seek re-election left the Coalition little time to introduce Ramsay who was even less effectual than Adair. The Communist was not expected to pull many votes away from Wheatley and consequently, the *Glasgow Herald* was forecasting that a Wheatley victory was a foregone conclusion. This prediction did not cause him to let up on his campaigning. He savaged the Government on the Health cuts.

'What can one think of a Government that spent £160,000 on clothing the guards and Household Cavalry and cannot find money for hungry babies.'[18] Of course housing and rents played a major part in his campaign and as usual there was that bitter irony in his speeches.

"From the first day that I raised my voice on behalf of tenants I heard the talk of those property owning widows and orphans that would be ruined by Labour's policy, but strangely enough I have never met any of them. I have investigated the histories of all the inmates of Barnhill Poor House and there was not one single property owner among them."[19]

A $7^1/_2$% increase in Labour's share of the vote at the Glasgow Municipal elections on the 7th of November sent the I.L.P. hopes soaring. There was only a slight worry in Gorbals where John McLean was standing in opposition to Buchanan as a Scottish Communist candidate. There had been the evidence however, from two recent Municipal elections, that McLean's appeal was not what it had been.

The results, when they were announced, greatly exceeded I.L.P. expectations and sent Glasgow delirious. Ten of the eleven seats had been taken. In addition, Kirkwood and Johnston had triumphed in Dumbarton and Stirling. 166,638 votes had been cast for the I.L.P. in the City of Glasgow, 43% of the electorate. Wheatley's majority was almost 5,000, but it was Central which provided the biggest surprise. Mitchell, although defeated, polled over 12,000 votes reducing Bonar Law's majority to 2,514. Buchanan, despite losing 4,000 votes to McLean, had a majority of 8,000 and Maxton also had a comfortable majority of 7,692.

In a statement to the press on the day following the result the Glasgow Executive of the I.L.P. said that the main issues on its platform had been housing and rents and the reason for their success was the rallying of the working class women.[20] It was a vindication of a policy Wheatley had initiated and pursued for ten long years. He would also take satisfaction in knowing that the Catholic vote, estimated at 20%, had gone solidly to Labour and six Independent Liberals lost their deposits. There had been no opposition to Labour from the pulpits and, indeed, it had been reported that many of the clergy had been sympathetic to Labour's cause.[21] What must have been a telling factor in the campaign was the character of the candidates themselves. Never has Glasgow had representatives so revered as this body of men who were later to put a new meaning into 'Clydeside'. Before the new M.P.s left for the opening of the new Parliament they attended a victory rally in St. Andrew's Halls. 8,000 gathered to hear them give a pledge to the people with this declaration.[22]

'We, the Labour Members of Parliament for the City of Glasgow and the West of Scotland, inspired by the zeal for the welfare of humanity and the prosperity of all peoples and strengthened by the trust imposed in them by their fellow citizens, have resolved to dedicate ourselves to the reconciliation and unity of the nations of the world and the development and happiness of the people of these islands.

The 1922 Election

We record our infinite gratitude to the pioneer minds who have opened up the path for the freedom of the people. We send to all people a message of goodwill and, to the sister nations of the British Commonwealth, fraternal greetings.

We will not forget those who suffered in the war and will see that the widows and orphans shall be cherished by the nation.

We will urge without ceasing the need for houses suitable to enshrine the spirit of the home.

We will bear in our hearts the sorrows of the aged, the widowed mothers and the poor, that their lives will not be without comfort.

We will endeavour to purge industry of the curse of unhealthy workshops and to restore wages to an adequate level of maintenance and eradicate the corrupting effects of monopoly and avarice.

We will press for the provision of useful employment and reasonable maintenance.

We will have regard for the weak and those stricken by disease, for those who have fallen in the struggle of life and those who are in prison.

To this end we will endeavour to adjust the finances of the nation that the burden of public debt may be relieved and the maintenance of national administration be borne by those best able to bear it.

In all things we will abjure vanity and self aggrandisement, recognising that we are the humble servants of the people and that our only righteous purpose is to promote the welfare of our fellow citizens and the well-being of all mankind.'

No group of elected representatives had ever given such a pledge to the people. As well as being messianic it gave recognition to the fact that not only was poverty the product of the Capitalist system, but also disease, loneliness and crime. That they were servants of the people they showed by example in that they themselves did not have an official leader, a fact of which they were proud. The spirituality of the evening led finally to the audience joining in the singing of the 'Lord is my Shepherd' and the 'Red Flag'. After the rally thousands flocked to the station where the new M.P.s were given an emotional send-off as they boarded the night train to London. The experience of that evening was to remain with Wheatley for the rest of his days. 'It proved to me,' he later said,[23] 'that the people were ready to respond to a Socialist lead.''

References

1. *Glasgow Evening Times* – 10/11/22
2. *John Wheatley–John Scanlon* (The Book of the Labour Party) Vol 3
3. *Forward* – 16/4/21, 26/11/21
4. *Glasgow Evening Times* – 5/5/30
5. *Beloved Rebel* – John McNair
6. *John Wheatley–John Scanlon* (Book of the Labour Party) Vol 3

7. *My Life of Revolt* – David Kirkwood
8. *Decline and Fall of the Labour Party* – John Scanlon – 1932
9. *Forward* – 19/8/22
10. *Glasgow Corporation Minutes* – 19/10/22
11. *Forward* – 17/10/22
12. *Scotsman* – 20/10/22
13. *Scotsman* – 12/10/22
14. *Decline and Fall of the Labour Party* – John Scanlon
    New Leader – 29/1/23
15. *London Times* – 28/12/22
16. Ibid.
17. *Scotsman* – 30/10/22
18. *Glasgow Evening Times* – 7/11/22
19. Ibid.
20. *Glasgow Evening Times* – 16/11/22
21. *Glasgow Evening Times* – 15/11/22
    London Times – 28/12/22
22. *The Clydesiders* – R. K. Middlemass – 1965
23. *Left Turn* – John Paton – 1936

Chapter Ten
Into Parliament

In the new Parliament the Tories, with only a third of the popular vote, had an overall majority of 80. National Liberals had 50 seats, Independent Liberals 55, and Labour with 142 seats was the official opposition.

It was assumed that Clynes, who had been Chairman of the Parliamentary Labour Party since 1920 and had strong T.U. support, would be named opposition leader. There were some, however, who had been dissatisfied with the effectiveness of Clynes' leadership of the Party in the previous Parliament and there were others, particularly among the left wing, who could not forgive him for his participation in the wartime Government. He was certainly not very popular on the Clyde on this account.[1] McDonald, whose opposition to the war had made him popular on the Clyde, decided to contest the leadership. He was nominated by Shinwell who had gained a seat at Linlithgow. Largely through the support of the Clydesiders and the Miners McDonald was elected by 61 votes to 57. There were 24 M.P.s absent on the day of the election, mostly through T.U. business. Many were uneasy at the outcome of this election and the manner in which McDonald went about canvassing support. Snowden, who gave his support to Clynes, felt that McDonald's passion for intrigue and compromise disqualified him from the leadership of a left wing Party.[2] Wheatley was also uneasy[3] and Maxton certainly had reservations.[4] Henderson prophesied that within six months the Clyde group would regret having given their support to McDonald.[5]

On the 23rd of November, the day the new Parliament opened, thousands of hunger marchers had converged on London in a bid to force the Government into some kind of action that would help to solve the unemployment problem. The King's speech contained little to suggest that the Government had any plans to deal with this problem. It was brief, referring to Ireland's new constitution, the Lausanne Conference, which the Allies had convened to negotiate a settlement of the Greco–Turkish war and 'the state of trade and unemployment which is causing us deep concern'.

In the debate on unemployment that followed the King's

speech[6] McDonald, ever eager to exhibit his Parliamentary skills, did little to impress the left wing of the Party on his handling of the unemployment question. Walt Newbold, the Communist Member for Motherwell, and Clement Attlee were much more convincing in their pleas on behalf of the unemployed. Attlee portrayed vividly the poverty of the people in his own constituency of Stepney. It was interjections from Lady Astor and Patrick Ford, Tory member for Edinburgh North, which provided Wheatley with the background for his maiden speech. After welcoming the air of reality that Newbold and Attlee had brought to the debate Wheatley turned to the remarks of the others.

'One of these remarks was an appeal to those of us from Scotland to remember that our opponents opposite have very good hearts, that they may not see eye to eye with us on the remedy for social evils, but that their intentions are of the best. Another was that the working men and women of this country believe that the government had a good heart. I am one of the representatives of a city in which the working men and women believe nothing of the kind. Our citizens sent two thirds of their total representatives to tell the Prime Minister they do not want him to occupy that position and seven days ago, if the citizens of Glasgow had had the opportunity, they would have voted themselves entirely and immediately and completely outside the Capitalist system of society of which the Honourable Lady Astor is a defender. During her little lecture she told us that she is very anxious to bring about the condition of society of which we claimed monopoly as propagandists. I do not doubt her good intentions. It is not her intentions which are at fault, it is the principles of which she is a defender. We have demonstrated, to the satisfaction of two thirds of the citizens of the second city of the Empire, that these principles are wrong. They have sent us here to tell you that, in their opinion, the system is a complete failure and they do not regard the collapse of the Government as being due to any imperfections in its personnel. They do not attribute unemployment to the fact that you have a Coalition government or a Conservative one. They believe that, if the front benches were occupied by Angels from heaven and these Angels defended the Capitalist system of society, you would still have the present deplorable conditions. I hope to be able to demonstrate that to the noble lady. Two questions have been mentioned. There is first the question of unemployment. You talk about solving it by improving trade with Europe and establishing commercial connections with Russia, but that is not the cause of unemployment. If your poverty and unemployment were due to the fact that you could not get certain goods from Russia or Europe you ought to be able to show us that there is a shortage of goods in this country. There is no shortage – unemployment is due to an embarrassment of riches. Shipyards on the Clyde are idle because you have too many ships. Miners in Lanarkshire are idle because you have too much coal. Textile workers in Leeds are idle because the markets and warehouses are glutted with the goods they produce. There is a shortage of only one thing in this country and that is housing accommodation and you do not import that from Europe or Russia. What is the cause of unemployment? It is due to the fact that your Capitalist system cannot distribute goods as rapidly as it produces them. During the war years industrial capacity was increased with new machinery and with a reduced workforce we were still able to meet the requirements of the people. After the war 7 to 8 million people were brought back into industry. Does it not appeal to your common sense that you are going to double the quantity of goods being produced and, if you are going to keep industry from becoming stagnant, there must be an outlet for this capacity. You are looking for markets in Russia and Europe. Has it ever occurred to you that you have reduced wages by £500 million and thereby cut off purchasing power to that extent and cut off a greater market at home than you are trying to get abroad? You talk about making credit facilities available to Europe. Why not give credit to the common people of this country and put the country back on its feet. The Capitalist system cannot provide a remedy for unemployment. Under that system, when an employer finds he has more goods than the people can purchase with the money at their disposal, he stops production.'

Wheatley then turned his attention to housing as another example of the failure of the Capitalist system. He spoke of the needs of Glasgow and the other great cities for houses, a need that the government recognised and for which they started a programme of building.

'Immediately they introduced this programme they found that all the necessary materials were controlled by Trusts and Combines and with the new demand prices started to increase. The Government being the defender of private enterprise could do nothing to prevent this. House prices soared and the Government could do nothing to stop the boosting of prices. The only thing they could do was stop building houses. That is Capitalism. The prices then dropped again. These Combines have the nation by the throat and you people sit there as the helpless defenders of this obsolete system of society. How long you will remain there will depend on whether other parts of the country become as intelligent as Glasgow.'

Wheatley's maiden speech brought him to the forefront of the wider Labour movement. Snowden, who had made a worthwhile contribution to the debate, singled out Wheatley from the other Clydesiders whose speeches, he thought, were lacking in maturity.[7] The press made no such distinction. One leading Scottish newspaper[8] commenting on the praise that was being heaped on Wheatley as a result of his speech had this to write, 'Mr. Wheatley was supposed by his friends to have achieved great success, but it was the success of the Glasgow Green type with platform rhetoric of the same calibre with the easy solution of Socialising the manufacture of material and eliminating private property.'

It was the Clydesiders use of the rhetoric of the Glasgow Green in the Commons which the organiser of the I.L.P. attributed to the increase in membership and new branches in the Party during 1923, not only in Scotland, but in many parts of England.[9] The Clydesiders were a new phenomena in British politics and the press was quick to seize on them as being good copy. While Maxton, Kirkwood, Shinwell and the others made themselves available to these news hounds,[10] Wheatley remained discreetly in the background. He was keenly aware of the damage the wrong type of publicity could do. He was distinctly unhappy with those new Labour members who were accepting invitations to the houses of the upper and middle classes. For representatives of the working class to be reported as wining and dining in the drawing rooms of the rich while thousands of their constituents were on the bread line could do nothing but harm to their image. There was also the danger that too much socialising with the opposition would erode the fighting spirit needed in the Commons.[11] Conscious of these dangers Wheatley, together with Maxton and Johnston, issued a memorandum, to which each Labour member was to give his signature, that called for a ban on the acceptance of such social invitations.[12] What also angered Wheatley was the Commons' lack of conviction in dealing with the question of unemployment. Before Parliament recessed for Christmas Wheatley had manoeuvred the Commons into its first all night sitting in protest at what he described as 'political fencing' on the question of unemployment.[13]

The recess was not an idle time for Wheatley. His arguments on the chronic lack of demand, which he first advanced eleven years previously, had now been formulated in a pamphlet entitled 'STARVATION AMIDST PLENTY'.[14] Criticism of his theories came from both right and left. The *Financial Times* held the view that the wealth of the rich was spent in one way or another and that transferring it to the poor would not increase purchasing power. Strangely, the Plebs held a similar view.[15] It was not surprising that Bonar Law, visiting Glasgow during the recess, should tell a deputation from the Trades Council that increasing wages or borrowing money was not the answer to unemployment.[16] Considering that Keynes' first publication did not appear until more than a decade later Wheatley's theories were unorthodox at the time. Nevertheless, his views were becoming widely known to such an extent that he and his group were being referred to as the Glasgow School of Economists.[17] During this recess Wheatley was also preparing for the launching of his own newspaper, the *Glasgow Eastern Standard*. The first edition of this paper appeared on the 3rd March under the editorship of Willie Regan. 'The policy of the paper,' wrote Regan,' was to boom the East End of Glasgow, to cultivate an interest in its people, its institutions and its history.' It was also going to keep a watchful eye on the local M.P.s' activities in Parliament.

With unemployment still close to the 1½ million mark the unemployed were again on the march to London for the opening of the new session of Parliament. A Council of Action had been formed to co-ordinate the activities of all the local unemployed committees. They had issued a call for reinforcements for the march on London 'to shake the attitude of callous and brutal indifference of Bonar Law'.[18] The King's Speech contained nothing that would alter the opinion of the marchers. There were three major Bills (1) Amendment to the Rent Restrictions Act, (2) The housing of the Working Classes, (3) Unemployment Insurance.

Following McDonald's reply to the King's speech the debate on unemployment[19] continued. During its course George Lansbury raised the question of the Hunger Marchers vis-à-vis their right to Poor Relief from the authorities of the various towns through which they passed. There had been a report of one group who had threatened to take over a town in which they had been refused relief.

'What is the position of the Hunger Marchers?' said Joynson-Hicks, Secretary of Overseas Trade – he was acting Health spokesman until Neville Chamberlain was returned to Parliament – 'It is not one of ordinary destitution. They are able to smoke cigarettes. These men are engaged in an attempt, on behalf of the Council of Action, either to break down the Poor Law in the towns which they pass through or else to take such action as could terrify the House into granting certain demands, notwithstanding the fact that we have had a recent General Election. The unemployed have elected representatives to put forward their case in Parliament. These Marchers are being brought to London for no purpose as the Minister of Health has stated that he has no intention of meeting them.' Hicks's statement brought a stinging reply from Wheatley.

'I wish that the outside public could see these benches opposite with only a score of members present. No doubt an investigation of the building would reveal a large number of enthusiastic Tory members interested in the consumption of champagne. Joynson-Hicks has referred to the terrible things that have been done by the Hunger Marchers. I wonder if it ever occurs to him how much society has injured these people and how it has contributed to the terrible conditions which have broken them physically and morally. I wonder what 1½ million of your people would do if deprived of income for 2 years and had no spare means. They would have done more than the Hunger Marchers had done. They would not sit contentedly listening to lectures on the proper way to starve. The Hunger Marchers had only threatened to hold up a town. I wish they would not just threaten, I wish they would do it and make themselves uncomfortable to you all.'

Wheatley then went on to criticise again the Capitalist system and the dishonesty of those who profited from it and who were continually searching for new fields in which to invest their surplus wealth. He condemned those who talked about the poverty of their country whilst they had invested £3 billion abroad not, he said, because of any desire to promote the interests of any foreign country, but because they were for ever on the lookout for cheap labour. He concluded by saying,' You people are the greatest enemies of the human race, you are responsible for the ruin of this country and you have the cheek to come here and talk about the character of the Hunger Marchers.'

The *Glasgow Herald* was not altogether wrong when it described the speech as a disjointed and iconoclastic harangue.[20] During the course of the speech Wheatley, in attempting to contrast the attitude of the British Government vis-à-vis the debts of its own people and that of foreign powers, had wandered to the subject of the Rühr and the French occupation there. He stated that it was his intention to make a thorough investigation of the facts concerning the Rühr. It was an investigation that almost put an end to a promising political career[21] and thwarted any ambitions he may have entertained in the field of foreign affairs.

The Allies had fixed German reparations at £6,600 millions, to be paid in goods. At the beginning of the year she had been in default with deliveries of timber and when shortly afterwards the Reparations Commission announced that she was again in default, this time with coal, the French occupied the Rühr. The French move was condemned by the European governments and European Socialists. Shortly before the I.L.P. Easter Conference of that year, Wheatley, accompanied by Maxton, Kirkwood and Campbell Stephens, went to the Rühr on a fact finding mission. On their return, Wheatley called for the Internationalisation of the Rühr and at a public meeting in Glasgow's Metropole Theatre put forward his arguments for this policy.[22]

'Capitalism has no constructive policy for dealing with the situation. The facts are, Germany is in debt and has admitted her debt and that debt should not be paid by lowering the standards of the German workers, but by confiscating the wealth of the German millionaires.'

At the Conference, a motion was put forward by Dollan condemning the French invasion and demanding the immediate withdrawal of all their forces. This motion represented the feeling of the Scottish Labour movement.

Speaking on his amendment, based on his earlier arguments, Wheatley warned the delegates to be careful lest they contributed towards an atmosphere which would result in British Capitalism leading the country to international war. In the debate that followed much emphasis was placed on the solidarity of European Socialists and particularly on the statements of leading German Socialists which had condemned French aggression. The Conference voted overwhelmingly against Wheatley's amendment for it would have been insanity on the part of the I.L.P. to ignore the feelings of its partners in the Vienna International whose conscience it claimed to be. Wheatley later said[24] that his proposal was more of a gesture to the French working class than any attempt to solve the problems in Europe. He was afraid that the return of the Rühr to Germany would throw the French workers into the arms of the reactionaries. He felt too, that the pacifists within the Party were as openly anti-French as the jingoists were anti-German. Despite Conference's antagonism towards his amendment he was elected to the N.A.C. together with McDonald, Jowett and Wallhead.

One of the pacifists to whom Wheatley referred and who was bitter in his opposition to his amendment, was Clifford Allen. A rising star in the I.L.P. Allen, in his short period as Treasurer of the Party, had impressed with his exceptional flair for organisation. He had also been instrumental in attracting large donations to the Party from wealthy pacifist families. Recognition of his qualities had come with his election as Party Chairman. With Fenner Brockway as Organising Secretary the Party was now much more professional. The official organ had undergone drastic surgery as a result of the influence of these two men. Its name had been altered from the *Leader* to the *New Leader* and, now under the editorship of Brailsford, had become more intellectual in character. Regular contributors were G.D.H. Cole, Attlee and McDonald. Arthur Ponsonby reported on Parliamentary affairs whilst Wheatley contributed from time to time. Circulation began to increase steadily as did membership of the Party. Between 1923 and 1925 the number of branches rose from 637 to 1028,[25] not all of this increase could be attributable to Allen.

One of Allen's notable innovations, one that Wheatley would have endorsed, was the 'MASSES STAGE AND FILM GUILD'. Designed to stimulate working-class art and express the spiritual concept of Socialism, the Guild aimed to personify the Party slogan 'BREAD and ROSES'.[26] Each I.L.P. branch was to have its own Arts Guild where, it was envisaged, the cultural talents of the workers would find an outlet. A fine example of this was the Arts Circle at Bath St. in Glasgow where encouragement was given to budding painters and sculptors.[27] Wheatley's own attempts to integrate politics and art in the Socialist Movement pre-dated Allen's Guild. He, himself, had written two one-act plays on working-class themes which had been produced a few years earlier by a Shettleston Workers Theatre group.[28] In his encouragement of the workers he advised them to ignore the highbrow in drama and not to stand in awe of middle class criticism.[29]

Scotland was now playing an increasing role in the affairs of the Labour movement. At the P.L.P. elections Johnston, Shinwell and Wheatley were voted third, seventh and eighth respectively.[30] An inner Parliamentary group of I.L.P. members was formed to discuss day-to-day topics and to organise cohesive action in the House on the most controversial matters arising from these discussions. Wheatley sat on this Committee along with Jowett, Johnston, Allen and Wallhead. It was thought that Wheatley's inclusion was necessary because of the influence he had over the Clydesiders.[31]

The first major piece of legislation to come before the new Parliament was the Rent Restrictions Bill. The Bill, primarily designed to de-control rents, also aimed to right what to the Government seemed a wrong emanating from the previous Bill. When rents were raised as a result of this Bill it was found, after the Scottish Labour Housing Association had taken a test case to court, that it was illegal for landlords to charge a higher rent without first abrogating the old agreement by issuing a 'Notice to Quit' to the tenant. This resulted in many landlords losing a year's rent and rates combined. This new Bill was to make provision for landlords to recover what was deemed to be owing to them. The new Act, which set the 1st December 1922 as the crucial date, stated that 'amounts paid by tenants before that date which the landlord has, he may keep. Any arrears cannot be recovered by the landlord. However, arrears which had been kept back from the landlord from that date either in respect of increased rents due after that date, or in respect of increases paid by the tenant before that date, the landlord can recover'.

'This clause,' Wheatley argued, 'is based on the Capitalist principle of possession. The good old rule, the simple plan, that he should take who hath the powers and he should keep who can.'[32] Wheatley also attacked the Government's argument that rent control had the psychological effect of frightening off investment in house building. "Why is it that private enterprise is not building in the private sector where rent restrictions do not apply?' The system of financing house building also came under criticism as did the financiers themselves.[33]

The Government's only attempt to boost the economy came with the Budget. £38½ million was given back by way of reductions in income and corporation taxes in what, said the Chancellor Baldwin, was an effort to stimulate trade. The Budget came under attack from the left wing of the Labour Party and again it was Wheatley who spearheaded it.[34]

'The Budget merely convinces the toiling multitudes outside that the richer sections of the community, for whom the Chancellor speaks, have put into the National Purse something which can be proved never to have been there. Forty years ago I stood open-mouthed on a village showground while a financier of those days took three half-crowns from his pocket and pretended to put them into a purse and then, having rolled up his sleeves, convinced the admiring multitude that everything was above board and he succeeded in selling the purse for half-a-crown to a man called Henry Dodd. When Henry examined the purse he discovered he had been deceived. What the conjurer had put in with one hand, he had taken out with the other. This is what happens to national finances. If you examine the National Purse you will find that the amount taken out by the interest drawing classes is approximately the amount of money contributed in income tax and super tax if you assume, as I do, that the class to whom we owe the National Debt is the same class who pay these taxes. The total estimated amount of tax for the ensuing year is £300 million, while the amount to be paid in interest is £310 million. To say the surplus which the Chancellor has at his disposal and which is being given to those who already hold the surplus will stimulate industry shows an ignorance of the situation. Can you tell me one single industry today which is depressed because of shortage of capital. It is not capital you want to stimulate industry, it is orders. I can take you to districts and show you where millions of pounds worth of capital is rotting. You have machinery rusting, workshops and warehouses depreciating and you talk about more capital being necessary and to give that as a reason for diverting £38½ million to the pockets of the rich is not paying a very high tribute to the intelligence of this House. You have an excellent opportunity to stimulate trade by diverting this money to the abolition of food taxes, and so increase the purchasing power of the people. This surplus wealth has, in any case, been obtained by robbing people of education, pensions and dole money over the past year.'

There were few critics of the Budget. Asquith was fulsome in his praise and McDonald, after mildly criticising the tax reductions, praised Baldwin for his provisions towards reducing the National Debt and said it gave him real pleasure to congratulate the Chancellor in this his first Budget. Snowden, Labour's chief spokesman on finance, condemned the 6d reduction on income tax as being too paltry to increase effective demand and he called for the introduction of a capital levy. He, too, praised the Chancellor on his provisions to meet the National Debt. Baldwin had used £50 million to create a new Sinking Fund. On the other hand Wheatley had criticised the Government over the management of the National Debt, particularly its failure to take the same advantage abroad, as it did at home, of an appreciating pound. Unlike Wheatley, McDonald and Snowden were content to stick to the Capitalist system of finance.

While Wheatley and J. A. Hobson saw under-consumption as the root cause of unemployment – Hobson's book *The Economics of Unemployment* had been published that year – the Labour Party, with the help of Hugh Dalton, was setting out deflationary policies. Public expenditure was to be reduced to allow for the repeal of food taxes. Dalton saw rising prices more as the cause of social unrest than unemployment. The National Debt was a prime cause of unemployment and Labour hoped to reduce this by means of an Accumulated Wealth Tax. The plan for this was outlined in the manifesto 'Labour and the War Debt' which was mainly the work of Dalton.[35] No doubt the Labour leaders would have sympathised with much of Chamberlain's proposals for housing.

It was a coincidence that the Government's major policy statements were on issues of which Wheatley had a degree of specialist knowledge. The most specific of these was on housing, it was the one that had carried the Clydesiders to Parliament and, as Maxton had said in a previous debate, if the problem could have been solved in Glasgow they would never have come to London. It was a tribute to the work that Wheatley had done in Glasgow that had given him the right to be the Opposition's Chief spokesman for housing.

When the Government's Housing Bill came before Parliament for its second reading Chamberlain was quick to point out that it was not proposed as a solution to the housing problem, but the beginning of a solution. He spoke of the prodigious efforts by previous Governments in trying to tackle this problem and which, he said, had achieved results disproportionate to the cost expended. Of the 215,000 houses provided by State subsidies, 161,000 went to meet the requirements of an increased population.[36]

'I am aware,' said Chamberlain, 'that much unrest and social discontent was caused by poor housing, although anyone familiar with the conditions in the poorer parts of our great cities must be filled with a feeling of admiration by the patience and good humour in which, for the most part, these evils are borne. However, it is not sufficient to pour out lavish expenditure in an effort to solve the problem as we have learnt to our cost. We have got to treat the problem with sense and sensibility.'

Chamberlain gave what he thought were the reasons for the present housing shortage which, he pointed out, were not solely as the result of the war.

'Private builders, responsible for the huge number of houses built before 1909, did not build to rent, but to sell, for which there was a ready market. This market was supported by an elaborate machinery of finance built up gradually over the years through the savings of small investors on the confidence that property was a sound investment. We must get back to similar conditions so that confidence can be restored to the builders. However, until private enterprise can gradually extend its operations from the larger type house to the less expensive, the Government will set up a scheme of State subsidies. The subsidy we propose is £6 per house per annum for 20 years and the scheme will last until October 1926. The subsidy will be paid only to the Local Authorities and can be used either for giving assistance to private enterprise or for the building of houses themselves.'

The houses were to be three and four apartments with bathrooms and the size of the rooms were to be scullery, 7'6" by 5'10", living room, 13'4½" by 12 ft and the parlour, which Chamberlain described as large enough for courting, 10'6" by 9'3". The bedrooms were to vary in size with the largest 13'3½" by 11'4½".

'The problem,' said Wheatley in his reply,[37] 'is not one of house building, but of finance. It is part and parcel of the great social problem by which, at every stop, we are baffled by poverty at the one end and exploitation at the other. I speak as one of many people on this side of the House who has studied the housing problem from the hard experience of living in the slums. I was one of eleven people who lived, not merely for a month, but for years in a single apartment. I am perfectly satisfied, if I attempted, I could shock even the Honourable Members on the opposite side by a narrative of what life was like under these conditions. The Honourable Members do not understand the housing problem nor do they understand the intense and imperishable hatred of your social order that is bred in the breasts of the victims of these housing conditions. It is a national disgrace to say that what is proposed is not intended as a solution to the problem. The time has come when the country wants a solution.'

Wheatley went on to give what he saw as the reasons for the housing shortage. Increased costs he blamed on the formation of trusts and combines. In the first three years of the existence of the Light Castings Company, prices of building materials had increased by 30%. Even if the government could control these trusts, he said, there would still be the question of £25 per annum to be placed by the money lenders of the country on the rent of the smallest house. He condemned as inequitable the burden that would be placed on local rates by this scheme and he also condemned the size of the houses proposed. By building houses of this size Wheatley accused the Government of attempting to stereotype poverty for the next fifty years. "Why do you propose these boxes for the people, are they less useful to society than yourselves?'

Wheatley's speech had little press coverage. *The Times*[38] allotted it three inches of space and the *New Leader*[39] while making mention of the fact that it was one of the great speeches of the session, printed not one word. The headlines in this paper were being reserved for McDonald and Snowden.

The aim of the Labour Party under McDonald's leadership at this time was for respectability. The boat was not to be rocked in case those Liberals, whom it was thought could be enticed to join the Party, were antagonised. In adopting this course the leadership was ignoring events in the country, something for which it was roundly criticised by Wheatley. At the beginning of June Bob Smillie, after an aggressive campaign, scored a resounding victory at a by-election in Morpeth. In the aftermath of the result Wheatley spotlighted Smillie's campaign as a lesson for the Party to learn.

'Some M.P.s had been saying that the electorate was not keen to send men with aggression to Parliament. Morpeth has demonstrated that the English electors desire more Scotch in their politics. These same M.P.s are of the opinion that a less aggressive Parliamentary policy might attract those wavering Liberals to our side. Liberalism is the last ditch of Capitalism and I for one do not want Liberals in our party.'[40]

The aggressiveness of Wheatley and the Clydesiders' Parliamentary tactics would not have encouraged many Liberals to their side of the House and towards the end of June their tactics had many on their own side shaking heads in disapproval. Prior to the annual debate on the Scottish Health Estimates Wheatley had forced Captain Walter Elliot, the Scottish Minister, to produce the figures for Glasgow of those children suffering from diseases related to malnutrition and asked what steps the Government proposed to take to restore the grant for the feeding of mothers and children which had been cut with Geddes. Elliot, in his statement, had said that it was impossible to determine whether the diseases in these cases came from organic causes or improper feeding rather than malnutrition due to poverty. In any case, the grant, had not been cut, only limited, he told the House.[41] It came as no surprise to the Clydesiders when the Scottish Estimates were announced to find that another £90,000 had been cut from Health spending.

It was Joe Sullivan who led the attack on the Estimates when the debate began on the 27th June, but it was Maxton, in what was described as the greatest appeal of his life for the children of the poor,[42] who took the debate to a climax. In an almost deserted House he harangued the Government on its treatment of the poor. He painted a lurid picture of poverty in his own constituency and contrasted the ratio of child deaths in Scotland to that of England and, while agreeing that the figures in England were bad enough, said that 1,035 children in his own constituency would have survived in English conditions. Turning then to the Scottish Office decision, brought about by Geddes, to limit the number of hospital beds for children at a time when disease was at its worst and child death at its highest, why he asked, in the interest of saving money were children condemned to death? I call the men who supported such a policy, murderers. Sir Frederick Bambury, Tory Member for the City of London, was outraged and called for Maxton to withdraw the word murderer. Maxton refused. McDonald, obviously unhappy with the situation, tried to take the heat out of it. ''I think that there is a great deal of misunderstanding about the use of a very harsh word. What Mr. Maxton really meant was that the result of the Government's action caused deaths.' Determined not to let McDonald smoothe things over Wheatley stood up and repeated Maxton's statement and refused to withdraw. The House then voted in favour of both being suspended. Following on this vote Campbell Stephen and Buchanan each in turn rose and reiterated Maxton's statement and they too were suspended. The whole episode had been contrived to publicise the scant importance given by the House to the Scottish Estimates.[43]

Wheatley and his band of wild men from the Clyde received the publicity and opprobrium they expected. 'Another of these regrettable and repugnant incidents,'[44] wrote a leading Scottish newspaper. This paper went on to tell its readers that the country should be congratulated on the manner in which destitution had been held in check during the Depression and consider itself fortunate compared to the people of Russia. Reaction within the Labour Party at first was anything but favourable. One leading member was mourning the loss of fifty seats at the next election.[45] With the delegates gathered at Queens Hall for the Annual Labour Party Conference the incident received much greater publicity. The Press had it that, because of their disloyalty, McDonald had issued the four with an ultimatum which demanded an apology and a guarantee as to their future good behaviour. McDonald was also reported as being prepared to resign if he failed to get the support of the Party on this matter.[46] There had been no talk of disloyalty to McDonald when Snowden and Wedgwood had joined the Six Point Group in the Commons, a group which was advocating against social injustices such as child abuse and sex discrimination in Government departments and which included Tory and Liberal Members.[47] In the event, at a specially convened meeting in Caxton Hall to consider the question of discipline a resolution was unanimously passed 'that the Labour Members of Parliament direct the attention of the Government and the country to the fearful infant mortality in our land and urge upon them the necessity of re-establishing Child Welfare work on at least the 1920 level.'[48] This result was a disappointment to the press 'the four suspended Labour Members had much need to congratulate themselves that they are under the benign rule of Mr. Ramsay McDonald and not the iron heel of Lenin and Trotsky' was *The Scotsman*'s verdict.[49]

The working class of the country took a different view from that forecast by the press and many of the Labour Members of the four's action. It was not just the Scots who appreciated their stand – before returning to Scotland Wheatley spoke to a huge audience in East London.[50] In Scotland they were accorded the welcome for heroes and for the first time Home Rule for Scotland became an issue in Scottish politics. Demonstrations in support of their action were arranged in all parts of Scotland.[51] On the Sunday after their arrival in Glasgow two meetings were held, one in the City Halls and the other in the Olympia Theatre. Despite the fact that Glasgow was experiencing abnormally high temperatures both these venues were packed to capacity.[52] In the intervening period the Glasgow press had heightened the campaign against the four and brought out statistics to discount Maxton's arguments. The severe Scottish climate was being given as the reason for its higher death rate. It seized upon the fact that in the quarter before milk and meals were curtailed the death rate was greater than the quarter following their curtailment. Maxton lamented the campaign of the Glasgow press.[53]

'I expected much greater sympathy for the children of Glasgow and I think it would be intellectually more honest, morally cleaner for them to aid those who were striving to raise the reputation of our city. Not one of us has any intention of withdrawing our remarks. If we had been inclined to waver, the cheap threats of some Tory M.P.s that our pay would be stopped would only have hardened our resolve. These threats show how little they understand the character of the people of the West of Scotland. My friends and I are leaders of a movement in which the rank and file work every day with the threat of their wages being withdrawn. Are the leaders to be deterred by what the rank and file are prepared to face?

When I was engaged as a teacher my soul revolted against the folly of the system which prescribed a school curriculum of Physical Culture to a class of children such as I had in which 20 of the 60 pupils had twisted legs, children who were so maimed before they reached school age. Glasgow holds the evil reputation throughout Europe as the city where there are more ricketty children to be found than any other place. We were right in saying that the men who were responsible for withdrawing the organised care of children were responsible for a murderous policy. I said what I said in the hope that the hearts of the people would be so touched that they may tackle this problem of the unnecessary loss of child life.'

Wheatley had his own answer to the press.[54] 'These critics,' he said, 'have not yet gone as far as saying that milk and meals kill infants and that the withdrawal of the same saves lives.' In answer to their arguments about the climate Wheatley's comment was that while Scotland might be a good place for a holiday and sport it was a dangerous place in which to be born and, he added, there was little difference in climate between Kelvinside and Govan, but there was a big difference in the death rate. The question of whether he apologised and returned to the House was of no importance compared to what is to be done about the unnecessary slaughter of Scottish infants. Had the mourning of these infants taken place in Buckingham Palace, the mansions of Britain or even among the middle class of Bearsden, Maxton's speech would have won for him a peerage.

Throughout the period of suspension the four had a complete disregard for the wishes of the Executive of the Labour Party. Maxton epitomised their attitude when he told reporters going into the Caxton Hall conference that their "constituencies would decide what action would be taken'. 'Neither sham respectability nor the fears of timid friends is going to disturb us,' Wheatley said[55] in the course of their campaign. This early Wheatley was making enemies within the movement. He was no fool, he must have been aware that McDonald had been placed in an invidious position and that he would never forget. What was his purpose? Was he aiming for the leadership or was he merely trying to have McDonald removed? Whatever, it was a mistake, McDonald had a better grip on the pulse of the Party and he was a much better infighter. Nevertheless, the popularity the four were gaining in the country was causing McDonald some concern.

Parliament was due to recess for the Summer on the 31st July and McDonald, prompted no doubt by the damage that could be done by the four during the break if still under suspension, made overtures to Baldwin to have the suspensions raised (Baldwin had replaced Bonar Law who had resigned the Premiership in May due to ill-health). Wheatley, informed that their suspensions were about to be raised, sent a letter on the 28th July to the Speaker of the House with a copy also to the press. In the letter he informed the Speaker that their constituencies could no longer afford to be without representation and that it was their intention to return to the House at 4.00 p.m. on the 31st to claim their seats. In the letter he had cited the case of a Tory who had been suspended for wilful remarks and who had been reinstated after three weeks without giving an apology and that Baldwin had himself voted in favour of this M.P.'s reinstatement.[56]

Taking a taxi-cab from their London hotel on the appointed day the four arrived at the House of Commons just before the end of Question Time as planned. On being refused entry by the policeman on duty, Maxton began to harangue him and the large body of reporters and photographers who had gathered.[57] Inside the House at the end of Question Time McDonald moved that the suspensions of the four be withdrawn. Baldwin agreed, stating that the four had served a suitable period of punishment.[58] In the middle of Maxton's harangue a messenger came running from the House with the news that the suspensions had been withdrawn. The four marched triumphantly into the House to the maximum publicity.

Shortly before Bonar Law's resignation Baldwin, in an address to the Women's Unionist Association, had indicated his preference for protectionist policies.[59] To pursue these policies would have meant his turning back on the Government's pledge at the election not to introduce tariffs. Consequently, when he assumed the Premiership, there was speculation that he would make an early appeal to the country for a new mandate. With the Liberals warning the electorate of the attempts that were being made to revive the 'Panacea of Protection'[60] the ground was being prepared for the battle between free trade and protection. Forecasting this battle Wheatley described it as nothing but a sham. It came as no surprise when Baldwin declared to the Tory Party Conference on October 25th that unemployment could only be fought by protecting the home market. Parliament was dissolved three weeks later and elections were set for the 6th December.

'Keep the Home Fires Burning'[61] was the Tories' slogan for, as the election got under way, protectionism became synonymous with patriotism. Unfair competition from abroad was the cause of unemployment the Tories claimed and Baldwin warned a Glasgow audience of the grave outlook for shipping because of the protectionist policies of foreign countries.[62] A tax on imported goods, particularly manufactured goods which were likely to have an adverse effect on employment at home, was the main plank of the Tories' six-point manifesto. Preference was to be given however, to imports from the Dominions. Also included in the manifesto was a promise to examine Health Insurance, Unemployment and Old Age Pension Schemes. The press was lukewarm in its support of the Tory policies.

The Liberal Party, now reunited under Asquith's leadership, had no definite plans for dealing with unemployment. Schemes such as afforestation, land reclamation, an improved transport system were mentioned in its manifesto. It also promised to develop colonial trade and establish trade relations with Russia, but its campaign eventually evolved around the issue of free trade.

As the election got under way the press conveniently forgot about the Liberal promise on trade with Russia and vigorously attacked Labour for its same proposal and warned the country of the Bolshevik influences within the Labour movement. Labour's old association with the Communist International was resurrected and it had a number of European countries suspending diplomatic relations with Britain should Labour come to power. Labour's Accumulated Wealth Tax overshadowed its policies on nationalisation and other public work schemes. Popularly called the Capital Levy it proposed a graduated tax on accumulated wealth over £5,000 to help reduce the War Debt. In his speeches around the country, right up to the eve of the election, McDonald plugged the necessity of this tax.

The I.L.P. was not caught unprepared for this election. It had organised a nationwide propaganda campaign which had begun at the beginning of September. The campaign had been designed to reach every town in the country. Thirty major demonstrations and 400 meetings were held each week and the Party's M.P.s were obliged to devote their summer vacation to the campaign. The campaign culminated in a huge demonstration on Armistice Day, the theme of which was 'Never Again'.[63] The I.L.P. manifesto had a Wheatley ring in calling for the organisation of the country's resources on a war footing to fight the problem of unemployment.

In Glasgow, the Federation of the I.L.P. published its own manifesto at the beginning of October. Not dissimilar to the national one the manifesto called for the creation of a National Emergency Committee with executive powers to deal with unemployment. It urged that the nation's credit be used to finance public work schemes and to reduce the unemployment in the city, it called for the building of 60,000 houses to be completed within 5 years. It was mainly in house building that Wheatley looked for an answer to unemployment, this was wealth, the creation of which would not embarrass the country. In the event, when the campaign began in Glasgow, much was made of the four's suspension from Parliament on the issue of the Health cuts. 'The Slaughter of the Innocents' and 'Save the Babies' were the headlines on posters and leaflets in support of a Child Welfare Scheme.[64]

The I.L.P. contested fourteen of the fifteen seats in Glasgow and in Kelvingrove the G.L.P. gave its support to the Communist candidate, Aitken Ferguson.[65] John McLean, whose name had gone forward for the Gorbals, withdrew before nomination day because of ill-health. By the time polling took place, John was dead.

Wheatley's opponent in Shettleston was a Liberal, J. F. Robertson. The Liberal Party was much better prepared for this election and conducted a vigorous campaign particularly in its attack on the Capital Levy. Wheatley introduced a personal note into the campaign when he condemned the alleged maladministration of the Russian Jewish Relief Fund of which Robertson was the organiser.[66] Since it was reckoned that Wheatley would have little difficulty in retaining his seat it is hard to understand him bringing this into the campaign considering his own reactions when he was subsequently to be the victim of a similar smear campaign. Contrary to the dismal prophecies of five months earlier, Labour gained 50 seats in this election. The result confirmed Wheatley's judgement that the working class was ready to respond to an aggressive Socialist lead, a fact confirmed with Captain Walter Elliot losing what was considered a safe Tory seat in Lanark. In Glasgow, while the I.L.P. lost Cathcart, its majority there at the previous election had been a mere 33, it had gained Partick and their overall share of the vote in the city had risen from 44.6% to 51.1%. 'Glasgow and Lanarkshire have been cleansed of Liberalism',[67] declared a jubilant Wheatley and this declaration contained a warning to the Labour leaders.

Labour now had 191 seats in a hung Parliament as against the Tories 259 and the Liberals 159. Despite McDonald's statement at the Labour Party Conference earlier in the year 'that it would be insane for any Labour Party to form a Government without an absolute majority'[68] it soon became clear that he was more than eager to form a minority Government and was willing to abandon Labour's foremost election pledge in order to do so. Speculating on the various coalitions that were possible *The Times* wrote 'It is thought that some of the moderate leaders of the Labour movement including, it is said, McDonald, Henderson and Thomas, would not be averse to some form of working arrangement with the Liberals, in which case it may be presumed that the Capital Levy would be allowed to slip quietly into the background'.[69] Three days later, at a meeting in Sydney Webb's house attended by the big five, McDonald, Henderson, Snowden, Clynes and Thomas, it was decided after a policy discussion to drop the proposal for a Capital Levy.[70] The following day Labour's National Executive announced that, if called upon, Labour was ready to form a Government. At the same time the press was questioning what the reactions would be from the I.L.P. section of the Labour Party to any agreement with the Liberals and pointed to the warnings that were coming from Glasgow.[71]

Wheatley's message to the Labour leaders was loud and clear.[72]

'There must be no coalition, no compromise and no watered-down policies. Appeals are being made to Labour that in order to break the stalemate there must be some understanding between two of the contending parties. The Labour movement was being exhorted to recognise, in the interests of the state, its great responsibilities, that the King's Government must be carried on. The movement that elected me to power sent me to establish a People's Government. There can be no agreement with Liberals, Liberalism stood for competitive capitalism and Labour regarded capitalism as the curse of Scotland. If the Labour movement, at this stage in its history, were to compromise its principles by allying itself with Liberalism, it would be the greatest betrayal in political history. They can take it from me that the men they elected for Glasgow would never betray them. He could understand a Labour Government being formed to promote bold Socialist policies with a view to soliciting for itself the support of the public, but it would be political madness to leave the impression on the public mind that the Labour movement is not a menace to vested interests. It is these interests that are keeping our people in the depths of poverty and which are threatening to throttle our national existence. We must destroy them rapidly in self defence.'

Wheatley was certainly not alone in his distrust of the Labour leaders. That year a book of essays on *Labour's Aims by Seven Men of the Labour Party*[73] was published. The authors, wished to remain anonymous not, they said, because they feared criticism, but because they did not want to be marked as sectional or schismatic. Their only reason for publishing these essays was a fear that Labour would abandon its fundamental principles, which were the abolition of capitalism and the establishment of the Socialist Commonwealth. In the book they warned of the danger of palliatives becoming obstacles in the march towards Socialism. Substance was given to these fears in an article which Thomas, leader of the railway workers, contributed to the *Railway Review* in which he warned Labour's supporters to keep their heads and not to expect Labour to do the impossible. 'It was Labour's policy to be fair and just to all,' he wrote.[74] These fears were further strengthened by the conciliatory tones of the press and some Tory leaders with assurances that the Labour leaders would be able to keep their wild men in check.[75] The possibility of a first Labour Government became a reality on the 18th December when Asquith, in a speech to the National Liberal Club, stated his intention to bring down the Government.[76] On the 17th January, nine days after Parliament reassembled, in the debate on the King's Speech Clynes moved a Vote of No Confidence on the ability of the Government to govern. The vote was carried by 328 votes to 251 and the King sent for McDonald to form a new administration.

References

1. *Glasgow Evening Times* – 5/3/20
2. *An Autobiography* – P. Snowden – Vols 1 & 2 – 1934
3. *My Life of Revolt* – D. Kirkwood
4. *Decline and Fall of the Labour Party* – John Scanlon
5. Ibid.
6. Debate on Address – *Hansard* – 29/11/22
7. *An Autobiography* – P. Snowden – Vols 1 & 2
8. *Scotsman* – 30/11/22
9. *Left Turn* – John Paton
10. *London Times* – 18/12/22
11. *Decline and Fall of the Labour Party* – John Scanlon
12. Ibid.
13. *London Times* – 14/12/22
    Forward – 3/2/23
14. *Starvation Amidst Plenty* – J. Wheatley (Reformers Book Stall)
15. *Forward* – 17/2/23
16. *London Times* – 27/12/22
17. *Forward* – 24/2/23
18. *Hansard* – 13/2/23
19. Ibid.
20. *Forward* – 24/2/23
21. *Decline and Fall of the Labour Party* – John Scanlon
22. *Forward* – 31/2/23
23. *London Times* – 3/4/23

Into Parliament

24. *Decline and Fall of the Labour Party* – J. Scanlon
25. *Inside the Left* – Fenner Brockway – 1942
26. Ibid.
27. *Forward* – 11/9/26
28. *Glasgow Evening Times* – 15/5/30
29. *Eastern Standard* – 6/3/26
30. *The Clydesiders* – R. K. Middlemass
31. Ibid.
32. *Eastern Standard* – 17/3/27
33. *Forward* – 7/6/23
34. *Hansard* – 24/4/23
35. *Call Back Yesterday* – Hugh Dalton – 1953
36. *Hansard* – 24/4/23
37. Ibid.
38. *London Times* – 25/4/23
39. *New Leader* – 27/4/23
40. *New Leader* – 29/6/23
41. *Eastern Standard* – 31/3/23
42. *Forward* – 7/7/27
43. *Decline and Fall of the Labour Party* – J. Scanlon
44. *Scotsman* – 28/6/23
45. *Decline and Fall of the Labour Party* – J. Scanlon
46. *New Leader* – 6/7/23
    Glasgow Evening Times – 6/6/23
47. *Glasgow Evening Times* – 6/6/23
48. *Scotsman* – 4/7/23
49. Ibid.
50. *Glasgow Evening Times* – 2/7/23
51. *Decline and Fall of the Labour Party* – J. Scanlon
52. *Glasgow Evening Times* – 9/6/23
53. *Eastern Standard* – 7/7/23
    Glasgow Herald – 6/7/23
54. *Eastern Standard* – 7/7/23
55. Ibid.
56. *Glasgow Evening Times* – 28/7/27
57. *Glasgow Evening Times* – 31/7/23
58. *Hansard* – 31/7/23
59. *Glasgow Evening Times* – 12/5/23
60. *Glasgow Evening Times* – 3/10/23
61. *First Labour Government* – R. W. Hyland – 1957
62. *Scotsman* – 29/11/23
63. *New Leader* – 21/9/23
64. *Forward* – 1/12/23
65. *Glasgow Evening Times* – 26/11/23
66. *Forward* – 1/12/23
67. *Scotsman* – 10/12/23
68. *New Leader* – 6/7/23
    Post War History of the British Working Classes – Allen Hutt – 1937
69. *London Times* – 8/12/23

70. *An Autobiography* – P. Snowden – Vols 1 & 2
71. *London Times* – 13/12/23
72. *Scotsman* – 10/12/23 quoted from speech at Metropole. *Forward* – 15/12/23
73. *The Labour Party's Aim by Seven Men of the Labour Party* – 1923
74. *London Times* – 20/12/23
75. *London Times* – 13/12/23 (see Lord Inchcape)
76. *London Times* – 19/12/23

Chapter Eleven
Minister of Health

'We have built our finer habitations away on the horizon. We are a Party of ideals. We are a Party that away in the dreamland of imagination dwells a social organisation fairer and more perfect than any organisation that mankind has ever known. We are not going to jump there. We are upon a pilgrimage. We are on a journey. One step is enough for me. One step, on condition that it leads to the next step.' This is what McDonald told the great Labour Victory Rally at the Albert Hall on the 8th January, 1924.[1] It became obvious, even before Labour assumed office, that the leaders were more intent on placating the opposition than in pleasing their own supporters. 'Labour in office would not attempt foolish things', Thomas told a Derby audience[2] and many of those chosen for office would be indebted to Lord Haldane who was not even a member of the Labour Party. Haldane, who a couple of years earlier had been advocating a merger of the Liberal and Labour Parties,[3] emerged as McDonald's chief confidant in the business of Cabinet making. To the older members of the Labour movement who knew of McDonald's attempt before the war to form an electoral agreement with the Liberals this would come as no surprise. Wheatley had no doubt as to the way the Party was being led.

Speaking to the delegates at the Annual Conference of the Scottish Division of the I.L.P. Wheatley cautioned them on the foolishness of confusing electoral victories with steps towards the emancipation of the working class. They would be fully entitled to judge the Labour Party in the House of Commons, not by the number of months or weeks they remained in Office, but by the output of their remedial legislation. They would be rightly condemned if they did not utilise the extra power now placed in their hands. He then issued a warning that the inception of a Labour Government would not mean the end of the aggressive activities of the Scottish Labour members in the House.[4]

It was a warning that had McDonald swithering, whether it would be more dangerous to have Wheatley in the Cabinet beside him or facing him on the back benches. It was a decision he left until the very last minute. *The Times* was accurate in forecasting which person would hold every major portfolio except Health, where it named Wheatley merely as a possible. When McDonald finally decided to give Wheatley the Health Ministry it was not without some misgivings for he was to write in his diary 'Wheatley finally fixed. Necessary to bring Clyde in. Will he play straight.'[5] Commenting on Wheatley's appointment *The Times* had this to say, 'A champion of more advanced views than those held by the majority of his colleagues, Wheatley represents a somewhat different, though by no means inexperienced, element in the Party.'[6] Considering the composition of the Cabinet this was something of an understatement.

McDonald, as well as being Premier, took over Foreign Affairs. Snowden was Chancellor of the Exchequer, Henderson was at the Home Office, Thomas in charge of the Colonies with Clynes as Lord Privy Seal. In addition, Lord Haldane became Lord Chancellor with posts being given to Lord Parmoor, Noel Buxton, Trevelyan and Wedgwood, all recent converts to Labour. Viscount Chelmsford, who was a Tory, was appointed First Lord of the Admiralty. Webb was President of the Board of Trade with Tom Shaw at the Ministry of Labour. The only other left winger besides Wheatley to be given a senior post was Jowett as Commissioner of Works. Of the other Scottish Members, Adamson was made Scottish Secretary with Jimmy Stewart as an Under Secretary at the Health office. Shinwell received a Junior appointment at the Board of Trade. The rest of the Clydesiders were ignored. Wheatley raised some eyebrows when he appointed Douglas Veale as his Parliamentary Secretary, Veale had previously served Chamberlain and Mond in the same capacity. Wheatley was under no illusions as to whom he owed his appointment. Speaking at a reception in Shettleston organised in his honour, he told his audience that,[7]

'he represented the Clyde men in the Cabinet and that the appointment was the Prime Minister's recognition of the magnificent lead in the direction of Socialism given by Glasgow to the whole country. During the past few days he had discovered he was a very clever man, that's what the papers were saying, but he was one of the people themselves and he could imagine some of his old Shettleston friends exclaiming that 'if John Wheatley is a clever man we ken where there's plenty.' He would never find finer minds nor better hearts than those of the working people among whom his life had been spent. For the future his supreme aim was to be able to declare that he had never broken a promise made by him to the people of Shettleston. Of the housing problem, he wanted to get people thinking of houses in millions instead of thousands. He was confident, given the goodwill and support of the British public, he would solve the problem. The Building Trusts, he promised, would no longer rob the people.'

Minister of Health

If Wheatley was a virtual unknown outside of Glasgow before his appointment there were two happenings, even before the Cabinet got down to business, which put him in the full glare of the public. The first incurred the displeasure of the King and McDonald and the second the wrath of the right wing and the press.

The King, who was imperial also in matters of court dress, had been assured by McDonald that, as far as his Cabinet was concerned, he had nothing to worry about on this score.[8] To his consternation, on the day that his Ministers were presented with their Seals of Office, Wheatley and Jowett appeared in lounge suits.[9] The King was upset by this refusal to conform and in order to reassure him for future occasions a formula was agreed between Lord Stamfordham, the King's Private Secretary, and the Cabinet. A panel of Ministers who possessed, or were prepared to acquire, the necessary uniform would be formed from which the three Ministers required to attend the King at Court functions would be drawn and that those Ministers who did not possess the uniform would be excused attendance at these functions.[10] The press made hay on Ministers appearing at Court in lounge suits as they did at the social activities of some Labour Ministers and their wives. A club, known as the Half-Circle, was formed to teach the social graces to the working-class wives of Junior Ministers. Amusing anecdotes were being circulated of the antics of some of these women. One story told of a Minister's wife being questioned as to why she was leaving a banquet while there was yet food and drink left on the table. She replied, 'My stays are tight, my shoes are tight and now my husband is tight.' Wheatley's wife steadfastly refused to accept invitations to the London homes of the upper and middle classes. Like her husband, she was more at ease among the working people of Glasgow.[11]

The second happening, of political importance, concerned the notorious Poplar Order. Prior to 1921, the entire burden of outdoor relief in London Boroughs was a charge on the local rates and no scale for the regulation of such relief had been laid down by the Ministry of Health. In 1920 Poplar, like most parts of the country, was badly affected by unemployment and found maintenance of the poor an intolerable burden on the rates. To highlight their plight and their demand for a large measure of equalisation of poor rates in London, the Poplar Borough Council refused to collect the rates for the London County Metropolitan Asylum Board and Police precepts, a sum which amounted to several hundred thousand pounds. Legal proceedings were taken against them and the High Court ordered the collection of the rates. The Council ignored the Order and 29 of its members, among whom was George Lansbury, were jailed for contempt. They served six weeks in prison before being released.[12] As a result of this conflict the Government, in 1921, introduced the Local Authorities (Financial Provisions) Act which put the burden of outdoor relief for Unions in London on to a Central Fund, the Metropolitan Common Poor Fund. Restrictions were placed on the amount that Poplar or any other Board could take from this fund, but local Guardians were free to give relief in excess of this amount out of their local rates. A section of Poplar's ratepayers considered that the amount the Guardians were taking from the local rates was excessive and appealed to the then Minister of Health, Sir Alfred Mond. Invoking Section 52 of the Poor Law Amendment Act of 1834, Mond issued an Order to Poplar that any payment in the way of relief in excess of the scale provided under the 1921 Act became automatically illegal. The Order, in fact, took away Poplar's right to give extra relief out of its local rates without the authority of the Minister of Health. The Poplar Board, which was Labour controlled, defied the Order and continued to submit records of the cases in which they had exceeded the legal amount. Although these amounts were estimated at around £2,000 per week no surcharge was made on them.[13]

Before the opening of Parliament Wheatley received a deputation from the Poplar Board of guardians requesting that (1) they be relieved of any obligation they might be under for having paid a section of their workers £4 per week; (2) to approve a special scale of allowances to be made for the earnings of children when estimating the grants to be made to necessitous families; (3) to rescind the Poplar Order and to remit any surcharges that might arise under that Order. With regard to the first request Wheatley made it clear that, as the matter was sub judice, it was impossible for him to interfere. To the second request, while expressing his sympathy with them, it would be necessary for him to consult the law as to his legal powers before he could make any decision. On the third request he told the deputation that he had already come to a decision to repeal that Order.[14]

The decision brought bitter criticism from the press and Tories and Liberals alike. 'Surrender to Poplar' were the headlines and *The Times* accused Wheatley of a dangerous and costly error of judgement.[15] Asquith gave notice that he was going to test the Government on this issue. 'In matters of principle he was not going to follow the tail of any dog, and Poplar was a matter of principle,' he stated.[16] Tempers were lowered slightly before the subject came up for debate in the Commons on the 26th February with the publishing of Wheatley's report[17] giving the reasons for his decision. Nevertheless, the atmosphere in the House was intense when the Liberal, Bryant, put forward his vote of censure.[18]

'That this House regards the action of the Minister of Health in cancelling the Poplar Order and in remitting any surcharge that might be made under it as calculated to encourage illegality and extravagance and urges that the real remedy for the difficulties of necessitous areas is to be found in the reform of London Government and of the Poor Law system.'

Bryant's speech in support of his motion was an attack on the principles by which the Poplar Guardians allocated relief and on the iniquities of the present Poor Law. He had no intention of joining in the violent abuse which had followed the rescinding of the Order, he said, but he did describe Wheatley's action in remitting surcharges before an audit was complete as dangerous.

In a speech which was to set him down as a politician of some stature Wheatley defended his decision.[19]

'I have been charged, both inside and outside the House, with having surrendered to Poplar, with having remitted a possible surcharge of no less than £100,000 which a gang of guilty Guardians had taken from the pockets of helpless ratepayers and with having encouraged extravagance and illegality among similar gangs of Guardians with which this unfortunate country is infested. What are the facts?

Three or four months after the Order was issued Mond left the Ministry of Health and the administration of the Order fell on three successive Ministers. Right from the beginning Poplar defied the Order and the Ministry of Health, aware of Poplar's illegality, made no attempt to force the law nor did they give the slightest indication that they intended to enforce it. Instead, in 1923, they took the first steps to alter the law. They withdrew the scale which had been imposed as a restraining influence in the 1921 Act and substituted a new instrument. It was laid down that the maximum amount which any Board of Guardians should take from the Central Fund was 9d per day per head of the persons relieved, but they made it clear that the Board of Guardians, Poplar excluded, were free to give relief in excess of that scale out of their local rates. Hence we had a position when the scale under the 1921 Act had been dropped by the Government itself. It did not apply to any Board of Guardians within the London area, or anywhere else, except Poplar and it would not have continued to in Poplar but for the fact that the Mond Order was still in force. We had a situation where what was legal in Bermondsey was illegal in Poplar. The Government had neither the courage to enforce the Mond Order nor withdraw it.

Why, if Poplar was breaking the law, was no action taken by my predecessors and why have the accounts of the Poplar Board not yet been audited, it is the only Board of Guardians in London whose accounts have not been completely audited. Here is the only Board breaking the law to an extent of £2,000 per week, surely the first step in dealing with a matter of this sort was to get the accounts audited. The business of the Ministry of Health was to see that this was done so that the Ministry was not brought into contempt. In all the agitation that has been going on in the country about my conduct I have been treated as though I had been an inexperienced countryman who has somehow or other wandered into the M. of H. and done the silliest possible things without knowing what I was doing.

I am not here defending Poplar, that is not my business or duty, my job is to emancipate my Department from a degrading situation. There were three courses open to me. I could have proceeded against the Guardians by having the audit completed, have the surcharges declared and proceeded to enforce them. If I had pursued this course it would have meant bankruptcy and prison for the Guardians, for doing in their own area what was legal in other parts of the country. Another course open to me was to supersede the Poplar Board altogether and appoint Commissioners to carry on their duties as I thought they should be carried on. If I had taken that course I would be saying to the people of this country who had been granted the powers of popular Government. 'You can have these powers as long as you exercise them in the manner I think you ought to exercise them, but immediately you exercise them according to your own views or that of your ratepayers then, ipso facto local Government is to cease'. In the course I did take I have been accused of making a friendly gesture to Poplar and in doing so injured the status of the M. of H. What this gesture amounted to was that I removed what I considered Poplar's legitimate grievance, that they were being treated differently from any other Board of Guardians in the country. I recognised that it was always difficult to carry on Government of this or any other country against the will of the people and if I could succeed in getting the goodwill of the people under my control then I would have achieved some success. Was this a wrong thing to do? The popular view is that I had wiped out every illegality in expenditure in excess of what would have been legal in Bermondsey during the currency of the Order. That is not the case. I laid it down quite clearly to Poplar that I was promising only to remit any surcharge that might be made under the Order, but I still left Poplar under the restrictions and limitations of the general Poor Law and Poplar understands this.'

Replying to the latter part of the motion Wheatley said that he welcomed the advice to reform the Poor Law. 'Since 1910, Labour Conference after Labour Conference has demanded the reform of the Poor Law system. We have been appealing in vain to successive Liberal and Tory Governments and we welcome the suggestion that we should have the assistance of both sides of the House in carrying out a reform which we demanded 14 years ago. I do not want to anticipate the provisions of any Bill that may be introduced, but if I am in Office and have to deal with it I shall appeal to this House that any reform is for the benefit of the poor and not merely for the convenience of officials.' Summarising he said,

'I have not surrendered to Poplar. I have rescued my Department from a state of degradation. I have put my Department in a position in which it can and will enforce the law and will do so impartially and fairly. I am willing and anxious to reform the Poor Law and particularly the Poor Law system of London at the earliest and in doing so I will see that the rights of the poor and the principles of popular Government are protected.'

In a lame attempt to justify Liberal opposition Asquith said that the Motion had been put down, not for the purpose of embarrassing the Government, but to get the assurance of the Prime Minister that the removal of the Order did not give licence to the Poplar Board to continue to act illegally. The Motion, supported largely by the Tories, was defeated by 295 votes to 228. Bryant and Asquith both voted against it.[20]

Wheatley's speech brought immediate praise from his most bitter adversary Joynson-Hicks. 'I have had the privilege of being in the House for a great many years and have seldom heard a comparatively new member make such an excellent speech.'[21] McNeill Weir went much further,[22] 'Delivered with his chubby Pickwickian face beaming cheekily behind his large spectacles, the speech, established Wheatley as a Parliamentarian of the first rank and, for one who had hitherto been little known outside Scotland, a possible threat to McDonald's leadership'. McDonald himself was generous in his praise of Wheatley's speech which, he told the King, was a masterpiece.[23]

Before the new Parliament opened on the 12th February the Cabinet had several meetings to discuss policy. There was quick agreement to recognise Russia. A special Committee on Unemployment and Housing was set up under Webb which included Snowden, Trevelyan who was Education Minister, Wheatley and Shaw and their respective Under-Secretaries, Greenwood and Margaret Bondfield. From this, two sub-Committees were formed. The one on unemployment was chaired by Shaw and Wheatley took charge of Housing with the assistance of Arthur Greenwood and James Stewart.[24] Both Committees reported back to the Cabinet within ten days.

With 1,800,000 unemployed, the worst hit areas being the North of England and the Clyde, the Committee on Unemployment showed a lack of urgency and of ideas. It advised the Cabinet that policies should be directed, not so much as for the relief of unemployment, but for the restoration of trade. Existing schemes for the relief of unemployment, it felt, had comparatively little effect and it advised against the Government drawing on large funds from normal channels for measures that would amount only to palliatives. The necessity of expenditure for subsidising schemes in direct relief of unemployment would be judged in relation to the greater necessity for maintaining undisturbed the ordinary financial facilities and resources for trade and industry. The sign-post to recovery lay in improving relations with foreign powers and a full resumption of trade with Russia and certain other countries, although with Russia it would be a slow development. It was hopeful that with a big housing scheme in operation unemployment would be reduced, not only in the building industry, but in related industries. This report,[25] which was the basis of the Government's policy presented to Parliament, showed clearly Snowden's influence. The Government's programme read in the King's speech, apart from its Housing policy, differed little from any previous administration. The only firm decision taken with regard to unemployment was to increase the existing loan grants from a limit of £20 million to £22 million.

By contrast, Wheatley, in his report to the Cabinet,[26] recognised the magnitude of the housing problem and presented evidence of its solution. On the 30th January he had engaged in informal discussions with representatives of building workers employers and before giving his report he and Shaw had again met and discussed with them as to the availability of labour and materials for a long term building programme on a scale of approximately 200,000 houses per annum. This was the figure he considered necessary to make good the accumulated shortage and also provide for normal population expansion and renewals.

The report defined the problem as being able to supply, over a period of 15 years, 2,375,000 houses which could be let at rents workers could afford from their wages. The Chamberlain scheme fails to meet this condition as to a large extent the houses are being built for sale and those which are being built by the Local Authorities for letting the rents are too high. Under the Chamberlain Act only 8,140 houses had been completed with 30,405 under construction.

The major difficulty to be faced in a programme of this size was the severe lack of skilled labour caused by the instability in the building trade which had resulted in a steady decline in the workforce over the years. There was however, a confidence in the industry that the estimated 300,000 additional men required for a programme of this size could be recruited. The report suggested two ways in which the number of skilled workers in the industry

could be increased.
(a) promoting men already engaged in the industry to craftsmen.
(b) Increasing the number of apprentices, the numbers at present being below strength.

Agreement would have to be reached with the Unions on this and also ensure against any cause for strikes. It was to be hoped that the launching of the new scheme would not bring a demand for wages that the workers would not have been able to secure without the scheme. The scheme itself would provide a guarantee of full employment within the industry for ten years provided houses were delivered according to a reasonable time-table. An assurance to the workers that the primary object of the scheme is the provision of houses at rents which the ordinary worker could afford should help bring their cooperation.

Shortage of materials was not a serious obstacle although there would have to be an increase in brick-making capacity. The report warned against any increased costs following on production increases and stated that manufacturers of materials should be asked to make agreements on profits. The Department would require to have accountants and other experts to carry out costing investigations. Statutory powers must be taken providing for severe penalties against profiteering. It also thought it may be necessary in the last resort to have powers to take over works closed down by an owner or to put down plant if supplies prove inadequate.

It was essential to the scheme that the houses provided were let at rents roughly equivalent to those paid by the working classes before the war and gave a figure of 8/- per week to cover rent and rates as a general estimate. On the basis of an average cost of £500 per house the annual loss would be £16 per year for 80 years, £38 million for the total programme. Generous arrangements will have to be made with L.A.s as to finance. It was essential that L.A.s have a definite financial interest in the scheme which, in itself, would provide a check against any undue increases of tender prices. Practical steps would have to be taken against profiteering which was mainly the reason for the collapse of the Addison scheme and in fact rings of all kinds must be prevented. It will be necessary for the Department to assist L.A.s in the matter of building costs by keeping detailed records of costs which will enable checks to be applied. It may also be necessary to have in reserve a power of direct building by the state.

Finally, the report stated that the Committee was making arrangements to meet with the manufacturers of building materials and to negotiate with the L.A.

The Cabinet accepted the report almost entirely. Only on the question of rents did it demur and Wheatley was forced to amend the figure of 8/- per week to 9/-. On the question of L.A. subsidy the Cabinet was averse to granting anything more than £9 per house for a period of 20 years. It did allow that should Wheatley have difficulty reaching agreement on this figure that he had the power to increase the period to 40 years.[27]

It was a bold Socialist programme and yet the Report was a bit demeaning to the workers and also demonstrated Wheatley's immaturity. In hoping that the workers would not demand increases was tantamount to saying that they were fortunate to have employment. To expect the full co-operation of the workers purely because they were building low rental houses was certainly naive. The proposal to promote unskilled or semi-skilled men to craftsmen in an industry where the workers had fought stubbornly against dilution since the end of the war showed that Wheatley did not fully appreciate industry's class structure.

On a question that had immediate concern for Scotland and Glasgow in particular Wheatley was less decisive. Evictions for non-payment of rent due to unemployment and the harshness of Chamberlain's Bill had steadily risen – almost 5,000 Eviction Orders had been granted in Glasgow in 1923[28] – and it seemed that, initially, Wheatley was loth to introduce any sort of legislation to alleviate the people's plight. At a Cabinet meeting on the 13th February McDonald asked Jowett to discuss with Wheatley on the advisability of introducing a Rents Restrictions Bill with a view to removing the injustices of the Chamberlain Act and to report back to the Cabinet.[29] In the light of the events that followed it is difficult to come to grips with McDonald's motive in approaching Jowett. Ben Gardner, a Labour Member, introduced a Private Member's Bill designed to amend the Chamberlain Act. Probably here Wheatley had the first whiff of betrayal.

Gardner's Bill, which received its second reading on the 22nd February, set out, amongst other things, to bring back under control all houses de-controlled after 1920, to narrow the existing grounds on which an owner could re-possess his house – he must require the house for himself and even then he must provide alternative accommodation for an existing tenant – to reduce 15% increase allowed on the standard rent to 10% and the repairs allowance from 25% to 15%. It also sought the abolition of tied cottages. The Bill was bitterly attacked by the Tories and an Amendment, put forward by Lt. Col. Freemantle, called for a full Government inquiry into the Act before any new measure was considered. Liberals' attitude in attempting to discredit the

Government while appearing sympathetic to the Bill could be summed up in Harcourt Johnstone's reply 'It is astonishing to find a measure of this importance brought forward as a Private Member's Bill. If it hadn't been a question of extreme urgency I would have found great difficulty in supporting it.' Johnstone also gave warning of the difficulties that could face the Bill at the Committee stage, particularly on the question of re-possession. Tory attacks were on the familiar grounds that private investment in housing would cease because of its unprofitability. Chamberlain also accused the Government of hiding behind a Private Member's Bill and then went on to tell the House that he represented thousands of poor tenants and, while knowing that he would not be popular with them for voting against the Bill he was doing so in their long term interests.[30] Wheatley, while not wholly enthusiastic in support of the Bill, condemned the hypocrisy of those who accused the Government of hiding behind a Private Member's Bill while they themselves were content to hide behind a Private Member's Amendment. Answering those who argued that the Bill would frighten off private investors, he said that anyone with a knowledge of housing knew that it was not Socialism that would frighten private enterprise away from the business of providing houses. "No one with ordinary business intelligence would advise investment in working-class housing'.[31] As Harcourt Johnstone forecast the Bill never got past the Committee Stage. Wheatley's absence from the Committee meetings was a measure of his apathy towards Gardner's Bill.[32]

While Gardner's Bill was still locked in Committee the Cabinet agreed[33] that Wheatley, after he consulted with Adamson, should use Gardner's Bill as a basis on which to draft new Amendments which would be 'consonant with Government policy'. Dragging his heels on the Cabinet's decision Wheatley eventually came forward with proposals for a short Bill[34] which would:

(a) Repeal or modify paragraphs 4 and 5 of section 5 of Chamberlain's Act so as to extend to persons who were landlords before 29th June, 1923 to prove either that there is alternative accommodation or greater hardship as a condition precedent to an eviction Order.
(b) Prohibit evictions owing to non-payment of rent in cases where non-payment is due to unemployment unless a Landlord can satisfy the Court that greater hardship would be caused by refusing to grant an Order than by granting it.

By quoting figures on the number of cases coming before the courts for non-payment of rents and the number of evictions ensuing, Wheatley was able to cajole the Cabinet into supporting these amendments.

'INSTALMENT OF SOCIALISM' was the opposition cry[35] when this ill-conceived Bill was presented to Parliament. He totally ignored the fact that, unlike Scotland, Poor Law Guardians in England took rent into consideration when granting relief. It was not a bold Socialist policy that would attract the British voter as a whole, nevertheless, the manner in which he presented the Bill brought praise from Chamberlain and Asquith[36] and his speech was formidable enough to allow the *New Leader* to print it in pamphlet form.

'The principal object of the Bill, said Wheatley, was to reduce the number of evictions and to stop evictions at once where Orders had been granted. He painted a distressing picture of a Sheriff Officer calling on a house to inform the mother that, if she and her children had not vacated the house by noon the following day, he would have no alternative but to force the law and put the parents, the children and their little bits of furniture on to the street. He recalled to the House of when he first joined the Socialist movement and being told that Socialism threatened the destruction of that sacred institution, the family. Here, you have an order of things that not only threatens, but does it. When these poor people steal away from their homes, when they are put on the street and it happens on scores and scores of occasions, it is frequently necessary for the parents to be separated from the children or the boys to be separated from the girls. He went on to say that it was in the interests of the state that, when trade revives that the workers were not broken and therefore unfit to enable it to compete with the world. He ended his speech in a tone which was unusual for a Government Minister. The people, to their credit, have borne these things patiently and are relying on you to come to their assistance, but there is a limit to human endurance, that even animals will fight for the protection of their young and I would have no faith in the future of this country if it contained, in a large degree, a population that was prepared to sit silently and see their families destroyed.'[37]

It seemed to be a speech designed to capture the leadership of the left rather than an attempt to persuade Parliament. The opposition pounced on what they claimed was the shifting of the onus of Public Relief on to the landlords and the unequal sharing of this burden with some landlords having a larger share of unemployed tenants than others. They also argued that the burden would be more evenly shared if carried by the State and that the position in Scotland could be eased if the Local Parish Councils took rent into consideration when granting relief. During the debate Clynes made a surprising intervention to say that the Government was willing to substitute the offending clause with one which would enable the unemployed in distress to obtain help with their rents from Public Funds. Kirkwood expressed the anger of the Clydesiders at this change of face when he remarked that 'we would be as well with a Tory Government'.[38]

Meeting to decide the shape of the face-saving clause it was the majority opinion of the Cabinet that there was no evidence to support the conviction that tenants were evicted on the grounds of non-payment of rent due to unemployment. The formula arrived at and agreed upon was 'Unless the Court is satisfied that the tenant has had a reasonable opportunity of applying to the Local Poor Law Authority for relief and the Authority has had an opportunity of considering any such application'[39] and which contained no evidence of the Government's intention to provide extra funds to meet this contingency. The Bill received little support from the opposition and was defeated. The Government hid behind a Liberal Bill 'Prevention of Evictions' that merely narrowed the grounds on which a tenant could be evicted. There were many on the Labour Back Benches besides Kirkwood beginning to wonder which class the Government represented for even its attitude to strikers was as obdurate as its predecessor's.

On the 16th February the dockers came out on strike and the Government was prepared to use troops to transport food supplies and then in March when London Transport was paralysed by strike action it introduced the hated Emergency Powers Act. Through all the industrial unrest the Government was searching for the Communist influence with little thought for the strikers,[40] Wheatley alone of the Cabinet had a concern for their welfare. In anticipating the hardship that could be caused by the Dock Strike and the difficult decisions which the Poor Law authorities would be faced with in relation to this strike he issued a memo to the Cabinet.[41]

'In the event of large scale applications for Poor Law Relief I shall certainly be asked to define my attitude on this question. The Cabinet will remember the question became acute during the Coal Trade dispute in 1920 and more recently in the Dock Strike of last year which was considered by the press to be the reason for the action in Poplar. Different interpretations could be taken by different Boards of Guardians – Contentions that strikes should not be supported out of Rate Funds against Statutory duty of Guardians to relieve destitution –. There can be no question of allowing persons on strike to starve.

It would be open for me to issue an Order under my existing powers requiring that all relief to persons directly affected should be given in kind. This could provide a clear cut line that could be followed by all Guardians. This form of relief could not be regarded as an inducement to persons on strike to remain out of work.'

It was a cleverly constructed memo, but it left no doubt whose side Wheatley was on. The Cabinet however, was more concerned in ending the strike and could only allow that the Ministry place itself in a position to be ready to assist L.A.s to the knowledge of the Law if enquiries were made.[42]

Wheatley realised the need for reform of the Poor Law and within two months of taking office he was pressing McDonald to sound out the other Parties on an all Party Conference that would be a prelude to setting up a Committee of Inquiry into the whole system.[43] He was content that such an inquiry should follow the recommendations laid down by the 1917 McLean Committee viz. the transfer of the Guardians power to L.A.s and the setting up of special bodies to provide specialised care to the mentally ill etc. The re-organisation of the Health Service was another priority.

'The most ardent individualist will not contend that the community should rely for its health on the unorganised, unaided and uncontrolled individual action. I think I may venture to go the length of saying that in the production and distribution of health we are all Socialists and that we are opposed to Free-Trade in disease.'[44]

He told this to an audience at the opening of the Social Hygiene Congress at the Empire Exhibition on the 12th May, ten days after he had reached agreement with representatives of the Medical Services and Approved Societies on the terms of reference for a Royal Commission to inquire into National Health Insurance.[45] Wheatley demonstrated his skills as a negotiator in dealing with these bodies, the medical profession had given evidence of being intractable. He showed an open-mindedness when receiving a deputation from a Birth Control Association which included Bertrand Russell and H. G. Wells. The Association wanted Wheatley to raise the ban that had been placed on doctors at Maternity Centres from passing on information on birth control in cases where it was considered medically advisable. In answer Wheatley said that 'a clear distinction must be made in allowing access to knowledge and actually distributing knowledge. No-one would maintain that access to knowledge should be forbidden, but public opinion on the question was not so definite that it would allow state or rate aided institutions to do more than direct people in need of advice to where it could be obtained.'[46]

While Wheatley was pursuing advancement in Health and in Housing for the workers the Government as a whole was adopting a Micawber-like attitude to the problem of the unemployed. Apart from the extra £2 million added to Unemployment Grants and a further £8 million towards major roadworks, nothing more tangible was offered in the way of job creation, money was to be made available only for revenue producing schemes and the Government seemed bereft of ideas in this direction. As early as the middle of April the Cabinet was reviewing the situation with pessimism. It had concluded that it would be impossible for the L.A. to embark on any major schemes as they were coming to the end of their resources. It piously hoped that a scheme for the electrification of the railways could be expedited.[47] By June, backbenchers were becoming impatient and angry at the Government's lack of ideas and response to the problem of unemployment. A typical Government reply to questions that were being put was 'You can't expect us to produce schemes, like rabbits, out of a hat.' It came from Shaw.[48] The I.L.P., backed by the *New Leader*, joined in the clamour for work and organised demonstrations for National employment schemes.[49] However, if the workers expected any crumbs of comfort from Snowden's budget they were bitterly disappointed.

Snowden seemed pleased that his budget had relieved the fears of the rich.[50] Certainly the press was quick to praise it. It abolished Corporation Tax, returning £12 million to the rich. There were no tax increases or any new taxes. Inhabited House Duty was also abolished, a concession of £2 million to the upper and middle classes. The meagre concession to the poor was to halve the duty on tea and sugar and abolish the duty on dried fruit. He abolished the McKenna duties, a tax on imported cars. This was a sensible tax affording protection to an infant motor car industry and one which a Socialist Government would have imposed. Snowden later refused to meet a deputation of workers from the motor car industry who were concerned about possible redundancies with the removal of this tax.[51] The poor had earlier received their crumbs from what the Government described as a stop-gap Unemployment Insurance Bill. Benefit had been increased from 15/- to 18/- for men and from 12/- to 15/- for women. Benefit age was lowered from 16 years to 14 years and the Child allowance was doubled to 2/-, the Gap was also abolished. In preparing the Cabinet for his Budget Snowden said that he would have liked to introduce a Valuation Tax on Land, but it was impossible after a few weeks in Government to submit a full and comprehensive scheme, we want our proposals to be thorough, practical and simple.[52] It was evident that, apart from Wheatley and possibly McDonald in Foreign Affairs, Labour Ministers were ill-prepared for governing. Indeed, the Cabinet was looking to Wheatley's Housing Bill as its only real hope of job creation.

After meeting with representatives of the Building Materials manufacturers Wheatley set up a National House Building Committee representing all sections of the industry, fifteen members representing the workers and nineteen representing the employers. Its terms of reference were to inquire into the state of the industry with regard to the availability of labour and materials for a programme of building working-class houses on a large scale over a long term. In a little over a month the Committee presented its report to Wheatley. 'Few of us thought that such a unanimous report as has been presented was possible' said John Winning, who represented the Scottish Building Crafts on the Committee. The report in itself was unique in that it was compiled only by those who were engaged in the industry.[53]

The report pledged the industry to a 15 year building programme to produce 2½ million houses. The manpower problem was to be solved by absorbing trained workers not already engaged in the industry and by increasing the number of apprentices. Contractors were to employ one apprentice for every three craftsmen and apprentices could be accepted up to twenty years of age. Apprentices would start with 40% of a craftsman's wage with 5% increases every six months. By adopting these measures it was thought possible to increase production from the present rate of 40,000 houses to 90,000 in the first year and then gradually increase the rate to 225,000 in ten years. This figure would be sustained for five years. It confirmed the industry's capacity to meet the material demands of the programme and it agreed that no foreign manufactured goods should be used for houses built on subsidy. Concerning price control the Committee felt, at the outset, it was best to rely on the goodwill of the manufacturers before adopting any restrictive measures. It did agree that a Statutory Committee be appointed under the Act to carefully monitor house prices. The report, from an industry not hitherto renowned for good relations, was, as Wheatley later told the Commons, extraordinary.

In the course of presenting this report to the Commons[54] Wheatley stated that it had been a fixed principle of all recent housing legislation that the housing problem could only be solved on the basis of a partnership between Government and L.A. He had summoned a Conference of representatives of all L.A.s and explained his proposals. The L.A.s then formed a small Committee to consider the proposals and to look into the financial aspect of the whole scheme. Agreement was quickly reached with nearly all the L.A.s, a notable exception was Birmingham, Chamberlain's heartland. It was Birmingham's belief that the housing problem could easily be solved if the industry was prepared to accept dilution. However, on reaching agreement with the L.A.s, Wheatley had to concede on a time limit of 40 years for the Government subsidy and a £12-10s per house for agricultural areas. The L.A.s were to contribute a sum equal to half of the government subsidy. The houses could only be rented to tenants who wanted to inhabit them and they could not be sold without the permission of the Ministry of Health. There was to be a fair wage contract written into contracts with builders and the rents were to be based on those of pre-war working-class houses in the same area. Wheatley also had to concede to the L.A.s their right to determine the size of houses which they insisted should be the same size as that laid down in the 1923 Act.

Wheatley's skill in negotiating with these separate bodies and the groundwork he had done stifled most of the opposition to the Bill by the time he introduced the Finance Resolution in the Commons on the 3rd June.[55] It had the backing of the entire building industry, sufficient to keep the Tories at bay. Even the Finance Resolutions were bound in such a way that left little room for discussion. It was as if he was presenting a package that the House dare not refuse.

'It was merely a continuation of Chamberlain's Act which had failed, because the short term aspect of it failed to bring the much needed stability to the building industry. This failure only added to the deficit in housing. He had not attempted to teach the building industry how to run its own business, he was aware of the industry's need of a long-term programme to restore confidence in itself. He had simply asked the building industry how many houses it could produce for the Nation in a year. They brought back proposals to him for a long-term building programme which they said was necessary to stabilise the industry and attract labour. In return for the Government accepting their proposals they were prepared to give guarantees on production and prices. The industry recognised the advantages of a long-term programme and was prepared to co-operate with the government in making the scheme work and had proposed the setting up of three committees towards this end; a Committee to represent manufacturers and merchants, one representing builders and operatives and the other on prices and survey. Each would have a representative on a National Building Committee set up by the Ministry of Health. In addition, there would be regional and local committees.

Building would go on for three years and at the end of that period the industry would take stock of its performance. If the average output is not maintained then, the agreement is terminated. If it is maintained then the agreement continues for a further period until at the end of fifteen years when we would have 2$^1/_2$ million houses. The output for the first two years is estimated at 190,000. However, if prices cannot be controlled the scheme will be discontinued.'

This was the basis of Wheatley's presentation. In the debate that followed criticism was directed mainly on the complex rents issue. The Liberal, E. Simon, argued that the Bill would create a class of privileged tenant living at a rather low rent because of the outpouring of Government money.[56] An Amendment by Simon to have the rents equated with those of houses of similar sizes and amenities in similar areas was seen by Wheatley as a wrecking Amendment and was strongly resisted.[57] The National Liberal Federation had previously taken the steam from any proposed Liberal opposition when it passed a resolution welcoming the Report of the Building Committee and declaring that it would support a Bill which provided safeguards on prices.[58] Masterman, the other Liberal expert on housing, assured the House that everything the Liberals wanted was contained in the four corners of the Bill, but thought the scheme should be combined with one that would allow for private ownership on a wider scale.[59] Wheatley's criticism of the size of Chamberlain's houses rebounded on him and he attempted to further justify himself by arguing that larger houses could mean subsidised housing for the middle classes, it was a lame excuse. To the argument that the building industry's failure to accept dilution had much to do with the housing shortage Wheatley countered with the burden placed on housing by interest charges. 'Over the 60-year loan period interest rates were double that of the combined cost of all other factors involved in production, his dilution would start with interest rates'.[60]

Praise for Wheatley's Parliamentary performance came from every side. Rayner, a Liberal, who claimed thirty years experience in the building industry as both worker and employer was wholesome in his praise of Wheatley.[61] Perhaps the greatest tribute came from that bitter adversary Joynson Hicks, "no matter whether one agrees with him or not, Wheatley is a great man, a great Parliamentarian'.[62]

The Government resisted two Amendments in the Lords and the Bill received the Royal Assent on the 7th August, six months after Wheatley had taken office. With this Bill Wheatley had demonstrated a single-mindedness, excellent negotiating skills and expert salesmanship. Even before he had set up the National House Building Committee he had put forward his proposals to the Cabinet and the end result showed little change from the original proposals. He introduced a Socialist conception to house building which had the minimum of government controls and, with consummate skill he sold this policy to men for whom the very word Socialism was anathema. Playing one set of interests against another he guided the Bill through Parliament encountering little opposition on the way. His boldness in putting through this measure was in stark contrast to the timidity of most of his

Minister of Health

colleagues. 'Wheatley, in his every day wear, had his bill worked out and passed through parliament before his colleagues had finished with their tailors.'[63] John Scanlon made this statement apropos the controversy over Court Dress. Indeed, after the passing of his Bill Wheatley confided to Scanlon that he would refuse to serve in the Cabinet after his Housing Bill No. 2 was passed for he had become aware of the futility of trying to remedy the defects of Capitalism in a Government composed of men who did not believe in Socialism.[64]

As a safeguard to the passage of his Bill Wheatley had omitted the proposals that were designed to control profits and prevent manufacturers creating shortages, these were to be included in a separate Bill. This Bill, introduced to the Commons on the 5th June, provided for Government powers to investigate any price increases of building materials, the restriction of supplies and, if necessary, to take steps to regulate prices and prevent artificial shortages aimed at boosting prices. The M.O.H. would have powers to take over production in plants where output was being unnecessarily restrained. Wheatley had already come to some form of agreement with the National House Building Committee on these measures and seemed confident that this Bill would go through. It was unlikely that he would receive Liberal support with such measures. However, before the Bill could be debated there were two events which coincided to bring about the downfall of the Labour Government and seriously impair its prospects of re-election.

On the 29th July the Communist newspaper, the *Workers Weekly*, printed an article which advocated against the intervention of the military in industrial disputes. Copies of this edition were thrown over the wall into Aldershot Barracks. The Attorney General, Patrick Hastings, on the advice of the Public Prosecutor, decided to prosecute the editor of the paper under the Incitement to Mutiny Act. The Attorney General was unaware that the Labour Party had conducted a national campaign a few years earlier in protest at the indictment of Tom Mann and Guy Bowman for giving similar advice to the troops. When it was asked in Parliament as to who was responsible for the Editor's indictment there were angry roars from the Labour Benches that a Labour Attorney General should institute such proceedings. Labour Member after Labour Member threatened to go back home and defy prosecution by making appeals similar to that which had appeared in the *Workers Weekly*.[65] A hasty Cabinet meeting was called to discuss the whole matter. In the course of the meeting it transpired that John Ross Campbell, the man facing the charge, had merely been sitting in for the regular editor who had been absent through illness. The Cabinet decided that Campbell could not be held responsible for the article. In addition, it was disclosed that Campbell had an excellent war record, being decorated for gallantry. It was decided that the Attorney General should not proceed with the charges and that in the future no public prosecutions of a political character should be undertaken without prior sanction of the Cabinet.[66]

On the day that the Cabinet met to discuss the Campbell affair the Government announced the signing of Treaties with Russia. Negotiations between the two countries had been going on for some time and were on the point of collapse over the question of a loan to Russia. Snowden and Wedgwood had both vigorously opposed the idea of a loan to Russia[67] and it was only through the late intercession of six Labour Members of Parliament that a settlement had been finally arrived at.[68] The media sounded the alarm bells. 'The Government had been taken over by extremists'. To a Government that had been prepared to use the Navy to man power stations in the event of a power workers strike and was willing to send gun boats up the Yangtse there was an element of farce to the hysteria that accompanied the signing of the Russian Treaties.[69] The seeds, however, had been sown to bring about the downfall of the Labour Government.

In September, a Lobby correspondent, while holidaying in the Highlands met McDonald for a chat. In the course of the conversation the Campbell case cropped up and McDonald put the entire blame on Hastings for both proceeding with and withdrawing the charges. The newspaper that published this interview with McDonald was also able to get an accurate account of the Cabinet discussions and scenting blood, never let up.[70] On the 30th September a question was put in the House as to why the Campbell case had been dropped. In a reply that was totally unsatisfactory Hastings stated that no representation was made to him to have the case dropped. McDonald was then asked directly what part he had played in the matter. His reply was that he was neither consulted in the institution of the prosecution nor its withdrawal. The whole matter had been left by him to his legal officers.[71] McDonald was aware now that he was in deep trouble and tried to extricate himself. According to John Scanlon, who was Hasting's Private Secretary, McDonald pleaded with Hastings to accept full responsibility for the whole business, resign from the Government and Parliament and re-contest his seat at Wallsend. Hastings refused and in this he had the full support of Wheatley who strongly objected to him being sacrificed to save

McDonald's skin.[72] A Tory vote of censure on the Government's handling of the Campbell affair was withdrawn in favour of a Liberal Amendment calling for the setting up of a Committee of Inquiry.[73] The Amendment was carried by 364 votes to 198 and McDonald, rather than face the inevitable result of such an Inquiry, decided to face the electorate. So ended 9 months of Labour Government in which only Wheatley emerged with an enhanced reputation. The date for the new election was set for the 29th October.

References

1. *London Times* – 9/1/24
2. *London Times* – 2/1/24
3. *Glasgow Evening Times* – 14/1/20
4. *London Times* – 7/1/24
5. *Ramsay McDonald* – David Marquand – 1977
6. *London Times* – 23/1/24
7. *Eastern Standard* – 5/2/24
8. *Call Back Yesterday* – H. Dalton
9. *Beloved Rebel* – J. McNair
10. Cab 10 (24) – 6/2/24
11. *Decline and Fall of the Labour Party* – J. Scanlon
12. *My Life* – George Lansbury – 1928
13. *Hansard* – 26/2/24
14. Ibid.
15. *London Times* – 7/2/24
16. *Glasgow Herald* – 20/2/24
17. Memorandum – C.P. 114 (24) – 8/2/24
18. *Hansard* – 26/2/24
19. Ibid.
20. Ibid.
21. Ibid.
22. *Forward* – 4/3/24
23. *Ramsay McDonald* – David Marquand
24. Cab 64 (23) 23/1/23
    Cab 8 (24) 28/1/23
    Cab 9 (24) 4/2/24
25. Cab 11 (24) Memorandum CP 83 (24) 8/2/24
26. Cab 9 (24) 4/2/24
    Cab 11 (24) Memorandum CP 89 (24) Appendix 18/2/24
27. Cab 11 (24) 8/2/24
28. *Hansard* 2/4/24
29. Cab 13 (24) 13/2/24
30. *Hansard* – 22/2/24
31. Ibid.
32. *London Times* – 12/3/24
33. Cab 17 (24) 28/2/24

34. Cab 22 (24) 26/3/24
35. London Times – 3/4/24
36. Ibid.
37. Hansard – 2/4/24
38. Hansard – 6/4/24
39. Cab 25 (24) 7/4/24
40. Cab 27 (24) 15/4/24
41. Cab 15 (24) Memorandum CP 122 (24) 20/2/24
42. Cab 15 (24) 20/2/24
43. Cab 21 (24) CP 173 (24) 17/3/24
44. *Eastern Standard* – 17/5/24
45. Cab 12 (24) 12/2/24
46. *London Times* – 10/5/24
47. Cab 27 (24) 15/4/24
48. *First Labour Government* – R. W. Hyland
49. *New Leader* – 6/6/24, 20/6/24
50. *An Autobiography* – P. Snowden
51. *London Times* – 19/5/24
52. Cab 28 (24) 29/4/24
53. *Forward* – 19/4/24
    New Leader – 18/4/24
    Cab 27 (24) Appendix 1 15/4/24
54. Hansard – 16/4/24
55. Hansard – 3/6/24
56. Ibid.
57. Ibid.
58. *London Times* – 15/4/24
59. Hansard – 3/6/24
60. Ibid.
61. Ibid.
62. *New Leader* – 6/6/24
63. *Decline and Fall of the Labour Party* – J. Scanlon
64. Ibid.
65. Ibid.
66. Cab 48 (24) 6/8/24
67. Cab 44 (24) 30/7/24
68. *The First Labour Government* – R. W. Hyland
    London Times – 27/8/24
69. Cab 37 (24) 30/5/24
    Cab 39 (24) 2/7/24
70. *Decline and Fall of the Labour Party* – J. Scanlon
71. Hansard – 30/9/24
72. *Decline and Fall of the Labour Party* – J. Scanlon
73. Hansard – 8/10/24

Chapter Twelve
Election and General Strike

'There is no room in British politics for three parties, politics is a conflict, not of parties, but of systems.'[1] Wheatley made this statement as a welcoming response to the tacit agreement of the Tories and Liberals not to oppose each other in constituencies where it seemed possible that Labour could win through the intervention of a third party.[2] 'The fight against Socialism is the common task' said Asquith.[3]

Going into the election the Socialism of the Labour Party was being painted a deep red by the opposing parties as well as by the media. There was no let up on the Campbell case and the Russian loan, which Churchill described as an accessory to Soviet crimes,[4] was bitterly criticised. Labour's failure to create new jobs was played up by both parties with the abolition of the McKenna Duties a special target for the Tories.[5] With the jobless figure standing at 1,300,000 when Labour took office and showing little reduction when it left, Labour's record on this front was hard to defend. On housing, the Tories were content to stand by the Chamberlain Bill which has demonstrated, they said, that it can produce all the houses for which labour and materials were available. The Liberals called for the utilisation of the unemployed in a housing scheme of which the advantages would be shared by both tenant and owner. 'The Wheatley Act', said Lloyd George, 'was the most portentous failure in history.'[6] The Tories played the patriot game in this election which Wheatley bitterly criticised in its aftermath. 'They struck a heavy blow at national unity when they adopted the Union Jack as their national emblem.'[7]

Labour tried to make capital on the leading role that McDonald played at the London Conference which had reached agreement on the Dawes plan for German reparations. This plan came in for heavy criticism by the T.U.C. because of the burden that would be placed on the German worker. On housing, Wheatley's Materials Bill was to be pursued and unemployment would be dealt with by a constructive policy of National Development. The benefits that the Russian loan would give to the country were also highlighted. From the outset of the campaign, the Labour leaders fought desperately to free the Party from the Bolshevik label that had been neatly attached to it. Thomas stated that he hated Bolshevism whether it be that of the Tsar or Lenin[8] and on an election tour McDonald condemned the Campbell article 'No good is going to come from mutinies in the army.'[9]

Wheatley's campaign was fought on the lines of the class war which brought a strong protest from the Marquis of Salisbury.[10] There was no way that Wheatley would condemn Campbell, he agreed with his sentiments.[11]

'Do not look at the technicalities of the Campbell case. Look at what was behind the author of the article. He is untrained in the Curzon-Birkenhead art of saying seditious things in a legal way. The difference of guilt between Campbell and Birkenhead was the difference between the poor man's street bet and the rich man's telephone bet. The reality of the Campbell article was that the military should not be used in a trade dispute. If it is a crime to express that view, then I am a criminal. The Liberals and Tories claim that troops should be used is class war run mad. If the landlords and capitalists wish to settle their disputes with the worker by physical force I have no objection, but they must do all the fighting themselves. Every candidate in the election should be questioned on whether they favour using the military in a trade dispute. If the candidates answer is yes, no worker should vote for him.'

Wheatley attacked the Free Trade of Snowden and of others, arguing that the precarious state of British industry made it vulnerable to foreign competition. 'With the cost of living largely controlled by the cost of production we are now at the mercy of the U.S.A. whose production costs are cheaper. British capitalism's only answer to this is to reduce wages.'[12]

In Shettleston, the campaign took a more sinister form. Wheatley's opponent in a straight fight was J. Reid Miller, a member of the local Unionist Party. Miller's tactics in this election were of the basest type. Sectarianism was crudely resurrected. Anonymous letters denouncing Protestants appeared in the local press purported to be written by friends of Wheatley. A smear campaign was got under way in which it was alleged in turn that Wheatley was a money lender, shareholder in a brewery concern, involved in the liquor trade, a financier of licence holders, a bookmaker and had an association with a firm of contractors who employed sweated labour. Despite the concern of his local party Wheatley refused to publicly rebut these charges. He took the view that his personal and public life was so well known to his constituents that any rebuttal was unnecessary.[13] He did condemn the obstructive tactics of the Fascists at this election.[14] In the main he fought his campaign on the issues which he saw as important, unemployment and housing. He defended his Housing Bill and promised the people that if he was returned he would show them houses built at a speed never before dreamed of by his predecessors.[15]

On top of this smear campaign came a blow that almost cost Wheatley his seat and one that sent Labour scattering and put paid to any faint hopes they had of being returned to power. The *Daily Mail* published the contents of a letter, signed by Zinoviev the President of the Communist International, in which Communists in Britain were urged to engage in revolutionary activities. Later proved to be a forgery, but with Labour cast in the Communist mould the letter had a debilitating effect on its campaign in the final run-up to the election. 'It is a Blue Plot, not a Red Plot' said Wheatley. 'It is a crude and mean election trick and the tactics of the Tories are no different from the tactics being used by my opponent in Shettleston.'[16] McDonald's silence on the matter added some substance to the allegations[17] whereas, said Wheatley,[18] what McDonald should have done was to jail the editor of the *Daily Mail* as would have happened in similar circumstances to a Labour editor. However, this statement by Wheatley was made in hindsight. The Tory tactics paid off in the country and almost succeeded in Shettleston.

The Tories were returned with 418 seats with Labour losing 40 seats. The Liberals lost heavily being reduced to a rump with a mere 40 seats. Wheatley scraped home with a majority of 630 and in nearby Camlachie Campbell Stephen also had a nail biting count. Partick was lost to the Tories and, with the exception of Buchanan, all the other Labour candidates in Glasgow had much reduced majorities. Johnston and Shinwell both lost their seats, but there was a surprise at Paisley where Rosslyn Mitchell captured the seat from Asquith. The results in Scotland as a whole must have been a disappointment to Wheatley in his dream of a Socialist Scotland.

After the 1923 election Wheatley was boasting that Labour only required to win a further 4 seats in Scotland to send a Socialist majority to Westminster. Yet, despite I.L.P. enthusiasm, Buchanan's Home Rule Bill[19] received little support in Parliament or from the Scottish people. Scotland was not, to all intents and purposes at the time, at the receiving end of some piece of English maladministration. There is no doubt that, outside the Cabinet, Wheatley could have created the necessary hysteria in the country to back Buchanan's Bill, but he did not look upon Home Rule as being a narrow Nationalistic creed. His newspaper, writing in support of the Bill stated,

'It is the expression of a definite desire for self-realisation, a definite principle of de-centralised organisation. We do not want Home Rule because Burns was born in Ayr or because there are fine hills in Rothesay. We want it because the special economic, cultural and moral development of the whole Scottish community can best be fostered by making Scotland a nation again. The time has gone when grown men should prate like schoolboys on Scotland's superiority over England. The exploited factory worker in Bridgeton has more in common with the sweated seamstress in Whitechapel than with the self-satisfied, vulgarly spoken plutocrat of Kelvinside.'[20]

There was no way that the Scottish people could be appealed to on these principles, there had to be an emotional appeal. McDonald the hard-headed Scotsman displayed little interest in Home Rule for his country, but McDonald was to prove, on more than one occasion, that his feel of the people's pulse was more sensitive than that of Wheatley the Irishman.

Whenever small groups of Labour M.P.s got together and talk turned to the election, McDonald's name figured prominently when reasons were being sought for the Party's failure at the election.[21] McDonald's stock had slumped both inside and outside the Party, his credibility was being questioned. He had come under suspicion for his relationship with Alex Grant, the biscuit manufacturer. Grant had supplied McDonald with a Daimler car and had also given him an income from shares in his company and in return, Grant had received a Baronetcy. Cries of 'Biscuits' were being directed at McDonald when addressing meetings.[22] At an election meeting in Glasgow McDonald was shouted down with cries for Wheatley and Maxton who were both on the platform. Shortly before the election there had been rumours in the press of a left-wing revolt in the Cabinet being led by Wheatley and Snowden.[23] Wheatley's stock in the Party was high and McDonald himself entertained fears that Wheatley might oppose him for the leadership.[24] On the surface there appeared to be a mood for a change in the leadership, but it was certain that Wheatley would never receive the necessary support from the Trade Unions[25] to effect a serious challenge to McDonald, Wheatley's brand of Socialism held little appeal for them. The one man who would have been acceptable to the Party as a whole was Henderson, but he spurned the approaches that were made to him.[26] In the event, McDonald was re-elected as leader without opposition.

Of the 151 Labour M.P.s returned to Parliament 26 had been funded in the election by the I.L.P. and approximately 40 others, including McDonald who was the I.L.P. nominee as Treasurer to the L.P., owed an allegiance to it, Snowden and Wedgwood had gone over to the Labour Party. At the election for the Parlia-

Election and General Strike

mentary Executive Wheatley and Maxton were voted fifth and sixth respectively and were now the effective leaders of the left wing in a Party which was giving indications that it wanted to distance itself far from the left.

In the post mortems that followed Labour's election defeat the leadership verdict was that Communism was to blame. The *New Leader* urged a 'Retreat From Moscow'[27] and Clynes spoke of the poisonous claws of Communism and revolution and their menace to Labour's progress.[28] Wheatley had reached a different conclusion and he spelled out the direction that the Party should take.[29]

'For a number of years Communism and Russia have been presented to the British public in the blackest possible colour. Even the recent Labour Party Conference* joined in the attack. The opponents of Labour shrewdly put us in the Communist corner and kept us there. Campbell and Zinoviev were our election companions and the British people who were asking for bread became interested in the Russian Treaty. Despite this, 5½ million people stood solidly in support of Labour. Now is the time to justify their political faith. Britain needs a new Blatchford. The Labour Party in the Commons is freed, and not too soon, from a difficult position. We can now return to a fighting policy. There can be no freedom for the toiling masses under Capitalism and knowing that we should fight to end it, not mend it. This is not the time for timid policies.'

Did Wheatley see himself as the new Blatchford or was this the role that Maxton was to play? Before Parliament met on the 12th December Baldwin's government had decided to drop the Russian Treaty. The King's speech, apart from a promised Commission to inquire into food prices, gave notice that the problems that beset the country would be left to the fate of free market forces. Housing was to fall into this policy which was to be solved by encouraging the private builder and the occupying owner, substantial progress having been made in this direction it was claimed.

Neville Chamberlain, back at the Health Office, seemed determined to abort Wheatley's Bill. Even before Parliament assembled he was aiming to drive a wedge into the agreements reached between Wheatley and the building trades. Addressing the Carlton Club, Chamberlain gave warning to the Building Unions that

*At this conference three resolutions were passed:
(1) That applications for affiliation by the Communist Party be refused.
(2) That no member of the C.P. be eligible for endorsement as Labour Candidate to Parliament.
(3) No member of the C.P. be eligible for membership of the L.P.
The first two resolutions were overwhelmingly adopted and the third by a narrow majority.

he intended, with or without their co-operation, to add several thousand new men to the industry.[30] In the debate that followed the King's speech he went even further by threatening to let Wheatley's Bill 'hang around until it hanged itself.'[31] Wheatley was contemptuous of the Government's plan to leave housing to the mercy of private enterprise.

'All those foul festering places in the centres of our great cities and towns are part of the wonderful work of private enterprise. Socialism is the purifying angel, but unfortunately the highest position our materialistic minds will allow us to obtain for it is to make it the scavenger of private enterprise.'

In the course of his speech he was interrupted by a Tory who asked him if there were any slums in Russia? 'I am never surprised,' he replied, 'that when we get down to a discussion of the social conditions of the people of this country that the Hon. Members opposite should try to divert our minds to the conditions at the ends of the earth.' At the conclusion of his speech Wheatley ridiculed the number of houses constructed under the Chamberlain Act, of the 30,000 houses completed 25,000 were for sale and in Scotland where just over 900 had been completed only 73 were for letting.[32] Chamberlain refuted Wheatley's charges by claiming that 110,000 had been completed by the end of September of which 86% were built by private enterprise with the large majority having rateable values of less than £26. A further 92,000 were under construction, he said.[33] According to M.O.H. figures given at a later date, just over 14,000 L.A. houses built by subsidy had been completed in 1924. By the end of 1928 almost 240,000 subsidised houses had been built by the L.A. for rent[34] and if the Chamberlain Government had not reduced the subsidy it was possible that Wheatley's target of 2½ million houses by 1939 would have been achieved. Wheatley's scheme had two advantages for the L.A. In addition to providing houses for the very poor it provided much needed work for the unemployed in the absence of Government financial aid towards Public Work schemes. Chamberlain had made it plain to a deputation from L.A. that there would be no more favourable terms for such schemes.[35] The debate on the King's speech provided the only colour to what was to be a dull first Session of the new Parliament, but in any case it was outside of Parliament that Wheatley was to take the fight that he hoped would capture the Labour movement for the left, particularly in the constituencies.

The beginning of 1925 saw the launching of the I.L.P.'s 'Backward Areas' campaign.[36] Devoted mainly to constituencies where Labour support had been weakest, the campaign in Scotland began in January almost simultaneously with the inauguration of the Scottish Federation's Guild of Youth.[37] Wheatley and Maxton were prominent in this campaign[38] which, by the time of the Annual Conference in April, had helped to bring I.L.P. branch membership past the 1,000 mark for the first time.[39] Allen's leadership of the I.L.P. was being questioned. His closeness to McDonald and his heel dragging on the new Socialist policies that were being debated within the I.L.P. had not endeared him to the rank and file of the Party.[40] The decision by Conference to adopt Maxton's proposal for a 'Living Wage' was an early warning of the strength of the left. The right wing opposed this principle, a principle that was to be the subject of bitter controversy, not only in the Labour movement, but in the country as a whole over the next year and already the battle lines were being drawn.

At the beginning of the year Sir Adam Nimmo, Coal Owner, told the National Liberal Club that 'The wages of the men engaged in the industry cannot permanently rest upon considerations of the cost of living or what the men call a "Living Wage." The problem of wages rested upon fundamental economic considerations which neither the miners' leaders nor anyone else would be able to change.'[41] The following month A. J. Cook, the outspoken Communist miners' leader, called a conference of Miners, Railways and Transport Workers Unions where it was agreed to support each other in the event of industrial action.[42] As was expected, the Coal Owners gave notice of the termination of existing agreements. In turn they proposed drastic wage reductions, abolition of the principle of a minimum wage and a return from National agreements to District agreements. Lock-out Notices were set for the 31st July. The miners refused to accept the owners' proposals and were backed by the other two unions who pledged the complete blacking of all movement of coal from the 31st July. At the eleventh hour the Government intervened in the dispute and a temporary agreement was reached with the owners. A special subsidy was to be given to the industry for a period of nine months during which period a Royal Commission would make a detailed inquiry into the state of the industry. Strangely, the Commission under the Chairmanship of Lord Samuels did not contain a single member of the coal industry.[43]

'Red Friday' was the name coined by the workers for a day on which they perceived a great victory had been won, but while the Union leaders were celebrating Wheatley issued a bleak warning.[44] He warned the workers to prepare during the next nine months on new lines and on a new scale for the greatest struggle in their history. The Capitalists, he said, will get their Fascisti ready to carry on a transport system that will make them independent of the workers during a general strike. The navy will be ordered to man the mines and the army and the police drilled to keep the locked-out miners in order. Wheatley sprang to the defence of Cook who, like himself, recognised the danger and was being criticised by Union and Labour leaders for his use of wild rhetoric. 'Cook has great qualities. He is basically honest and cannot coin words to conceal his thoughts. He preached a very old and now neglected doctrine 'Workers Unite' and Capitalists began to howl at this man from Moscow. He preached a triple alliance as if it were a fact and the workers began to believe in themselves. Until then the Labour movement was sick, and some people believed, until death.'[45]

Of the Government's subsidy to the industry Churchill was forthright,[46] 'There is no element of finality in this settlement, the Government decided to pay the subvention in order to gain nine months breathing space'. Wheatley was even more forthright and dangerously so;[47]

'WORKERS, LOOK OUT! MASTERS MOBILISING.'

The Mining Association operating through the press is to expose the Reds to the public, how they work and control the Miners' Federation and other Unions.* When this exposure takes place the decent Pinks and Whites among the working classes are expected to blush for the Trade Union connection with the Devil's own Reds. The Government is also warning that the Unions will lose their legal rights. Will the workers be cowards or will they rally in 1925 as they did in 1914. They are the same men and women, the danger is no less serious, the cause is just as great. Every non-Unionist worker should now be regarded as an enemy of the State. Workers must be prepared to make sacrifices in the struggle. Every Labour Organisation in Britain should proceed immediately to obtain pledges from millions of workers that, in this hour of destiny, they will not desert their class. We want ten million men who are prepared to suffer rather than see Britain made a land of coolies.'

Wheatley was advocating a Workers Defence Corps and in this respect his ideas had changed little in 20 years. Strangely, Wheatley's bellicosity went unregarded by the press for whom Cook was the bogey-man.

By the end of September the Government's strategy had become obvious. Much undue publicity was given to the army manoeuvres at Andover.[48] An unofficial Organisation for the Maintenance of Supplies was set up under the Presidency of Lord Hardinge and composed of prominent figures like Lord Jellicoe

---
*The Communist Movement (Trade Unions and Moscow), written by Dr. Arthur Shadwell was serialised in The Times during September and October.

and Lyndon Macassey.[49] The purpose of the Organisation was to provide technical training for would-be strike breakers. Offices were opened in every part of the country and 100,000 people were quick to answer the call.[50] The Home Secretary, Joynson-Hicks, admitted that the Government had made no objection to the setting up of this organisation when approached by the organisers, but the organisers had been told that it was the Government's duty to preserve order and maintain supplies during an emergency and plans for such a contingency had been made.[51] The Government's secret plans were to divide the country into ten areas or divisions, each with its own Commissioner and military staff. These Commissioners were to be given extraordinary powers and would act outside Parliament.[52]

Wheatley was not ignorant of the Government's plans. At Atherton,[53] he warned the people that they were on the eve of a great social struggle, a struggle that would not take place in Parliament. 'Joynson-Hicks' said Wheatley, 'is a candidate for the first Mussoliniship in this country. For the first time in the history of Britain a strike-breaking class war organisation has been taken into the bosom of the Government.' To all these signs, and the warnings of Wheatley and Cook, Union and Labour leaders paid little heed.

Leaders at the T.U. Congress in September urged the members to caution and a check on extremists.[54] The Labour Party Conference at Liverpool was conciliatory. In his Chairman's address,[55] C. T. Cramp, while recognising the existence of class conflict and a society that was torn with strife, maintained that conditions could not be changed by substituting one class for another. 'Labour,' he said, 'should transcend class warfare and the destructive policies of the left wing.' McDonald, for whom this Conference was a personal triumph, made a statement which lent credence to Dr. Shadwell's theories. The issue of individual Communist membership was raised again at this Conference and, despite an eloquent plea by Harry Pollitt, opposition to it was even more pronounced. Wheatley, who had been opposed to Communist expulsion[56] in the first instance, hit out at this further rejection and also the mood of the Conference.[57]

'The country is not on the road to ruin because of anything the Reds have done, but because there is a super-abundance of goods and insufficient purchasing power. Improvement can only come about with a change in the industrial system.'

The Government seemed intent on isolating trouble before a final showdown. Two weeks after the Labour Party Conference the headquarters of the Communist Party was raided and twelve members of the Party, including Gallacher and Bell, were arrested and charge with conspiring to publish seditious libel. They each received sentences sufficient to distance them from any future conflict. In Glasgow, attempts were made to minimise Wheatley's influence. Sunday meetings in City Halls, which had been arranged by him, were banned by the Corporation on the grounds that they were being organised by the Party to raise funds to make propaganda (meetings of other Labour leaders were not subject to a ban). Wheatley ignored the ban and spoke to capacity audiences. 'Democratic rights,' he said, 'were given provided that they were not used to the detriment of Capitalism.'[58]

On the 10th March the following year the curtain was raised for the most dramatic conflict in the history of industrial Britain when the Samuel Commission published its report. Little was offered to the miners in return for less wages and longer hours. The Miners' Federation sought reassurance of support from the T.U.C. in the event of the Coal Owners enforcing unacceptable conditions on their members. The Central Committee, which at first was equivocal with its offer of support, stiffened its attitude when the Coal Owners announced their intention to negotiate with the miners at District level only. Negotiations between the T.U.C., the miners and Baldwin ended in stalemate. Baldwin's solution to the problem was for the miners to accept a reduction in wages and an increase in the working day. The expected showdown was now inevitable. On the 29th April lock-out notices were posted and the T.U.C., rather reluctantly, decided to draft plans for a General Strike. According to Clynes, the majority of the T.U.C. leaders, including himself, had been against the strike and they had only acted for fear of being looked upon as traitors.

A State of Emergency was proclaimed on the 30th April and thousands of Special Constables were enrolled. Army tanks and armoured cars began to move into all the major cities and troops in full war kit marched through the streets. The Strike began at midnight on the 3rd May and despite the Government's massive show of strength support was solid. In the face of extreme provocation in the shape of the huge army of O.M.S. personnel that was recruited to help the army maintain essential services the workers displayed a remarkable discipline. Only in the East End of Glasgow was rioting reported. Greater uncertainty appeared in the ranks of the leaders with a statement by Sir John Simon in the Commons that the Strike was illegal and that every man was liable to be sued by his employer for damages and that the leaders were liable to great personal loss. It soon became obvious that the T.U.C. had little heart for this fight and the escape hatch that they were seeking came on the 11th May when Lord Samuel drafted a memorandum which was merely a touch up on his original report. That evening the T.U.C. Chairman, Arthur Pugh, informed the Miners' leaders that the Council considered Samuel's Memorandum as a fair basis for negotiating a settlement. The Miners disagreed, but notwithstanding, the General Council called on Baldwin the following morning to announce the strike was over. No reassurances were sought and none were given, the leaders had surrendered unconditionally and those closely involved in the struggle were stunned.[59]

The Times[60] hailed the General Council's action as a victory for the nation: to Wheatley it was 'THE GREAT SURRENDER'.[61]

'The response to the call for a General Strike was magnificent and electric. It startled and staggered not only the Capitalists, but the Labour leaders. The discipline shown by the workers was perfect. For the first time in history political differences disappeared. Tory working men whom we had regarded as reactionary declared in the most emphatic manner that they would not let their fellow workers down. Highly respectable middle class railway clerks who had never struck in their lives stood shoulder to shoulder with grimy workers. Everywhere among the strikers there was order, determination and confidence. A Fifth Estate appeared in the realm. It was a wonderful and unforgettable spectacle which put fresh hope and courage into the hearts of men whose lives had been devoted to the cause of working-class unity and intelligence. To the consternation of the country the strike was called off without apparent rhyme or reason. Those of us who had left London thought, on hearing the news, that a great victory had been won. Early reports had left the impression that, while the reputation of the Government had been saved, so had the position of the workers. Then came the horrible revelation that workers were being selected for victimisation. It suddenly dawned on us that there had been an abject unconditional surrender. Not only had the T.U.C. deserted the miners, but they had gratuitously thrown their members to the wolves. The Bosses were snubbing and insulting the Trade Unions with calculated offensiveness. The T.U.C. had given Baldwin more than he asked and a great deal more than he expected. All Baldwin had demanded in his public statements was a return to the position of the 1st May. Cowardice will occupy a central place when the reasons for the surrender become known. The qualities which distinguish men in a drawing room, palace or debating society are of little use in a vital struggle. Even before the struggle began prominent Labour men were whining and grovelling. The real tragedy was that the workers were deserted in their hour of trial by those in whom they put their trust. Now that the Trade Unions have been mortgaged to their enemies a new form of organisation may be necessary.'

What form of organisation did Wheatley have in mind? Was the thinking behind his subsequent tactics clouded by this unique response of the workers? He had never expressed any great enthusiasm for the Trade Union Movement, but any hopes he might have entertained of alienating the workers from their leaders were bound to be dashed on the pillars of the establishment. Nurtured in an environment where hatred of the establishment was endemic, Wheatley was to find it difficult to come to terms with the collective thinking of the British people. It is possible that he shared part of Trotsky's analysis[62] 'that the British people will turbulently liberate themselves from the national conservative discipline, working out their own discipline of revolutionary activity. Faced with pressure from below the upper ranks of the Labour Party will quickly change their colour. McDonald and company will be replaced by Wheatley, Lansbury and Kirkwood. However, these men would prove to be only a left variety of the Fabian type.' His personal assessment of Wheatley was that he was a left winger directed by a personal morality which in itself was based on religion.

The Miners' Federation rejected Samuel's proposals as a basis for peace talks and decided to fight on much to the annoyance of the T.U.C. and the Labour leaders. Indeed, McDonald's main concern was that those who had helped the Government during the strike should not be made to suffer because of their actions.[63] Wheatley backed the miners in every possible way. His newspaper opened a Relief Fund to which Wheatley made a personal contribution of £8 per week, a sum equal to his Parliamentary salary. He addressed meetings all over the country in their support.

'There were no words that could convey his admiration for the miners and their leaders, they were his ideal of a fighting industrial army. They were the National Guards who were fighting Britain's battle. If they were defeated Great Britain would again become poor Britain.'[64]

When the Government introduced a Bill to repeal the 7 Hour Act (Mines) Wheatley launched a bitter attack on Baldwin for taking sides in an industrial dispute.[65]

'He is the most reactionary statesman of the modern age. Other Tories have merely put the brake on progress, he has reversed the engine. Our class right or wrong is the basis of Tory policy. The owners now do not need to break the law, Baldwin will simply change it to suit their needs. This Act is not an intelligent solution to the problem, the problem is not a mining or coal problem it is a great National problem and if the miners are forced to accept an 8 hour day, one in every eight miners would be out of work.'

Election and General Strike

The miners stubbornly resisted for nine months until increasing hardship forced their surrender and a return to work on the basis of District Agreements. Help from the Russian miners[66] and the I.L.P. was not sufficient in the face of the Government's Board of Guardians (Default) Act brought in at the end of the year. This Bill gave the Ministry of Health power to remove those Guardians whom they considered were too generous in giving relief. Labour gains at the Municipal elections in November were attributed to the generosity of Labour Guardians by the National Union of Ratepayers.[67] Chester-Le-Street gave an example of how the Government intended to use this Act when twelve elected Labour members in this area were superseded for allegedly making extravagant payments. It was Buchanan who brought this case to the notice of the Commons[68] in the March following the passage of the Bill. In a bitter attack on the Government Wheatley defended the Guardians and accused it of testing Socialist Guardians by Tory standards.[69]

'The Guardians had not been reckless, but had displayed a sound public policy in regard to subsidising wages. They were being charged not with giving general treatment to an ordinary destitute person, but to a miner's dependant and it was obvious that it was Government policy that when a district deserted Toryism it should be disenfranchised.'

Chamberlain's reply was that they had had trouble with these Guardians before the General Strike, they had given a scale of relief that was extravagant.

Following this attack on the Government Wheatley made the final break with McDonald and company – he announced his decision to retire to the back benches where, he said, he would have greater freedom to speak his mind.[70] He was not at all happy with Labour's present policies.

References

1. *Glasgow Evening Times* – 15/10/24
2. *London Times* – 22/10/24
3. *Scotsman* – 24/12/24
4. *London Times* – 21/10/24
5. *Glasgow Evening Times* – 13/10/24
6. *Glasgow Evening Times* – 20/10/24
7. *Glasgow Evening Times* – 25/10/24
8. *London Times* – 22/10/24
9. *Scotsman* – 20/10/24
10. *Glasgow Evening Times* – 13/10/24
11. *Scotsman* – 20/10/24
12. *Scotsman* – 21/10/24

13. *Eastern Standard* – 19/9/25
14. *Glasgow Evening Times* – 25/10/24
15. *Glasgow Evening Times* – 25/10/24
16. *Glasgow Evening Times* – 27/10/24
17. Ibid.
18. *Glasgow Herald* – 12/3/28
19. *Hansard* – Vol 1973 – May 1924
20. *Eastern Standard* – 10/5/24
21. *Decline and Fall of the Labour Party* – J. Scanlon
22. Ibid.
23. *Eastern Standard* – 7/9/24
24. *Diaries* – Beatrice Webb – 1952
25. *Glasgow Evening Times* – 17/11/24
26. *Glasgow Evening Times* – 17/2/25
    Decline and Fall of the Labour Party – J. Scanlon
27. *New Leader* – 14/11/24
28. *New Leader* – 21/11/24
29. *New Leader* – 7/11/24
    Eastern Standard – 8/11/24
30. *Hansard* – 16/12/24
31. Ibid.
32. Ibid.
33. Ibid.
34. *London Times* – 15/10/29
35. *Glasgow Evening Times* – 27/1/25
36. *New Leader* – 2/1/25
37. *Glasgow Evening Times* – 1/1/25
38. *New Leader* – 2/1/25
39. *Inside The Left* – F. Brockway
40. Ibid.
41. *Glasgow Evening Times* – 22/1/25
42. *Glasgow Evening Times* – 26/2/25
43. *Post War History of the British Working Classes* – A Hutt
44. *Eastern Standard* – 8/8/25
45. Ibid.
46. *London Times* – 7/8/25
47. *Eastern Standard* – 15/8/25
48. *London Times* – 22/9/25
49. *London Times* – 25/9/25
50. *Memoirs* – J. R. Clynes
51. *London Times* – 1/10/25
52. *Memoirs* – J. R. Clynes
53. *Glasgow Herald* – 7/10/25
54. *London Times* – 9/9/25
55. *London Times* – 30/9/25
56. *Decline and Fall of the Labour Party* – J. Scanlon
57. *Glasgow Herald* – 13/10/25
58. *Glasgow Herald* – 17/10/25
59. *Memoirs* – J. R. Clynes

Election and General Strike

Inside the Left – F. Brockway
Post War History of the British Working Classes – A. Hutt
Emergency Press
60. *London Times* – 13/5/26
61. *Glasgow Herald* – 21/5/26
    Eastern Standard – 22/5/26
    Forward – 22/5/26
62. *Whither England* – Leon Trotsky – New York – 1925
63. *London Times* – 14/5/26
64. *Eastern Standard* – 30/10/26
65. *Eastern Standard* – 3/7/26
66. *London Times* – 5/11/26
67. *London Times* – 4/11/26
68. *London Times* – 30/3/27
69. *London Times* – 31/3/27
70. Ibid.

Chapter Thirteen
Challenge from the Backbench

Not only was Wheatley not happy with Labour's policies, but also with the machinations of its leaders. Towards the end of 1926 he had been ready to respond to Henderson's plea for unity within the Party, but when he was out-manoeuvred by the Leadership from a place on the Executive he began to doubt even their spoken word.[1] Despite these manoeuvrings Wheatley was voted into thirteenth place in the elections for the Executive. The man who beat him for the vital twelfth place was Hugh Dalton. Dalton, a future Labour Chancellor of the Exchequer, stood in awe of Wheatley's expertise on finance.[2]

Wheatley's decision to leave the Opposition Front Bench was met, no doubt, with a sigh of relief from McDonald and company. Although he was respected by them, there is evidence that many disliked, not only his views, but the man himself and even distrusted him. His business success brought envy and suspicion although he was a man of simple tastes. He did not mix readily and was little understood. In conversation his voice was soft and amiable, but could be vitriolic in debate whether in the Commons or at P.L.P. meetings.[3] Wheatley's decision however, demonstrated once again his failure to understand the fundamental arts of British politics and in this he could have taken a lesson from McDonald. McDonald held the view that one should never resign, but that the other person should be manoeuvred into taking the unpopular step of expelling you.[4] This view explains his continuing association with the I.L.P. when their policies took on a different shape from those of himself and the Labour Party.

At the Whitley Bay Conference, a month before the General Strike, the I.L.P. had taken decisive steps towards the left. Maxton superseded Allen as chairman and the document 'Socialism in our Time (The Living Wage)' was adopted as Party policy.[5] Mainly the work of Hobson and Wise,[6] the document pledged a living income for all workers and payment by the State of children's allowances. Industry would be reorganised with the nationalisation of key industries and the bulk purchasing of essential imports. The Bank of England would be nationalised and credits and investments controlled. 'This is the wisest and most opportune programme that has ever been presented to the people'[7] Wheatley told the Conference. By contrast, McDonald derided the Document, 'Socialism is not going to come by a legal declaration of a nominal living wage and the consequential nationalisation of bankrupt industries. 'Socialism in our Time' is a sanctification of phrases of no definite meaning.'[8] The Labour Party had earlier produced its own policy document 'Labour and the Nation', a policy of national reconstruction and reform which McDonald declared was not a programme, but just an attempt to let the people know Labour's frame of mind. Thomas said that the whole idea of a programme was superfluous as it would only hamper the leaders from adapting to circumstances.[9] Other changes in the organisation of the I.L.P. which strengthened the grip of the left came with the appointment of Brockway as editor of the *New Leader* and John Paton as National Organiser. In Parliament, Wheatley and Maxton controlled the Party's inner group which met each week to decide on the strategy to be adopted on issues likely to come before the House.[10] It was perhaps the strength of this base that persuaded Wheatley to end his association with his right-wing colleagues.

'Socialism in our Time' was to be used to capture the soul of the Labour Movement and perhaps for Wheatley the leadership of that movement. All his utterances in support of this policy contained veiled attacks on the incompetence of the leadership to solve the country's problems.

'The collapse of Capitalism was not due to the incompetence of the Capitalists, but to the inherent difficulties in a system that only produced goods for profit. A Labour Government could not control that system any better than the Capitalists themselves indeed, Britain's Capitalists are the finest in the world outside of the United States. The country's problems could not be solved with nationalisation by instalments. The old idea of dealing with an industry or a group of industries would have to be abandoned. In the interests of the people one industry was dependent on another. All the Bishops and Baldwins in the world could not out of coal alone obtain a decent standard of living for the miners. Britain should be treated as one workshop and every industry looked upon as a department of that workshop. I am happy that, for the first time, we are going to the people with a policy that would end the competitive system of fixing wages and prices and one which would improve production through nationalisation so as to meet the increasing demand for higher living standards.'[11]

Wheatley's bid to have McDonald replaced as leader had the support of his friend Maxton. In a statement issued prior to the Scottish Divisional Conference in January 1927 Maxton said that a Labour leader other than McDonald would be necessary if the aims of the I.L.P. were to be furthered.[12] An alternative to McDonaldism or Communism was the disguised heading given by the media to Maxton's statement. A resolution at the Conference calling for a change in the leadership of the Labour Party was narrowly defeated by 61 votes to 57.[13] There is little doubt that the Tories took Wheatley's challenge for the leadership seriously and were concerned. Lord Birkenhead had no doubts,[14] 'McDonald's position has been challenged and if Wheatley is to be the new leader of the Labour Party – even new Prime Minister – it shows the complete and ludicrous incompetence of the Socialist Party to guide the fortunes of the Empire.' Birkenhead had previously denounced Wheatley for his defence of the Chinese Liberation Army under the command of Chen.

Parliament re-assembled on the 8th February, 1927, as China was enmeshed in civil war. Shanghai was threatened. In the King's speech the Commons was informed that the Government had despatched sufficient troops to protect British and Indian subjects from the violence of the mob. The majority of the Labour Members were opposed to the sending of these forces and any proposals to increase these numbers. It was to the ambivalent that Wheatley's words were directed of whom McDonald and Thomas were the most prominent.[15]

'There can be no room for compromise in the Labour Party's policy towards China. Chen has a dream of an independent Socialist China and already in his march he has raised wages and abolished the private ownership of girls. When he begins to nationalise the cotton mills, mostly foreign owned, the cries will become louder. The Labour Party should not allow itself to be stampeded by all the talk of British lives being in danger. There are only a few thousand British in China altogether. Very few belong to the working class and would have no difficulty in getting about the world. Chen has declared more than once that British residents and British property will be treated exactly as Chinese lives and property are treated in this country.'

'I regard as vile a man who asks British men and women to what class they belong,' said Birkenhead, 'I hold the man vile when he distinguishes between one class and another. It was our pride and boast, in the days before Mr. Wheatley and men like him, that all those who were English and stood for England would have the resources of the nation to assist them if their lives were imperilled.'[16]

A month later when the Government proposed to send additional forces to China Wheatley again showed his anger. He called on the British worker to show the same determination to prevent intervention in China as they had shown when Russia

Challenge from the Backbench

was in danger.[17] The only reason for a British presence in China was to protect British investments, investments that did nothing to help the British people. Every poor cotton worker in Shanghai earning a penny an hour is a menace to the cotton workers in Lancashire.' Labour forced a division on the Government's proposal in which four of their members abstained from voting, McDonald and Thomas being among the four.[18]

While Wheatley made no open bid for the leadership of the Labour Party his guns were being directed at the present leaders. Speaking in the debate on Churchill's Budget, which he said was prominent only in that it gave nothing and promised nothing to the poor, Wheatley warned that a Labour Government would be compelled by the forces of the country behind it to produce a Chancellor who would be a menace to the power, the privilege and the income of those who lived in a parasitical manner on the industry of the country.[19] It was a direct attack on Snowden's performance while in Office. However, the most serious attack on the leadership came at the I.L.P. Conference at Leicester in which the *Daily Mail* cited Wheatley as being the villain of the piece.[20] Abandoning the custom of the previous fifteen years the N.A.C. resolved not to nominate McDonald for the Treasureship of the Labour Party. The reason given for this snub was that the I.L.P. could not have, as a representative to the L.P. Conference, someone who had consistently opposed and criticised its policies. Sixty nine members of the I.L.P. signed a memorandum disassociating themselves from the Council's decision.[21] The Conference debate on the resolution was dominated by the Wheatley and McDonald factions, the Wheatley faction triumphing with the resolution being adopted by an almost two to one majority.[22] In reply to this rejection McDonald said 'They are angry with me because I do not shout Socialism from the housetops. In any case, the I.L.P. does not represent the bulk of the Labour Party, they are but a cave within a Party.'[23]

In a statement issued seemingly to dispel press reports of deep divisions within the Labour Party Wheatley reminded McDonald that the Party represented its majority and criticised him for failing to respond to the will of that majority.

'Never has there been an absolute united Party. Labour thinks aloud and pools these thoughts to mould policy. Unity is maintained by the acceptance of majority rule and freedom to anyone who abstains on conscience. For example, McDonald and three of his colleagues declined to vote in the recent debate on China, but not one of the 119 Members who obeyed the Party decision has complained. The majority is the only leader of the Labour Party and the Chairman is but its servant.'[24]

Included in that majority were the Trade Unions and any

attempt to remove McDonald from his position would require their support and given the rapturous welcome he received at the T.U. Congress that year[25] this support was unlikely to be forthcoming. It would certainly not be given to a man like Wheatley who had condemned the Union leaders for their timidity and foolishness.[26] It may have been even then that Wheatley was considering making a direct appeal to the workers for he had already spoken of their need to resort to unconstitutional action in any future conflict, conflict that the Government hoped to avoid with the introduction of its Trades Disputes Act. The support of the workers was paramount to Wheatley in his bid to rid the Party of McDonald and company for the base from which he was operating was too narrow and too fragile and it was already being chipped at by his adversaries. However, Wheatley's challenge almost came to an end, and with it his political career, in the summer of that year because of belated action he had taken to defend himself against the slanderous allegations that had been circulated at the time of the General Election.

His earlier decision not to defend his character had not only nearly cost him his seat, but the confidence of many of his supporters. The local branch of the I.L.P. had made it clear to him that if the slanders were to go unchallenged then it would withdraw its support from him.[27] As a result, Wheatley had issued a challenge in his newspaper offering a reward of £1,000 to anyone who could testify to the truth of the stories that had been circulated about him.[28] Reid Miller replied immediately with a letter which Wheatley described as scurrilous. Following his refusal not to publish the contents of the letter Reid had it published in the *Eastern Argus*. Wheatley then filed an action suing Miller and the publisher of the *Argus* for slander and seeking damages of £3,000. The letter not only accused Wheatley of an association with nefarious trades but also contained allegations that were even more damaging including (a) That he had used his position as a Cabinet Minister to have the prison sentence of Thomas McVey, his former partner, reduced. McVey had been jailed for fifteen years for forgery and in 1924 had this sentence reduced to five years. (b) That he had refused to toast the King at public functions thereby dishonouring the oath he had taken as a Privy Councillor.

The case came before the High Court in Edinburgh on the 5th July, 1927 at which the Defence argued that Miller had been challenged and the subject of his letter was fair comment on matters relating to the pursuer in his public capacity and that Miller could not be expected to pay damages for transgressing the broad aspect of fair public criticism. Most of the allegations Wheatley was able to disprove, but on the question of the oath the defence brought forward two witnesses who testified to an occasion at a civic luncheon when Wheatley remained seated while the toast to the King was being proposed. Much to Wheatley's distress the decision of the Court went against him. The judge in his ruling said that the contents of the letter were hard-hitting rather than defamatory.[29] Wheatley's immediate reaction was to appeal, but on legal advice decided later to withdraw the motion.

For a man who had said that his reputation was all that he had, the judgement was a bitter pill for Wheatley to swallow. Under the circumstances he felt that he had no other option but to resign his Parliamentary seat. Despite pleas for him to reconsider taking such action Wheatley announced to a special meeting of the local Branches at the end of September his decision not to contest the seat at the next election.[30] The reasons he gave for this decision were the recent court action and continuing ill-health.

References

1. *Decline and Fall of the Labour Party* – J. Scanlon
2. *Call Back Yesterday* – H. Dalton
3. *Left Turn* – J. Paton
4. *Ramsay McDonald* – D. Marquand
5. *New Leader* – 9/4/26
6. *Inside the Left* – F. Brockway
7. *New Leader* – 2/4/26
8. *Forward* – 26/3/26
   London Times – 6/8/26
9. *London Times* – 30/9/25
   Post War History of the Working Classes – A. Hutt
10. *Inside the Left* – F. Brockway
11. *Glasgow Herald* – 2/8/26
    Eastern Standard – 15/1/27
12. *Glasgow Evening Times* – 6/1/27
13. *Glasgow Evening Times* – 10/1/27
14. *Glasgow Evening Times* – 9/4/27
15. *Eastern Standard* – 19/2/27
16. *Hansard* – Vol 203 – February – 1927
17. *Eastern Standard* – 26/3/27
18. *Eastern Standard* – 3/4/27
19. *Forward* – 16/4/27
    Glasgow Evening Times – 29/4/27
20. *Forward* – 23/4/27
21. *Forward* – 6/4/27
22. *Glasgow Evening Times* – 18/4/27

23. *Glasgow Evening Times* – 19/4/27
24. *Forward* – 23/4/27
25. *Glasgow Evening Times* – 8/9/27
26. *Eastern Standard* – 30/10/26
27. *Glasgow Herald* – 8/7/27
28. *Eastern Standard* – 19/9/25
29. Wheatley v Anderson & Miller – *Glasgow Herald* – 6th–13th July 1927
30. *London Times* – 27/9/27
    Glasgow Evening Times – 26/9/27

Chapter Fourteen
A Manifesto for Socialists

'Disruptive elements have, to some extent, blurred the vision of the electorate and temporarily embarrassed the forces of Labour. The Labour movement will not be blindly led by the servants of reaction no matter their colour.'[1] F. O. Roberts' opening address to the Labour Party Conference at Blackpool in October reflected the thinking of Party and Union leaders and answered the calls for peace that were coming from both sides of industry. Wheatley, who had gone missing for two months from the political scene,[2] re-appeared to condemn the mood of the Conference.[3]

'Nothing happened at Blackpool to excite the workers. The starving and oppressed are looking for bread and liberty, but they will look in vain for either in the proceedings at Blackpool. The workers are in a state of apathy, almost of hopelessness, and there is no doubt in my mind that there is a close connection between this and the industrial policy now being advocated. The Labour Party is in danger of becoming the police force of Capitalism. There is more criticism directed at Russia than our own competitive system and there are many Labour leaders more interested in making peace with the employers than in peace with Russia. The idea that you can have peace in industry under the competitive system of fixing wages and prices springs from ignorance. In this system neither employers nor workers have free will.'

After the General Strike Baldwin's Government made it clear that it was determined to curb the power of the Unions and by the Summer of 1927 its Trades Dispute Bill has passed through Parliament. This Bill not only made illegal General Strikes and some forms of sympathetic strikes, but was intended to cripple Union finances by altering the contractual law on political levies. Even before this Bill was presented to the Commons, Union and Labour leaders seemed determined to avoid industrial conflict. From the beginning of 1927 Union leaders were engaged in what Ben Turner described as sensible talks with industry.[4] McDonald lent weight to these talks by calling for a round-table conference on industrial peace[5] while at the same time Henderson and Thomas were condemning the futility of strike action.[6] The passing of the Trades Dispute Act put pressure on the Labour leaders and in September the T.U. Congress resolved to co-operate with the employers in a policy 'that would secure the efficiency of industry and improve the standard of life for the workers'. This resolution was moved by Ernest Bevin and seconded by Thomas.[7] As if to impress the Government and the employers as to its sincerity Walter Citrine announced to the Congress that the T.U.C. had broken its relations with the Russian Unions.[8] The Government had previously terminated the Trade Agreement with Russia[9] following on the Arcos Raid.*

The movement towards peace in industry, the initiative for which had been wrongly ascribed to George Hicks, accelerated on the 25th November when the Unions received a letter from Sir Alfred Mond, Chairman of I.C.I., inviting them to a conference to discuss the entire question of industrial re-organisation and industrial relations. Reference was made to the problems of redundancies which would have to be faced with the introduction of new methods and new machinery.[10]

The Conference took place on the 12th January, 1928 where it was agreed that each body would set up a sub-committee which would meet at regular intervals for further discussion. Turner, for the Unions, and Mond, for the employers, were the principal figures in these committees.[11] It was mainly because of these talks, the contents of which were supposed to be private, that led Wheatley to go back on his decision not to contest his seat.

From the outset Wheatley had condemned the whole idea of Peace in Industry talks. He was bitter on Snowden's call for purely negotiated settlements in industry through the help of Tribunals.[12] 'The only time the workers have gained through negotiations was when the right and the will to strike was in the hands of those who negotiated,' was his reply. In the Commons he quoted the Insurance Bill as a practical example of how the Government sought to achieve Peace in Industry. This Bill, based broadly on the Blanesborough Report, gave benefit to boys and girls of between 16 and 18 years, 6/– and 5/– respectively and to men and women of between 18 and 21 years, 10/– and 8/–. The object of the Bill said Wheatley, was to force young unemployed men through the process of starvation to break T.U. rules in order to work in industry at lower rates.[13] It was while the actual peace talks were in progress that Wheatley announced to a meeting at Bridgeton that he intended to again contest his seat at the next

*The raid on ARCOS (All Russian Co-op Society) took place following the alleged disappearance of a document from a Govt. dept. The Home Secretary, reported to the Commons after the raid that he was satisfied that the document was or had been in the ARCOS building. 'A Govt. of burglars' was Wheatley's verdict on the raid, 'Why a document of such importance was not properly guarded is as mysterious as the Zinoviev letter.'

election.[14] At this meeting he told the people that all the talk of Peace in Industry was merely an attempt to keep the workers quiet and content with their lot. 'It is one thing to tell the workers not to fight or strike when they are not in a position to do so,' he said, 'but when they are not in a position to do so, as I believe is the case now, they should spend the time well building up the sinews of war.' Two months later Wheatley set out to build up these sinews.

Cook, when he had been elected to the General Council of the T.U.C., had stated openly that, while he remained a member, the proceedings of the Council and its committees would no longer be secret.[15] True to his word he began to leak accounts of the Peace talks and was being threatened with expulsion from the General Council, he had described the talks as farcical.[16] Eager to make capital from Cook's inside knowledge of the Peace in Industry talks Wheatley and Maxton invited him to a meeting in the House of Commons. Also present at this meeting were Kirkwood, Buchanan, Stephen, Gallacher and John Scanlon. It was intended to be an exploratory meeting, but before they adjourned it was agreed to issue a manifesto addressed to the workers, warning them of the course on which they were being led by their present leaders. On the 21st June, 1928, the manifesto appeared in the press.[17]

TO THE WORKERS OF BRITAIN

For some time a number of us have been seriously disturbed as to where the British Labour movement is being led. We believe that its basic principles are:-
(1) An increasing war against poverty and working class servitude. This means an increasing war against Capitalism.
(2) That only by their efforts can the workers obtain the full product of their labour.

These basic principles provided the inspiration and the organisation on which the Labour movement was built. They were the principles of Hardie and the other pioneers who made the Party. But, in recent times, there has been a serious departure from the principles and policy which animated the founders. We are not being asked to believe that the Party is no longer a working class Party, but a Party representing all sections of the community. As Socialists we feel we cannot represent the views of Capitalism, Capitalism and Socialism have nothing in common. As a result of the new conception that Socialism and Capitalism should sink their differences, much of the energy which should be expended in fighting Capitalism is now expended in crushing everybody who dares to remain true to the ideals of the movement. We are convinced that this change is responsible for destroying the fighting spirit of the Party. We now come out openly and challenge it. We can no longer stand by and see 30 years of devoted work destroyed in making peace with Capitalism and compromises with the political philosophy of our Capitalist opponents. In furtherance of our effort we propose to combine in carrying through a series of conferences and meetings in various parts of the country. At these conferences the rank and file will be given the opportunity to state whether they accept the new outlook or whether they wish to remain true to the spirit and ideals which animated the early pioneers. Conditions have not changed, wealth and luxury still flaunt themselves in the face of the poverty stricken workers who produce them. We ask you to join in the fight against the system which makes these conditions possible.

While the manifesto was signed by Cook and Maxton, who emphasised that they were acting on their own responsibility, it was Wheatley who had complete control over the campaign.[18] In an effort to pre-empt charges of disloyalty to the Labour movement Wheatley told a meeting at Shettleston why he supported the manifesto.[19]

'I was sent to Parliament to bring about Socialism in our time. Cook and Maxton said that the competitive system is responsible for poverty and that a Socialist system should take the place of Capitalism. If any Labour leader challenges them it would not be on these points. Cook and Maxton say the Labour movement is being led into Liberalism and Mondism towards a Liberal-Labour alliance in politics and a Capitalist-Socialist coalition in industry. Those who think that the lot of the worker can be improved within the competitive system of wages and prices should join the Liberal Party.'

The campaign was ill-conceived and ill-prepared and the fundamental differences between Wheatley and Maxton as to its main objectives were exposed at the first meeting in Glasgow's St. Andrews Hall. Wheatley held that under Labour's present leadership there was no hope for Socialism and that the worst thing that could befall the Labour movement would be a government composed of men who would do nothing to satisfy the aspirations of the workers, it could cause disillusionment and set the movement back twenty years. To bring about a change in the leadership would require half the Labour back-benchers being removed and replaced with members committed to Socialism. To bring about this change the constituencies would have to be controlled by the left. Maxton, on the other hand, believed that the workers would be unlikely to support anything that would seem damaging to Labour's chances of winning the election, but if the rank and file were convinced of Socialism they would demand it and McDonald would have no option but to meet that demand. Consequently, Maxton, who was extremely nervous, refused to say anything at this first meeting that could be interpreted as being divisive to the Labour movement and his speech lacked its usual fire. Cook, who was first to speak on that occasion, was also a bitter disappointment. Instead of revealing the secrets of the Peace in Industry talks he chose to read a typescript dissertation on Marx. With speakers of the calibre of these men the capacity audience was expecting an evangelical revival type meeting. It was disappointed and so too was Wheatley who later in the evening tore up a cheque he had written to finance the campaign.[20]

Wheatley acted quickly to try and put bite back into the campaign by addressing an open-air meeting at Springfield Rd. the following evening.[21] Here he launched into a fierce assault on McDonald and Thomas. McDonald, he said, was a Socialist in theory, but a Tory in practice who believed that Socialism was a state of society to be enjoyed by our grand-children. Thomas, who made no claim to be a Socialist, was the real leader of the Labour Party because of the influence he had on McDonald. Maxton apparently had a change of mind because he too began to openly criticise the leaders of the Party and their speeches resulted in their being asked to appear before the P.L.P. 'to answer certain statements which bore upon the actions of certain members of the Party.'[22] They were both unconcerned with Wheatley expressing the opinion that the leaders did not have the courage to tackle them. Clynes and Thomas were the chief inquisitors at the hearing[23] and in the face of the pair's refusal to detract the statements they had made in public the P.L.P. merely recorded a resolution 'that the machinery of the weekly meetings of the P.L.P. and the provision of special meetings together with the annual Conference provided the proper opportunities for discussing the policy of the Party.'[24] Although Thomas gloomily forecast that the Campaign would cost Labour 50 seats at the election[25] McDonald had good reason not to make Wheatley a martyr, the campaign had entrenched him in the leadership of the Party.

According to some, what Wheatley envisaged if the campaign was successful was the emergence of a new political organisation representing all elements of the working class that would include the I.L.P.[26] It never really got off the ground after St. Andrew's Halls. Maxton was partly correct for, with an election so close, the campaign was viewed by many as damaging to Labour and turned some, formerly diffident, closer to McDonald. In Scotland Wheatley and Maxton lost many friends. Dollan said 'that local Labour leaders were hostile to the idea of a new Party' while Johnston wrote of 'the reactionary folly of reckless folk who temperamentally must ever be fishing in troubled waters.'[27] For-

ward began advocating the gradualism of McDonald and at Birmingham Lansbury was opting for the cautious approach as opposed to rapid change.[28] Perhaps the greatest tragedy to come out of this campaign was the damage that was done to the I.L.P., particularly as to its credibility.

That year the I.L.P. was struggling to maintain its membership amidst questions that were being repeatedly raised as to its efficacy, McDonald and Snowden had been among those putting these questions.[29] The argument for the dissolution of the I.L.P. was that since the Labour Party allowed for individual membership and had adopted a definite Socialist policy the I.L.P. had lost its raison-d'être. It sounded plausible enough, but in fact there were fundamental differences between the two Parties. As well as being different in structure and in function the I.L.P. looked on Socialism, not merely as an economic policy, but as a whole way of life and there were large numbers committed to this ethic. Given responsible leadership the I.L.P. could have survived the membership crisis. One could imagine loyalty to the Party being stretched when it was found that its chairman had given his signature to a Manifesto without even bothering to consult his executive.[30] Not only were Maxton and Wheatley cocking a snoot at the leaders of the Labour Party, but they were guilty of disloyalty to their own Party. Despite this breach of faith the N.A.C., with the exception of Shinwell, Stanforth and Scurr, endorsed the Manifesto as being in the spirit of Socialism in our Time.[31] Nevertheless, there was no doubt the I.L.P. had been seriously wounded, yet such was the affection in which Maxton was held within the Party that it was not he who was being blamed for inflicting that wound.

There were many on both sides of the house who would no doubt have agreed with Hore-Belisha's description of Wheatley at that time,[32] 'A Parliamentary Brigand, whose collected and impassive demeanour only intensifies the appearance of cruelty. A broad immobile face, set in the serenity of satisfaction with sunken, narrow and expressionless eyes. Nothing, not even the sight of blood, ruffles his composure.' Wheatley's enemies within the I.L.P. could not understand the close relationship between him and Maxton, described as unique in British politics.[33] They assumed that Maxton had fallen under the evil spell of Wheatley and made an attempt to break that spell. English M.P.s who retained an allegiance to the I.L.P. organised a meeting to discuss ways of removing the power of the Clydesiders. The meeting was closed to all Scottish M.P.s with the exception of Shinwell. This meeting expressed its dissatisfaction with the actions of the

A Manifesto for Socialists

Clydesiders, but excused Maxton who they felt had been vitriolised by his Glasgow colleagues.[34] Shinwell, more so than the others, should have known better than to try and drive a wedge between Wheatley and Maxton. It was to become evident that the Manifesto campaign had reduced the Wheatley faction to a rump. Besides Maxton, he could only be assured in the Commons of the solid backing of Kirkwood, Buchanan and Stephen.

References

1. *London Times* – 4/10/27
   Glasgow Evening Times – 3/10/27
2. *Glasgow Evening Times* – 26/9/27
3. *London Times* – 17/10/27
   Eastern Standard – 22/10/27
4. *Glasgow Evening Times* – 10/1/27
5. *Glasgow Evening Times* – 17/1/27
6. *Glasgow Evening Times* – 7/3/27
   Glasgow Evening Times – 12/1/27
7. *London Times* – 6/9/27
8. *Glasgow Evening Times* – 8/9/27
9. *Glasgow Evening Times* – 25/5/27
10. *Glasgow Evening Times* – 26/11/27
    Glasgow Herald – 28/11/27
11. *London Times* – 14/1/28
12. *Eastern Standard* – 25/6/27
13. *Glasgow Herald* – 12/11/27
14. *Glasgow Herald* – 23/4/28
15. *Glasgow Evening Times* – 8/11/27
16. *Glasgow Evening Times* – 13/1/28
17. *London Times* – 21/6/28
18. *Decline and Fall of the Labour Party* – J. Scanlon
19. *London Times* – 26/6/28
20. *Decline and Fall of the Labour Party* – J. Scanlon
21. *Glasgow Herald* – 10/7/28
22. *Glasgow Herald* – 20/7/28
23. *Decline and Fall of the Labour Party* – J. Scanlon
24. *Glasgow Herald* – 20/7/28
25. *Decline and Fall of the Labour Party* – J. Scanlon
26. *Inside The Left* – F. Brockway
27. *Forward* – 28/7/28
28. *Glasgow Herald* – 2/10/28
    London Times – 9/1/28
29. *Glasgow Evening Times* – 9/4/28
30. *Inside the Left* – F. Brockway
31. *Glasgow Evening Times* – 30/11/28

32. *Eastern Standard* – 12/5/28
33. *Decline and Fall of the Labour Party* – J. Scanlon
34. *Glasgow Evening Times* – 30/11/28, 1/12/29

Chapter Fifteen
1929–30

Take your harp, go round the town,
you poor forgotten whore.
Play and sing your songs again
to bring men back once more.
ISAIAH 23:16

What may have influenced Wheatley on the course that he took was the impotence at that time of the I.L.P. within the Labour movement to combat the pragmatism of the right-wing leaders and the power of the Unions. One of the things about the Cook/Maxton Manifesto that had angered Labour's leaders was that it had appeared at the same time as their policy document 'Labour and the Nation' thus reducing much of its impact. In consultations preceding the drafting of this document the Labour executive had ignored major amendments put forward by the I.L.P. representatives.[1] It lacked commitment to Socialism, its one concession was the Nationalisation of the Mines. McDonald had previously told a Labour Conference that any programme produced would be the work of the Executive and the P.L.P. and on resolutions passed at Conference which they thought fit to include.[2]

At Birmingham in October, in what would be the last Conference before the election, 'Labour and the Nation' was presented for approval. The document, which McDonald claimed was pregnant with programme after programme,[3] was vague on how it proposed to tackle unemployment. 'There was no lack of sound schemes for which the urgent need is generally admitted' the document stated. Schemes such as afforestation, satellite towns with their own services, major roads and bridges to meet the demands of modern transport were mentioned without any indication as to how they were to be financed. It did promise the restoration of the seven-hour day for the miners and the raising of the school leaving age. Equally vague was the promise that National Insurance benefits under a Labour Government would be humane and adequate. Wheatley and Maxton were the most prominent of the left in attacking the document which Maxton said could in no way be called a programme and he warned the conference that its approval of this document would be tantamount to giving free rein to any future Labour Government.[4] The document was approved by a majority which Wheatley declared was the result of the cold, machine-made card vote of the Unions which in no way reflected the spirit of the Conference.[5] The growing confidence of the right wing was reflected at the Conference with the passing of a resolution that was an attempt in fact to gag Wheatley and Maxton. 'Only those who were prepared to advocate the principles of the Labour Party should be engaged by constituencies to speak on public platforms.'[6]

The only thing likely to gag Wheatley was his health and this was already causing some concern among his friends. His blood pressure was a cause for anxiety sufficient for his doctor to send him to Bath at the beginning of 1929 for hydrotherapy. By February he had recovered sufficiently to join his friend Maxton on the platform at the Olympia Theatre where Fenner Brockway was the guest speaker.[7] Brockway had tremendous respect for Wheatley and was one of the few English M.P.s in the I.L.P. who approved of his Parliamentary tactics.[8] The three met up again at Carlisle at the end of March for the I.L.P. Annual Conference. Shortly before the Conference Baldwin had announced that Parliament would be dissolved on the 11th May and that new elections would be held on the 30th May. The Conference met in a buoyant mood. Almost on its eve Jenny Lee had recaptured Joe Sullivan's old seat at Lanark North for Labour and added to the sweeping gains at the local elections the previous November the delegates had every reason to be optimistic of Labour's prospects in the new elections. In his Chairman's address[9] Maxton dampened the enthusiasm by warning that success could only be a means to an end. Wheatley gave his own warning[10] when he told the delegates that the only alternative to Socialism in our Time was Liberalism.

Despite the pre-election mood the divisions within the Party were evident. Dollan and Shinwell made an unsuccessful bid to have Maxton ousted from the chair.[11] The efficacy of the Party was again being questioned and suggestions were made that the Party renounce its Parliamentary role and concentrate its energies on education and propaganda. These divisions were evident too in the constituencies, McLean had split with the I.L.P. in Govan and was standing as an Independent Socialist.

Ignoring 'Labour and the Nation' the I.L.P. went into the election with its own manifesto. It re-iterated the demand for a Living Wage and it stated that 'the accummulated wealth of the nation produced by the co-operative effort of all must be treated as the product of common services and made available for common needs. The nation can no longer allow its key sources of economic power to remain in the irresponsible control of the profit maker.'

'Labour and the Nation' was the framework for the Labour Party's manifesto. It was a policy which only Winston Churchill could describe as one of Socialist plunder.[12] McDonald made appeals to the Liberal voter and he warned that there would be no early cure for unemployment. It was a problem that Snowden said in a broadcast should be the matter for an all Party conference. McDonald did promise to repeal the Trades Dispute Act and also to restore Wheatley's Act to good health.

On the basis of some good by-election results the Liberals were also confident going into these elections. With Lloyd George now in control they produced a pamphlet 'We can Conquer Unemployment' which promised massive spending on local government, roads, drainage, railways and telephones. Their campaign received a setback when the Tories, in a move which was unprecedented, produced a White Paper drawn up by the heads of government departments which questioned the financial provisions of the L.G. scheme.

The Tories produced, what Baldwin called, a programme of Social Welfare. They proposed to introduce maternity benefits, clear the slums, give relief to agriculture and develop the Empire. Baldwin also added that he was content to be judged on the Government's performance. Two other pieces of major legislation that had passed through the Commons were the Housing Act in 1926 and the Representation of the Peoples Act. The former reduced the subsidies on houses built under the 1923 and 1924 Acts by £2 and £1.10/- respectively. A money resolution was pushed through, to become effective in October 1929, which abolished completely the subsidy on the 1923 Act and reduced by a further £1.10/- the subsidy on Wheatley's Bill. The Representation of the Peoples Act extended the franchise to women over 21 years thereby increasing the electorate by $5\frac{1}{2}$ million. In Shettleston, the Tories were looking to these new voters to overturn Wheatley's slender majority.

Captain H. J. Moss a shy, handsome young man was Wheatley's only opposition. Early election reports were that he was wooing, not only the flappers, but the matronly types as well and the press was hinting at a sensational result in Shettleston.[13] It seemed that all Captain Moss had to offer the electorate was a handsome profile for there were no reports of anything he had to say. Strangely, little was being reported about Wheatley either and it looked as if the local Tories were betting also on a low key campaign and the apathy of the workers. The poor attendance at the May Day rally in Glasgow Green may have suggested that the workers lacked enthusiasm for this election.

Wheatley's opening meeting[14] of the campaign however, attracted such a crowd that the Shettleston Town Hall and the adjoining Lesser Hall were unable to contain it. Partly responsible for this turn out was the appearance of Jennie Lee, who along with Maxton and Kirkwood shared the platform with Wheatley. Jennie Lee had enlisted Wheatley's support, which must have been invaluable, in her by-election campaign where birth control had somehow become a prominent factor and the Catholic press was urging Catholics to vote for the Liberal who was unequivocal in his opposition to birth control. Nevertheless, her appearance on his platform was taken as an indication by the press that Wheatley, concerned as to the outcome, required to bring in all the vote-winning aids that he could muster.

As election day drew close the Tories in Glasgow themselves showed concern when they crudely attempted to introduce sectarianism into the contest. Leaflets were distributed outside Catholic churches which quoted extracts from a speech by Cardinal Bourne in which he stated that a good Catholic could not vote Labour.[15] The quotations had been taken out of context. Following this Sir John Gilmour made a promise that, if the Tories were returned, they would legislate to deport all Free State Irishmen who were now seen to be a burden on the rates.[16] The press took this a stage further by pointing to the many jobs that were lost to the Scots because of these Irish.[17] These incursions looked damaging to Wheatley as right up to the eve of the election the press was rating his chances of retaining the seat as no better than evens.

The forecasters could not have been more wrong, Wheatley was elected with his highest ever majority, 6,724. Maxton too increased his majority to nearly 11,000. Labour in Glasgow, with a 53.84% share of the vote, now held 11 of the City's seats. Whatever the Manifesto Campaign had done it certainly did not harm Labour at the polls because, instead of losing the 50 seats that Thomas had forecast, it had gained well over 100 seats. Labour had 289 seats in the new Parliament as against the Tories 260 and 58 for the Liberals and once again McDonald agreed to form a minority Government.

As was expected, there was no place for Wheatley in McDonalds Cabinet. The press, while not surprised at his omission, thought McDonald was taking something of a risk by leaving Wheatley on the backbenches to lead the left. Both Henderson and Snowden shared this view,[18] but McDonald was intent to let the country see that the left had no influence on Labour policies, the inclusion in the Cabinet of nine former Liberals testified to this.

McDonald did not, this time, assume the extra responsibility of the Foreign Office, the post going to Henderson. Snowden returned to the Exchequer and Clynes was given the Home Office. Thomas was made Lord Privy Seal with overall responsibility for unemployment. Working under his direction were Oswald Mosley, Lansbury and Johnston, the latter pair being rewarded for their loyalty during the Manifesto Campaign. Margaret Bondfield, who had not endeared herself to the rank and file for her acceptance of the Blanesborough Report, was Minister for Labour and Greenwood was promoted to Wheatley's old job at the Ministry of Health. Wheatley was less concerned about his role in Government than that Labour, without an overall majority, should govern at all.

Before the opening of the new Parliament the P.L.P. met in a mood of triumph to salute McDonald for guiding the Party to victory. Wheatley quickly put a damper on the atmosphere.[19]

'There were whispered criticisms as he began to speak of the danger that could befall the Labour Party taking office, no doubt inspired by the thoughts that he resented being omitted from the Government. His sheer forcefulness of character and logic compelled the M.P.s to listen. He forecast that the country would soon be faced with a grave economic crisis. Fundamental changes would be required to overcome this crisis, changes that a minority Government would not be allowed to make. For a Labour government to adopt orthodox Capitalist measures would mean introducing repressive cuts, reducing still further the already low standard of the workers. Was a Labour Government prepared to accept the responsibility for these cuts? Far better to let the Tories, who believe in the system, deal with it and accept the responsibility. Labour should have the courage to wait until it had a working majority and then make fundamental changes. That was his own view and since Labour had already decided to govern it was academic, but then he put forward the views of the I.L.P. which were that Labour, on taking office, should introduce short-term popular reforms and then legislate for more fundamental changes. The Tories would be faced with the responsibility for rejecting these changes and the Labour Party would then have the confidence to go forward to face the electorate.'

Wheatley had his audience momentarily convinced until McDonald restored the atmosphere by dismissing Wheatley's policies as cowardly. 'Labour will show the country that Labour was fit to govern,' McDonald told the cheering M.P.s. The King's Speech did little to demonstrate that Labour was prepared or fit to govern. There were none of the popular reforms demanded by Wheatley. The Speech was full of McDonaldisms. 'Schemes and Bills were being prepared. Inquiries will be undertaken, general surveys are being conducted' were the phrases used to convey that the Government was on the point of bringing forth a comprehensive package that would be the solution to unemployment. No mention was made of the pledge to restore the 7-Hour Act. In fact, the only concrete measures introduced in the summer session were amendments to the Widows and Orphans Pension Act and the Housing Act. In the former, the pension age for widows was reduced from 60 to 55 years. On the Housing Bill, contrary to McDonald's promise, the amendment proposed only to maintain that part of the subsidy due to be cut in October. This brought an angry response[20] from Wheatley who reminded McDonald of his promise and he also warned the government not to play with Tory fire.

The failure of the Government to bring forth its proposals on N.I. in the first session was bitterly criticised by the Wheatley group – *the bad five* – and none was more vehement than Maxton.[21] These criticisms upset not only the Government, but the majority of the Labour Members. McDonald had warned that the greatest danger to a Labour Government lay in sniping from within the Party and the consensus of opinion was that the Government should be given every chance to prove itself.[22] Wheatley defended the actions of the group when he claimed[23] that they had the support of their constituents and that it would be hypocrisy to have one policy for their constituents and another for Parliament. He did not believe in the sincerity of the Labour leaders and expressed this opinion openly. When asked why he did not believe in their sincerity he often replied[24] 'of course they are sincere, they sincerely want office and they will make any sacrifice to stay there, but I doubt if some of them are as sincerely concerned to help the working class as is Baldwin.' Wheatley had had the advantage of working closely at Government level with these leaders. Within a few months many of the Labour M.P.s were ready to share Wheatley's opinion.

The first signs of discontent came when Margaret Bondfield produced her U.I. Bill. The least that the Labour Members expected from this Bill was that it would satisfy the Minimum Demands put forward by the Party to the Blanesborough Committee[25] i.e. weekly benefit of 20/– and 18/– for men and women over 18 years respectively, 15/– for youths of between 16 and 18 and 10/– for those under 16 years. Her proposals fell far short of these. All that distinguished it from the Tory Bill was that there was an increase in the adult dependant rate of 2/–, of 4/– for the 18 to 21 year olds and the minimum age for entitlement had been reduced to 15 years. Benefit of 17/– and 15/– for men and women over 21 remained the same. What was more, the humiliating clause 'Not genuinely seeking work' had not been withdrawn. This was a clause whereby the unemployed person had to prove that he or she had made a genuine effort to find work before entitlement to benefit. The unemployed still did not have the right, without losing benefit, to refuse a job where rates and conditions were below standard. The proposals were hotly debated at the Labour Party Conference in October and a resolution to refer them back to the Government was only narrowly defeated.[26] The Wheatley group did not let the matter rest there and contrary to a majority decision of the I.L.P., Parliamentary Party pressed amendments to the Bill in the Commons. These amendments, Maxton was the prime mover, were greeted with cries of disloyalty and received little support. The 'not genuinely seeking work' clause was removed, but this amendment had Union backing. The group was becoming more isolated, being looked upon more as a disruptive element within the Labour movement.

It was at the Brighton Conference that Wheatley first began sniping at Thomas's efforts to find work for the unemployed. During the summer recess Thomas had gone to Canada on a job-finding mission. On his way home he had sent a cable to say that he was satisfied with his mission and that he was certain that work for the unemployed would result. Arriving home he told the country that he had the complete cure for all those who were willing to work. Consequently, as Parliament re-assembled there was much speculation as to the good news Thomas had to give to the House. Wheatley had no illusions, he was convinced, despite his cable, that Thomas's trip had achieved nothing.[27]

Thomas began his much awaited report by warning[28] that there was no magic cure for unemployment. He then went into great detail on the work schemes which had been given Cabinet approval, schemes for land drainage, for the electrification of Liverpool Street station and for a mid-Scotland Canal. £9½ million was to be spent on trunk roads over a five year period and the railways, one part of the transport system not mentioned in 'Labour and the Nation', were to receive £7 million towards modernisation. As the House began to show its impatience Thomas turned to his mission in Canada, a prosperous country whose granaries and storehouses, he said, were bulging with grain. He had reached agreement with the Canadian Government on a resettlement scheme whereby 3,000 men would be trained in this country before going to work on Canadian farms. There were prospects of the Canadians ordering five 7,000 ton ships and he had an agreement that Canada would import 600,000 tons of British coal. It transpired that Canada was already importing that amount. The speech was a bitter disappointment for the vast majority of the Labour M.P.s who, unlike Wheatley, were eager to believe that Thomas was the man with the initiative to find work for Britain's 1,300,000 unemployed.

Over the next two months Wheatley teased and tormented Thomas on his promises of jobs until he had stripped him completely of all credibility. Finally, in December in what proved to be his last major speech in the House, Wheatley made a savage attack on Thomas, Government policy on jobs and the whole economic system.[29]

'Government policies are making no impression on reducing the numbers of unemployed. Every proposal to help the situation is purely a makeshift one. Every scheme is merely an overdraft on labour requirements over the next few years. Has the Government got any long distance plans for dealing with the situation? We are not dealing with a temporary industrial dislocation. We recognise the Lord Privy Seal's sincerity and energy, but you need more than that for his job. What has happened to the raw recruits of the Lord Privy Seal's stage army? What has become of the steel sleepers for the railways? I read that the G.W. railway company, with whom the Honourable Gentleman has had a long and honourable connection, has placed an order abroad for 200 sleepers. Did he explain the advantages of buying sleepers in this country? Is that the response the Government gets to the granting of aid? What about the coal marketing scheme for Canada? I have found that there has been a substantial increase in exports of coal to France, Belgium, Norway, Sweden and Finland, places that Thomas has not yet visited. He has been to Canada and brought home good cheer. What about the five ships? Are these to be regarded as 'ships that pass in the night'? Thomas has told Canadian journalists that Britain should be supplying Canada with labour and capital to enable it develop its own resources. Does Thomas not realise that a great part of our difficulties arise from our having supplied labour and capital to other people.'

Wheatley went on to question the Government's £20 million land drainage scheme when the country already had millions of acres of reclaimed land not being used and of money being spent on training the young in trades for which thousands could not find work. He appealed to the House to give serious consideration to the country's present industrial problems.

'I want you to realise that one half of the outlet for goods at home is closed just at a time when the potential output is doubled. I want you to see whether the system of distributing wealth which suited the 19th century suits the 20th century. I claim it is obsolete. Why should we have at this moment of crisis a condition of things where our great industries are engaged in cut-throat competition which may bring down the lot. Why not have a national policy that will bring all our industries together, making them mutually helpful rather than mutually destructive.'

The control of imports and exports Wheatley perceived as essential to any plan for national economic recovery. He condemned foreign traders who refused to discriminate between personal gain and the needs of the country.

'What a benefit it would be if we could have something like national organisation of our imports and exports. Our exports are governed by our imports, I mention this to the Liberals who talk about the value of free imports and others who speak of safeguarding duties on exports. If the quantity of imports governs the quantity of exports, the governing factor of the situation is the purchasing power of the people at home. The greatest menace to this country today is poverty. I appeal to gentlemen of all parties to put their mind to this problem, it is a problem that transcends all party differences. It is not only the workers and the capitalists who are going to go down, but the morale of the nation.'

Lloyd George praised[30] the speech as a brilliant exposé of the economic situation. Wheatley saw clearly the economic catastrophe that was to come and more, he recognised the causes. He saw the solution as a new economic structure and perhaps he was the only person capable of bringing this about. He may not have been a theorist like Lenin, but he had the ruthlessness of Stalin necessary to change the existing order. However, as he himself said in his speech, he was now regarded as an extremist, an impossibilist without a constructive mind and not one likely to be considered fit as an alternative to McDonald. He had taken himself and his group beyond the pale.

Small though the group now was, Wheatley made a pledge that it would continue to fight, both inside and outside Parliament, for a new order of society. He would quit politics, he said, if he thought the I.L.P. would agree to accept policies just because they were initiated by a Labour Government. In a speech at Bridgeton[31] he attacked Snowden's orthodox views on finance. 'The people were being led to believe that when Budget time came round in April a certain amount of money was put into the national till and that was the total sum the Chancellor had to meet his obligations. There never is any money in the till, what was in the till was National Credit. The only difficulty the Chancellor faced was that of finding the money and he should go to where the money was. He certainly won't find it in the tenements of Bridgeton.' In this speech, in what may have been a premonition of his death, he gave acclaim to the work of Maxton whom, he said, 'would soon be regarded as the greatest figure thrown up by the Labour movement in the present generation.' It was as if he was publicly handing over succession.

At the beginning of April 1930, Wheatley made his final intervention in Parliament on behalf of the people to whom he had devoted all his life in the Socialist movement.[32] During the debate on Greenwood's Slum Clearance Bill he criticised not only the construction of the Bill which, he said, provided no safeguards against the size of houses, but also the mental attitude of the House to slum dwellers.

'The improvement area of one year will be the clearance area of another year. It is no use approaching the question as if there were a given number of slums and that when we had dealt with them the problem would be solved.

Slum dwellers are not an inferior type of human being to be treated like Crown Colonies, as a section of humanity not fit for self-government, but to be taken by their superiors and coaxed and led to a higher plane where they may be allowed to run loose.

Under this Bill we are laying down that, in order to get a house, you must first of all pass through the slums.'

On his way to Birmingham for the I.L.P. Easter Conference Wheatley collapsed at Crewe Station. He was taken to a hospital in Birmingham where he was later allowed home. After a holiday in Ireland where he seemed to have made a good recovery he returned to his work. He went to the House of Commons on Thursday the 8th May and returned to Glasgow the following day. He called into his office in Broad St. that same day and seemed to be in good health, but then on the Saturday morning he collapsed at home with a cerebral haemorrhage. He lost consciousness that afternoon and died on the Monday at 11.20 p.m.[33]

Wheatley's body lay in an upper room of his house at Sandyhills where hundreds called to pay a final tribute. As the cortège made its way to Dalbeth cemetery thousands of bare-headed men and shawl-cladded women lined the streets to pay homage to the man who had kept a promise not to betray them. Father McCarthy of St. Joseph's Church conducted a simple interment service at the graveside. His friends, Maxton, Stephen and Kirkwood, who wept unashamedly, were there. No dignitaries from the Roman Catholic Church were in attendance, but the Church of Scotland honoured Wheatley with the presence of its most senior representative, the Right Reverend Dr. John White, Moderator of

1929–30

the General Assembly[34]. John Wheatley would have been proud of that.

References

1. *Forward* – 28/7/28
2. *London Times* – 5/10/27
3. *Glasgow Herald* – 3/10/28
4. Ibid.
5. *Glasgow Herald* – 4/10/28
6. Ibid.
7. *Eastern Standard* – 5/1/29
8. *Inside The Left* – F. Brockway
9. *London Times* – 1/4/29
10. *Glasgow Herald* – 2/4/29
11. *Glasgow Herald* – 1/4/29
12. *Glasgow Herald* – 9/5/29
13. *Glasgow Herald* – 16/5/29
    Glasgow Evening Times – 29/5/29
14. *Eastern Standard* – 18/5/29
15. *Glasgow Herald* – 26/5/29
16. *Glasgow Evening Times* – 25/5/29
17. *Glasgow Evening Times* – 27/5/29
18. *An Autobiography* – P. Snowden
19. *Inside The Left* – F. Brockway
    Aneurin Bevan – Michael Foot – 1962
20. *Eastern Standard* – 20/7/29
21. *Hansard* – Vol 231 – June 1929
22. *Aneurin Bevan* – M. Foot
23. *Eastern Standard* – 19/10/29
24. *Decline and Fall of the Labour Party* – J. Scanlon
25. *Glasgow Evening Times* – 12/2/27
26. *Glasgow Herald* – 2/10/29
27. *Decline and Fall of the Labour Party* – J. Scanlon
28. *Hansard* – Vol 233 – December 1929
29. Ibid.
30. Ibid.
31. *Glasgow Herald* – 16/12/29
32. *Hansard* – Vol 237 – April 1930
33. *Eastern Standard* – 16/5/30
    Glasgow Observer – 17/5/30
34. *Glasgow Evening Times* – 16/5/30

Other Recent Spokesman Titles

Spreading the News
by Frank Allaun

The next few years will be a crucial time for the British media. In television and radio, the advent of satellite and cable broadcasting continued with the present government's 'free market' policies could lead to a drastic lowering of standards in an industry which has attracted world acclaim.

In the press, the technological revolution *could* lead to a reverse of today's stranglehold by just five huge press groups. But, those powerful proprietors are also major shareholders in TV and radio companies.

Frank Allaun, for many years a distinguished politician who made reform of the media one of his principal concerns, and before that a successful journalist, surveys the state of both press and broadcasting and explores the opportunities and dangers that now present themselves.

120pp 210 × 140mm
cloth 0 85124 488 2 £17.50
paper 0 85124 498 X £4.95

Wales in Closed
by Ralph Fevre

As the job losses gathered pace, the graffiti on the Severn Bridge announced that "Wales is Closed". But it is not just the drastic reduction in *volume* of employment that has had such a devastating effect on the workforce of the steel industry. Insecurity and *under*employment through the mechanism of casual or temporary work with private contractors are now conditions necessary to the production of steel. In the Port Talbot steelworks since 1980, the author traces what might be called the quiet privatisation of British Steel.

164pp 210 × 140mm
cloth 0 85124 466 1 £17.50
paper 0 85124 476 9 £5.95

Britain's Regions in Crisis No. 4

Idle Hands, Clenched Fists:
The Depression in a Shipyard Town
by Stephen Kelly

There were people watching the Toxteth riots of 1981 who had seen it all before. In the Autumn of 1932, those on the dole in Birkenhead had reacted similarly, venting their anger against the police as their frustration finally reached breaking point. Many stories of those earlier riots have been passed down by word of mouth, but little that is accurate has actually been written about them. This book, for the first time, records in detail the events of that Autumn on Merseyside.

**106pp 210 × 140mm
cloth 0 85124 436 X £15.00
paper 0 85124 446 7 £4.95**

Hanging on by your Fingernails:
The Struggle at Lea Hall 1984-87
**Photographs and design: Nigel Dickinson
Text: Jon Williams & Liliane Jaddou**

From almost the start of the Strike at Lea Hall Colliery, Nigel Dickinson began taking photographs which were exhibited on the walls of the Strike Centre, or regularly passed round and discussed. They came not only to represent a collective point of view, but to help build that point of view.

By the end of the strike there was a photographic record which was perhaps unique in Labour Movement History. 151 photographs from it are published in this book together with a commentary produced in much the same way as the photographs, under the ultimate editorial control of those who had been involved in the Strike.

**56pp A4
paper 0 85124 486 6 £4.25**

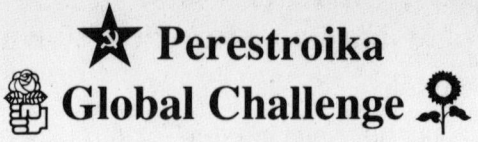

★ Perestroika
Global Challenge
Our Common Future
edited by Ken Coates

A serious crisis of the environment has assumed the proportions of a global menace. This has been pinpointed by the UN Commission headed by Mrs Brundtland, the Norwegian Prime Minister, whose report, *Our Common Future*, was published last year.

The Global Challenge involved in this crisis is aggravated in the economic crisis of monetarism and debt, brilliantly analysed in the programme of the Socialist International.

Now Mikhail Gorbachev has addressed the same themes in a powerful message to the United Nations. The power of separate nation states is now insufficient to meet this world-wide threat. Can the peoples join their forces to prepare joint international action on the necessary scale?

This is the agenda of this important book featuring contributions by Mikhail Gorbachev, Michael Barratt Brown, Keith and Anne Buchanan, Luciana Castellina, Ken Coates, Andre Gunder Frank, Stuart Holland, Bob de Ruiter, Marek Thee, Maarten van Traa, Joop den Uyl, Norbert Wieczorek,

It is introduced by Neil Kinnock.

"Should command attention and be widely discussed"
Neil Kinnock

"We can speak till we are blue in the face . . . Nothing will change till we start acting"
Mikhail Gorbachev

Cloth £17.50 Paper £4.95
from Spokesman, Bertrand Russell House, Gamble Street, Nottingham NG7 4ET